Student Agency and E

This book offers fresh perspectives on the challenges of assessment and feedback in higher education. A must-read for university leaders, academics, and educational developers, it asks 'what if' questions to unlock some of the systemic problems of assessment and feedback. It shifts the debate to focus on students' experience at a programme level, introducing a different way of thinking about assessment and feedback, and advancing the value of theories of alienation and engagement.

Based on the 'Transforming the Experience of Students through Assessment' (TESTA) project, the book discusses a method for understanding the impact of assessment and feedback on student learning. Drawing on evidence from TESTA, it provides practical insights about changing programme assessment patterns to foster student agency and engagement. The book gives impetus to changing the design assessment and feedback, inviting academics, educational leaders, and students into more transparent, open, and shared decision-making about assessment and feedback beyond the module level.

This key title is designed to support academics and educational leaders in making sustainable and systemic improvements to the pedagogy of assessment. It expands on good principles, practices, and theories about how students learn from assessment and feedback by paying attention to a programme level perspective of the student experience.

Tansy Jessop is Pro Vice-Chancellor for Education and Students at the University of Bristol. She leads 'Transforming the Experience of Students through Assessment' (TESTA), a research and change project which has challenged education leaders across the sector to re-imagine assessment and feedback from a student perspective.

The Staff and Educational Development Series
Series Editor: James Wisdom

Written by experienced and well-known practitioners and published in association with the Staff and Educational Development Association (SEDA), each book in the series contributes to the development of learning, teaching and training and assists in the professional development of staff. The books present new ideas for learning development and facilitate the exchange of information and good practice.

Titles in the series:

For more information about this series, please visit: https://www.routledge.com/SEDA-Series/book-series/SE0747

Student Agency and Engagement

Transforming Assessment and Feedback in Higher Education

Tansy Jessop

Routledge
Taylor & Francis Group

LONDON AND NEW YORK

Designed cover image: © Getty Images

First published 2024
by Routledge
4 Park Square, Milton Park, Abingdon, Oxon OX14 4RN

and by Routledge
605 Third Avenue, New York, NY 10158

Routledge is an imprint of the Taylor & Francis Group, an informa business

© 2024 Tansy Jessop

British Library Cataloguing-in-Publication Data
A catalogue record for this book is available from the British Library

ISBN: 978-0-367-36669-8 (hbk)
ISBN: 978-0-367-36671-1 (pbk)
ISBN: 978-0-429-34796-2 (ebk)

DOI: 10.4324/9780429347962

Typeset in ITC Galliard Pro
by KnowledgeWorks Global Ltd.

To Sam, Jonty, and Tommy

Contents

Foreword

Some of the most powerful research into students' experience of assessment, and some of the accompanying insights concerning the obstructions assessment puts in the way of engaged student learning, was published half a century ago. To an extent, some of the fundamental ideas are not news. They have been summarised and added to in an incremental way over decades, with piecemeal developments in theory (e.g. about feedback) without any overarching conceptual framework with a solid evidence base. There has been an enormous volume of piecemeal advice about specific assessment practices, often devoid of a coherent underlying rationale. And there has been very, very little evidence that assessment works better to support student learning today than it did 50 years ago.

Rarely has any of this research and practical advice acknowledged just how difficult it is to change assessment or revealed an understanding of change processes: how you get from here to there in an academic environment. Much of the advice on changed practice has focussed on the limited actions that can be taken by individual teachers within the highly constrained context of their own course unit or module, rather than address the much thornier question of how you get everyone to move forward together, in step. This has often produced incoherent innovation and led to more confusion on the part of students, not less.

This book provides a much-needed overarching conceptual framework for the whole enterprise. It understands that students experience not just assignments, exams, and feedback, the focus of almost all research, but entire assessment regimes. It places individual assessment events in their proper context. In the UK, quality assurance and the metrics that accompany it that are designed to inform those choosing where it is best to study, the focus is not on teachers or course units but on degree programmes. There are bigger differences between undergraduate degree programmes about assessment than about any other aspect of students' education, and these metrics about assessment have proved stubbornly difficult to improve despite nearly 20 years effort. Programmes have global assessment characteristics that create environments that profoundly affect students, whatever individual course they are studying, or assignment they are working on. Changing entire degree programmes is notoriously difficult, and assessment regimes are perhaps the most intransigent part of degree programmes. The early research showed just how dominant assessment is in determining students' approaches to their studies, so programme level assessment regimes are the proper focus for serious attempts to improve student learning.

The TESTA (Transforming the Experience of Students Through Assessment) programme took on the difficult and massive task of changing entire assessment regimes. TESTA is informed by qualitative and quantitative data collected in order to illuminate students' experience of their degree programme, underpinned by credible theory that helps teachers to make sense of this data. It is implemented through change processes that stand a chance of moving whole departments forward. And against all the odds, it has succeeded. More than a decade after the original small-scale project funding ran out, its implementation has continued to spread at an extraordinary rate, not just as a 'here today, gone tomorrow' project but by embedding itself in institutional quality assurance and enhancement policies and efforts. It has done this across many disciplines, in all kinds of universities, traditional and modern, managerial and collegial. It has spread far beyond the UK and operates in very different cultural environments, in different kinds of universities, in different higher education systems, facing different problems. It is evidence based and it is possible to tell if, by following the TESTA process, the assessment changes you have made across the degree programme have produced the improvements in student learning you had hoped for. It is the nearest to a comprehensive conceptual and practical framework for change in universities I have ever encountered. Tansy Jessop is the person responsible for the success of this extraordinary achievement, and this book is her testament. I wish I had been able to read it at the start of my career: it would have saved a lot of misdirected effort.

Readers with a penchant for theory have plenty to get their teeth into in the early chapters. Those who prefer to let student voices take the front seat have a rich tapestry to explore in the later chapters. It is not a 'how to do it' book but a 'how to understand how it works' book.

The research into assessment, as students experience it, that provided the underlying rationale for TESTA was undertaken in the context of conventional face-to-face higher education. The evolving implementation of TESTA as a research-based change process, intended to improve the learning environment for students by changing assessment practices, also took place in this face-to-face context. None of the case studies in that research were from the Open University, a distance learning university, for example. Of course, assessment regulations and briefings to students about assignments, criteria and marking, are usually written down, and are often expected to be understood and acted on without the need for face-to-face encounters. This is often a forlorn hope as informal social processes oil the wheels and frame students' responses. Many university teachers have also introduced elements of online and remote teaching and assessment practices into their courses in all kinds of blended variations, but they have usually still relied on students having idiosyncratic face-to-face access to teachers and to each other, even if more and more of the whole system was becoming mechanised and impersonal. But then the pandemic struck, and suddenly, many of these conventional assessment practices, and even the blended variations, were impossible to implement. Academic departments operate like 'communities of practice' and the mechanisms through which a novice student comes to understand the workings of their discipline or profession, and its values and standards, so they are able to focus their efforts on the important things, are predominantly social. The final section of the book looks to the future, examining the implications of the online assessment practices that emerged out of the challenges of COVID. If you want to avoid the student alienation, confusion and disengagement that often accompanies conventional assessment regimes and practices, then you need to try that much harder in online environments. The same principles apply, even if the details of effective practices are somewhat different. It is these underlying principles about the overwhelming influence of assessment on student learning that are at the core of this brilliant book.

Graham Gibbs

Acknowledgements

This book has been long in the making. I signed the contract in May 2019, but the idea dates to the early years of a project funded by the UK's Higher Education Academy (now Advance HE) in 2009. For more than a decade, 'Transforming the Experience of Students through Assessment' (TESTA) has encouraged universities to develop programmatic approaches to assessment and feedback based on evidence from its research process. TESTA's empirical research has given rise to theoretical advances in understanding student learning, reaching beyond 'approaches to learning' theory to more sociological interpretations of student learning. While most of TESTA's work has taken place in the UK, the themes of TESTA and its findings have had wider resonance globally, as interest in programmatic forms of assessment has grown.

I am grateful to the Higher Education Academy for funding TESTA and enabling us to lead a Change Academy to embed its programmatic approach in a group of institutions. The Staff and Educational Development Association (SEDA) promoted TESTA and hosted national and international events, which sustained its growth. As a result, TESTA gained momentum and became a self-sustaining project, led by a community of assessment enthusiasts who gather periodically to discuss its impact and interpret findings in their different contexts, most recently at its tenth anniversary in Dundee, Scotland. TESTA's funding ceased in 2012, and it has been kept alive because university leaders, academics, and academic developers recognise its value, can access its resources, and have developed it in their own contexts. TESTA would be nothing without the participating programmes, programme directors, academics, and students who have contributed thoughtfully to understanding the practice of assessment and feedback on their programmes.

There are many people whose insights, ideas, and research are reflected in the pages of the book. Graham Gibbs shared a lifetime of experience in educational development with me and the TESTA community. This project was his idea, and he is the architect of its approach. I have learnt more than I can say from his wise, humorous, and honest counsel, and I am grateful for his unstinting support. Yaz El Hakim, former co-leader, was energetic, insightful, and great fun to be with on our road trips. Both he and Angus Paddison supported me to embed TESTA in quality assurance processes at the University of Winchester. TESTA researchers and academic developers at Winchester made it a joy to collect data: I am grateful for the way they shaped the project, and particularly glad that Juliet Winter was able to lead and influence assessment practice at Winchester through TESTA. At Solent University, researchers brought fresh insights to TESTA, conducting a comparative analysis of formative assessment in different types of universities. At Bristol, Isabel Hopwood Stephens grasped all the opportunities of adapting TESTA's Assessment Experience Questionnaire, and colleagues from the curriculum enhancement programme have made the process and its evaluation ever more sophisticated. Judith Squires, the University of Bristol's DVC and Provost, has been unstinting in her support of TESTA as an enhancement initiative, and strengthened my resolve to complete this book.

Ronan O'Beirne will be pleased to see that the book proposal that he commented on in late 2018 has finally come to fruition. Ann McLoughlin copyedited many of my early chapters. The book is much better for her forensic eye on my grammatical lapses. I am grateful to Mark Allinson for his thoughtful, current, and often humorous comments on the book. The SRHE editors recommended revisions that have improved the clarity and scholarly quality of the manuscript before you. In revising the book, I was enormously grateful to Alan Penny for his wisdom, encouragement, and the kindness of his critical comments. I am equally grateful to Sabine Bohnacker for her thorough, exacting, and encouraging feedback.

Sarah Hyde at Routledge and James Wisdom, the Editor of the SEDA Series have offered their expertise and support to make the book more readable, scholarly, and contemporary. I am grateful for their patience, encouragement, and confidence that the book would see the light of day in the end. Thanks also to the production team especially Dueata Menon for their meticulous work in bringing the book to fruition.

Finally, I am appreciative of all my friends and family who have been long-suffering and supportive. Sam and Jonty read the book from cover to cover, keeping me grounded and pointing out clumsy rhetorical flourishes that needed to go. Tommy was constantly kind and empathetic and avoided reading the book. After a wealth of commentary from colleagues, friends, and family, the infelicities that remain are all mine.

April 2023
Tansy Jessop

Part I

TESTA's research and change process

Introduction

Why another book on assessment and feedback?

If you have picked up this book, there is a good chance that you are interested in assessment and feedback and want to make it more engaging for your students – either as a teacher, a programme director, an educational leader, or an academic developer. There is also a good chance that you view assessment and feedback as challenging and are concerned that students are dissatisfied with their experience of it. This book responds to the challenge by stepping back and asking 'what if' questions about improving assessment and feedback. What if the conventional approach of teachers designing assessment and feedback on their modules is the wrong place to start? What if assessment and feedback worked better for student learning when designed at the programme level? What if assessment and feedback developed student agency and engagement, and motivated students to make a personal connection with their work? This book sets out new ways of understanding assessment and feedback which are programmatic and encourage students to be agents of their own learning.

'Transforming the Experience of Students through Assessment' (TESTA) is a research and change process which uses an alternative starting point for addressing the challenges of assessment and feedback. Based on the premise that many problems with assessment and feedback have their roots in programme structures, TESTA draws on evidence, theory, and analysis to demonstrate the value and potential of taking a programme approach to designing assessment and feedback on modular degrees. TESTA has been widely used in UK universities, and has shown its applicability beyond the UK, in India, Australia, New Zealand, Ireland, and Malaysia, among other countries. While this book is based on research conducted mainly in the UK, it speaks more widely to common issues and problems.

TESTA introduces a different way of thinking about assessment and feedback, a method for understanding the impact of assessment and feedback on student learning, and practical insights about changing programme assessment patterns to foster student agency and engagement. Most assessment and feedback texts provide guidance for academics about design decisions made at the individual and module level, but there is very little guidance for academic leaders wanting to understand the impact of assessment and feedback

DOI: 10.4324/9780429347962-2

on the overall experience of students. TESTA provides insights into students' experience of assessment and feedback across their whole programme. It gives impetus to changing the way academics design assessment and feedback, traditionally a solitary and invisible pursuit, usually occurring at the module level, often behind the scenes of the more public activities of teaching (Forsyth 2023, pp. 5–6). It invites academics and educational leaders into more transparent, open, and shared decision-making about assessment and feedback beyond the module level.

A book about assessment and feedback requires careful demarcation of its purpose, audience, and value for the reader. Readers want to be reassured about the authority of claims about assessment and feedback, and how theory, evidence, and arguments come together to provide a compelling story which has resonance and practical application. In the following sections, I set out the basis and rationale for this book, establish its unique contribution to debates about the practice of assessment and feedback, and outline its structure so that the reader has an overview of what lies ahead.

Rationale

Most good ideas begin with a hunch, sometimes arising as an intuitive sense of what is happening beneath the surface of a problem (Polanyi 1966). The research underpinning this book began with a hunch that poor student experience of assessment and feedback was related as much to the structure of their degrees as to assessment pedagogies. TESTA was funded by the Higher Education Academy (2009–12) to investigate this hunch, underpinned by findings from small-scale exploratory work on the distinguishing features of assessment patterns across degree programmes in different types of institution (Gibbs and Dunbar-Goddet 2009). Chief among these findings was that the combination of modular design and learning outcomes was driving up assessment that measured student achievement in preference to assessment which helped students to learn:

> If alignment of assessment and learning outcomes is stressed, within a modular course, this almost inevitably increases the variety of assessment, increases the use of summatively assessed coursework, increases the total number of summative assessments, and in doing so, reduces the resources available for formative-only assessment.
>
> (Gibbs and Dunbar-Goddet 2009, p. 488)

The thesis that underpins TESTA is that modularisation has had negative consequences for student learning from assessment and feedback. The book sets out to explore and analyse the effects of modularity on student learning, proposing that it is not sufficient for individual teachers to design good assessments without attending to the structures in which assessment and feedback are embedded. Structures can play havoc with the best of pedagogic intentions, yet may go unnoticed as an assumed, almost invisible part of the way things are done. For example, the design of a brilliant and compelling formative assessment which helps students to learn but does not count towards students' overall grades may be ignored by students who have a competing summative assessment, which does count, on a concurrent module. In this example, structures have interfered with and invalidated good pedagogy.

Modularisation has operated in the United States for over a century and is used in New Zealand, Sweden, Scotland, and most European countries linked to the Bologna Process of transferable credits. Modules are designed with the purpose of enabling choice, flexibility, and student mobility between universities, courses, and countries (French 2015). They were widely adopted in UK universities in the 1980s and 1990s. Modules are units of content disaggregated from traditional linear degrees to form smaller blocks of teaching, often semester long, which can be sequenced to form a degree programme. While the amount of student choice varies depending on the nature of the degree, modular structures offer students the opportunity to study areas of interest to them, building a sense of agency and engagement as students curate their own degrees.

This book analyses evidence from TESTA to examine the impact of modular systems on student learning from assessment and feedback. In many countries, modular degrees have become the normal way students learn, with compelling arguments supporting their value. The following proposition statements outline a contrary view, that modularity has had negative consequences for student learning:

- Modules diminish the impetus for staff to plan and sequence assessment and feedback in an integrated way across a programme of study, making it more difficult for students to see the connections in their learning.
- Modular structures lead to higher summative assessment loads for students to validate relatively small blocks of teaching in credit-based systems.
- Formative assessment and feedback suffer because they compete for student attention with summative assessments on concurrent modules.
- Assessment and feedback designed in isolation on different modules lead to perverse effects for students, for example, repeated varieties of assessment types, competing deadlines, and uneven assessment demands.
- Students see feedback as confined to each module, making it more difficult to apply it to assessments on subsequent modules because of the timing of feedback and/or the variance in assessment types.
- Modular structures increase the variability of assessment and feedback practice, impeding consistency and leading to incoherent, uneven, and even unfair assessment loads for students.
- Students find it difficult to internalise standards where shared standards are assumed across and between modules, which may impede conceptions of progression between levels of study.

- Students often engage in frequent, small assessments on modules which feel routine and repetitive, and discourage ownership and engagement.
- Students may graduate with a fragmented understanding of their discipline because the whole programme is less than the sum of its modular parts.

Assessment and feedback matter for student outcomes and they influence the kinds of jobs students get and the futures they have. In a context where assessment and feedback have serious ramifications for students, this book aims to support academics and educational leaders to make sustainable and systemic improvements to the pedagogy of assessment. It expands on good principles, practices, and theories about how students learn from assessment and feedback by paying attention to a programme-level perspective of the student experience. It uses research from TESTA to seek to unlock some of the systemic problems of assessment and feedback, shifting the debate and the starting premise to students' experience at a programme level.

TESTA's contribution to the field of assessment and feedback

TESTA has contributed to the field of assessment and feedback in significant ways over the last decade. Its research findings call to a different approach in the design of assessment and feedback, with an emphasis on systematic and student-centred approaches at the programme level. Evidence from students has also advanced theoretical developments about alienation and engagement in students' learning from assessment and feedback.

TESTA's first contribution has been to place more emphasis on a whole programme perspective of assessment and feedback, in contrast to the prevailing focus on individual and modular best practice. This emphasis overlaps with and overarches thematic areas of assessment and feedback, for example on evaluative judgement, peer assessment, and authentic assessment. TESTA research investigates the whole assessment and feedback process as it operates on a programme of study, crossing the boundaries between modules and academic years to examine the nature of the assessment environment from a student perspective.

Taking a programme approach involves developing a shared philosophy of assessment and feedback linked to educational principles and best practice. It requires teams to work together on balancing assessment loads, varieties of assessment, sequencing feedback and summative tasks to maximise student learning and manage staff workloads. It may involve academics sacrificing successful modular approaches to ensure that the programme works well from a student perspective, for example, changing a regime of graded continuous assessment on one module to create time for students to engage with developmental tasks on other modules. Adopting a programmatic approach to assessment and feedback brings benefits in coherence, develops consistency, and connects core concepts across students' degrees. Translating instances of one-off brilliant assessment design on individual modules to the programme level raises the bar of assessment pedagogy more generally, as does trouble-shooting modular assessment which does not work well for students.

The second contribution has been a focus on understanding students' experience of assessment and feedback as the primary driver of the programme approach. TESTA research methods collect data from students, through a questionnaire and focus groups. These methods examine how patterns of assessment and feedback influence students' learning, their engagement and sense of agency, choices about managing workloads and exercising effort, understanding of assessment expectations, and their active use of feedback. TESTA explores how modular design of assessment and feedback influences students' dispositions to learn, persist, and exercise autonomy, all features of student agency (Stenalt and Lassesen 2022). The ecosystem of assessment can facilitate students' sense of agency by creating a coherent narrative and opportunities for them to shape their own learning. These structural features of assessment and feedback go beyond students' psychological state of being, encompassing the assessment environment within universities, and wider socio-cultural and political factors which may foster or impede students' sense of agency (Nieminen et al. 2022).

A programme approach positions assessment and feedback as central to designing a curriculum that makes sense for students, enabling and challenging them to become insiders in the discipline. It sees beyond the walls of modules, and is cognisant of sequencing, timing, volumes, and types of assessment, and the role of feedback for learning over time (Tomas and Jessop 2019). As part of a curriculum design process, a programme approach attends to how students learn and reflect, how and when they exercise agency; it creates opportunities for students to learn from misconceptions and mistakes, balances high- and low-stakes tasks, and uses assessment as the means to integrate conceptual and thematic ideas in the discipline.

The third contribution to the field of assessment and feedback is theoretical. TESTA advances a more contextual approach to understanding how students learn from assessment and feedback, drawing on sociological theories of alienation and engagement (Barnhardt and Ginns 2014; Case 2008; Mann 2005; 2001). It emphasises the influence of context on assessment and feedback practices including disciplinary traditions, modular degree structures, quality assurance regimes, and different institutional cultures. TESTA contributes to a deeper understanding of why students feel disconnected from their studies than *approaches to learning* theory. Its focus on students' sense of alienation and lack of agency in assessment and feedback is a prompt to action. The TESTA process engages with students, teachers, and programme teams to create engaging assessment environments and practices that enable students to regain a sense of connection and agency in their learning.

The socio-cultural context in which assessment and feedback take place is broader than university systems and processes (Nieminen et al. 2022).

Theories about alienation and engagement in higher education prompt wider analysis of the influence of social, economic, and cultural factors on students' experience of learning from assessment and feedback. This book provides an introductory analysis of wider factors and trends which contribute to student alienation in their assessment and feedback, such as the effect of mass higher education on student learning.

TESTA's fourth major contribution is to create an evidence-based and systematic change process involving programme teams and influencing university processes and pedagogic practices. There are few assessment and feedback projects that take a programme approach to changing assessment and feedback patterns, and even fewer where bottom-up research influences quality assurance processes to adopt pedagogically principled approaches. TESTA's student-centred and programmatic research enables programme teams to discuss fresh insights, both contradictory and confirmatory evidence about their students' experience as part of a developmental process. The facilitated debriefing initiates discussion with members of the programme team, who identify actions flowing from the TESTA case study that will be most beneficial for students and lead to more engaging assessment and feedback across the whole programme. The key feature of the change process is a programme team commitment to principled actions in response to evidence in the TESTA case study.

TESTA's work with programme teams has evolved into a theory of change based on practice and scholarship. It provides real-life examples of negotiating and sustaining systemic educational change in universities. The challenge of securing sustained change in response to evidence is magnified when working with academics, whose strengths lie in critique and argumentation, and who hold dear the value of autonomy (Buller 2015; Fullan and Scott 2009; Pfeffer and Sutton 2000). TESTA's theory of change explores the challenges of working with groups of academics who have different vested interests and personal commitments to their own practice. It presents strategies based on the experience of securing meaningful changes rooted in evidence and discussion, and offering guidance for those readers seeking to implement systemic assessment and feedback changes at scale (Jessop 2016).

How the book is organised: a guide for readers

Part 1: *TESTA's research and change process*

- The Introduction provides an overview of the book for the reader and sets out the unique contributions TESTA makes to the field of assessment and feedback.
- Chapter 1 explains the research methodology, outlining the research traditions that inform TESTA, the specific data sample on which the book is based, exploring ethical questions raised by the research, and walking the

reader through the process of data collection, analysis, and strategies used to represent data.

- Chapter 2 takes the reader through each element of the TESTA research method, outlining its value in evidencing programme patterns of assessment and feedback, as seen through the eyes of students. It explains and discusses both the research and the change process involved in conducting TESTA. The chapter directs the reader to appendices which elaborate aspects of TESTA, including various research instruments and anonymised examples of research outputs.

Part 2: *Alienation and engagement*

- Chapter 3 offers an alternative theoretical explanation for findings from TESTA about students' experience of assessment and feedback. Evidence from students resonates with ideas of alienation, in their depictions of passivity, repetition, meaninglessness, and lack of agency over their assessment, and their disconnection from feedback. This chapter outlines key sociological and psychological theories of alienation, and the revival of interest in alienation as a concept for understanding features of learning and teaching in higher education. It summarises pedagogic approaches which have the potential to shift students from a state of alienation to engagement.
- Chapter 4 provides an introductory overview of sources of alienation that arise from the policy and regulatory context that influence students' experience of, and the practice of assessment and feedback. It identifies four factors that contribute to student alienation: mass higher education; marketisation, modules, and metrics.

Part 3: *Engaging assessment and feedback: from analysis to practice*

- Chapter 5 analyses TESTA data about key design features of assessment: the balance of summative and formative assessment, varieties of assessment, and the proportion of examinations. It draws out the implications of these assessment patterns on student learning, engagement, and sense of agency, using qualitative data from TESTA research. The chapter proposes programmatic and pedagogic tactics to overcome alienation and strengthen student engagement with assessment and feedback.
- Chapter 6 examines the transactional and mechanistic relationship with feedback that students describe and critique in TESTA focus groups. It highlights four themes from the data: transmission of feedback as 'telling'; impersonal, mass-produced feedback devoid of relationship; episodic, one-off feedback lacking transferability; and a breakdown in trust about the quality of feedback. The chapter proposes practical solutions to the feedback impasse for each of these problems.

- Chapter 7 explores the pervasive influence of commonly accepted theories about how students internalise standards, including telling students what the standards are, transparent criteria, and positivist assumptions about objectivity. It examines barriers that stand in the way of students knowing what good looks like (marker variation, over-reliance on criteria; students having limited practice at making evaluative judgements). It proposes strategies that students identify as helpful in developing a nose for quality (dialogue, practice, observation).
- Chapter 8 engages with the challenge of change. It presents a theory of change based on conducting TESTA in universities with distributed and devolved structures. It draws on scholarly literature about academic cultures, resistance to change, and organisational change. The chapter offers principles for bringing about educational change with programme teams.

Part 4: *The future: new horizons and challenges*

- Epilogue: this brief closing section reflects on the relevance of TESTA in a post-pandemic world. It examines developments that have occurred and reflects on tensions that the pandemic brought into focus, suggesting ways in which programme approaches to assessment might help to address them.

References

Barnhardt, B., and P. Ginns. 2014. An alienation-based framework for student experience in higher education: New interpretations of past observations in student learning theory. *Higher Education* 68: 789–805.

Buller, J. L. 2015. *Change Leadership in Higher Education*. San Francisco, CA. Jossey-Bass.

Case, J. M. 2008. Alienation and engagement: Development of an alternative theoretical framework for understanding student learning. *Higher Education* 55: 789–805.

Forsyth, R. 2023. *Confident Assessment in Higher Education*. London. Sage.

French, S. 2015. 'The Benefits and Challenges of Modular Higher Education Curricula'. Issues and Ideas Paper. Melbourne Centre for the Study of Higher Education. University of Melbourne.

Fullan, M., and G. Scott. 2009. *Turnaround Leadership for Higher Education*. San Francisco, CA. Jossey-Bass.

Gibbs, G., and H. Dunbar-Goddet. 2009. Characterising programme-level assessment environments that support learning. *Assessment & Evaluation in Higher Education* 34 (4): 481–489.

Jessop, T. 2016. 'Inspiring transformation through TESTA's programme approach'. In D. Carless, S. Bridges, C. Ka Yuk Chan, and R. Glofcheski. (Eds) *Scaling up Assessment for Learning in Higher Education*. Singapore. Springer.

Mann, S. J. 2001. Alternative perspectives on the student experience: Alienation and engagement. *Studies in Higher Education* 26 (1): 7–19.

Mann, S. J. 2005. Alienation in the learning environment: A failure of community? *Studies in Higher Education* 30 (1): 43–55, DOI: 10.1080/0307507052000307786

Nieminen, J. H., J. Tai, D. Boud, and M. Henderson 2022. Student agency in feedback: Beyond the individual. *Assessment & Evaluation in Higher Education* 47 (1): 95–108, DOI: 10.1080/02602938.2021.1887080

Pfeffer, J., and R. I. Sutton. 2000. *The Knowing-Doing Gap*. Boston MA. Harvard Business School Press.

Polanyi, M. 1966. *The Tacit Dimension*. New York, NY. Doubleday and Co.

Stenalt, M. H., and B. Lassesen. 2022. Does student agency benefit student learning? A systematic review of higher education research. *Assessment & Evaluation in Higher Education* 47 (5): 653–669, DOI: 10.1080/02602938.2021.1967874

Tomas, C., and T. Jessop. 2019. Struggling and juggling: A comparison of student assessment loads across research and teaching-intensive universities. *Assessment & Evaluation in Higher Education* 44 (1): 1–10, DOI: 10.1080/02602938.2018.1463355

Chapter 1

A research methodology for transforming students' experience

Setting out the challenges

Transforming the Experience of Students through Assessment (TESTA) is a large multi-disciplinary higher education project with a wide reach and a relatively long history. Writing a scholarly book on a complex and distributed project is methodologically challenging. TESTA has run for 14 years in more than 50 universities, many of which are in the UK. This chapter sets out the project leader's position in the research, outlines the research traditions which inform TESTA's approach, and explores the influence of multiple researchers working in and across different institutions on the overall approach taken. It describes the data sample on which the book is based, explores ethical questions posed by the research, and outlines the process of data collection, analysis, and representation.

The rationale for TESTA is to improve student learning through analysing assessment and feedback patterns on programmes of study in different disciplines from a holistic student perspective (Jessop et al. 2014a; Jessop and Tomas 2017). Evidence from TESTA is the catalyst for systemic and educationally principled changes to patterns of assessment and feedback on whole programmes of study. TESTA researchers collect qualitative and quantitative data from students about their experience of assessment and feedback. This illuminates themes about key aspects of assessment and feedback and, when triangulated with data about the planned curriculum in the audit, highlights contradictions, problems, and ambiguities, and invites discussion about best practice. The dialogic conversation with programme teams over the data surfaces pedagogic insights about assessment and feedback and is intended to lead to change-oriented actions (Jessop et al. 2014b; Jessop 2016, 2017). Actions most often include rebalancing formative and summative assessment (Wu and Jessop 2018), sequencing varieties of assessment, developing strategies to encourage students taking agency and using feedback, and strengthening students' capacity to evaluate the quality of their own and others' work (Jessop 2019). A critical element of changes made is that they occur at the programme-level rather than only on individual assessments or within single modules (Jessop 2017).

DOI: 10.4324/9780429347962-3

The nature of a programme approach presents its own set of theoretical challenges. In undertaking the process, TESTA facilitators grow in their understanding and familiarity with key areas in the literature, becoming well-versed with debates about and educational principles related to assessment design, feedback, and internalising standards. They acquire the skills to engage programme teams in principled assessment and feedback design, to challenge practices which lead to fragmented, disconnected, and superficial learning, and to suggest alternative approaches to realise student learning from assessment. There is a further challenge, which is that TESTA facilitators become familiar with disciplinary practices, 'ways of thinking and acting' (Kreber 2010; Shulman 2005), and their effect on assessment and feedback (Jessop and Maleckar 2016). Respecting disciplinary approaches to assessment and feedback requires discernment: there is a distinction between unique approaches which are the best and only way to assess in a discipline, and practices which are valued simply because they are 'the way it has always been done'. TESTA facilitators grow in their capacity to distinguish between the two, and in their sophistication and confidence at nudging, suggesting alternatives, asking questions, and teasing out the disciplinary rationale for approaches. Given this wide-ranging hinterland, this book necessarily draws on a range of theory and practice literature about assessment and feedback and educational change.

The challenge of 'positioned' research

TESTA is a higher education research project which has drawn on the collective wisdom, knowledge, and experience of its team members, and of experts in the field (Gibbs and Dunbar-Goddet 2009; Jessop et al. 2011, 2014b). While TESTA has been conceptualised and delivered by a team of academics, researchers, and academic developers, it is nevertheless positioned: 'a view from somewhere' (Diversi 1998). There is an expectation of social researchers in the qualitative tradition to make clear their positioning so that readers are aware of subjectivities in interpretation (Dean et al. 2018; Denzin and Lincoln 1994; Lincoln and Guba 1985). Even so, 'positioned' research often carries a stigma as those who conduct it are seen to be too close to the subject or participants to maintain the necessary critical distance to be objective in their findings (Jones and Bartunek 2021). However, being positioned has some advantages. A researcher's personal connection brings experience, expertise, and depth which can add to its trustworthiness and enhance the quality and impact of research, rather than detract from it (Jones and Bartunek 2021). Responsible research practice overturns notions of proximity or position by providing a transparent account of method. This allows the researcher and writer 'to know "something" in depth, without claiming to know everything' (Richardson 2000, p. 928), as argued here:

In some ways, "knowing" is easier, however, because postmodernism recognizes the situational limitations of the knower. Qualitative writers are off the hook, so to speak. They don't have to try to play God, writing as disembodied omniscient narrators claiming universal, atemporal general knowledge; they can eschew the questionable metanarrative of scientific objectivity and still have plenty to say as situated speakers, subjectivities engaged in knowing/telling about the world as they perceive it.

(Richardson 2000, p. 928)

Richardson (2000) takes transparency one step further in arguing that researchers from every tradition need to reflect on their stances, for all knowledge generation entails making choices, selection, and the handling and interpretation of data. It is a mistake to assume that research decisions in the sciences are somehow value-free and without human mediation (Palmer 1993; Polanyi 1966). Based on both qualitative and quantitative methods, TESTA's research processes are explained in this chapter to assure readers of their trustworthiness and in the spirit of seeing research as a partial, human enterprise.

TESTA is a mixed methods approach with triangulation between a psychometrically validated questionnaire (Batten et al. 2019; Wu and Jessop 2018), a programme audit, and qualitative data from students. The nature of TESTA data has required choices about focus. The focus on qualitative data in the book is deliberate: it is the most powerful way to bring the voices of students to life and illuminate themes in the data. These themes are supported by quantitative findings from the audit and AEQ which have been published previously (Jessop and Maleckar 2016; Jessop and Tomas 2017; Jessop et al. 2014a). Choices about data lead to stylistic choices about representation. In the book, I prefer the active voice over the passive; to use metaphor to illustrate points; and to write in the first person where it is necessary to show the hand of the agent (Richardson 1990; Richardson 2000). These stylistic decisions are intended to make the book more readable (Becker 2007; Goodall 2000; Sword 2009; 2013). They also hint at epistemological framing in a book about agency. However, I have sought to balance the idea of authorial agency with the need not to get in the way of telling a compelling yet scholarly story.

Research traditions underpinning TESTA

TESTA research draws on three traditions in the collection, analysis, and interpretation of qualitative data. The first is grounded theory with its data-driven and inductive emphasis (Glaser and Strauss 1967; Strauss 1987). The tools of grounded theory are used in TESTA: simultaneous data collection, analysis, coding, and memo-writing. The derivation of codes and categories from data is central to TESTA researchers' thematic analysis, building up a picture of students' experience of assessment and feedback. Grounded theory reveals invisible assessment processes by making them transparent through this iterative process of constant comparison, from the detail of data to developing a more holistic picture or storyline (Charmaz 2017). Grounded theory is commonly used in educational research, arguably the 'paradigm of choice' for qualitative researchers in education (Thomas and James 2006, p. 768). Our analysis uses some of the techniques of grounded theory but does not follow the original and rigid framing of grounded theory to its logical conclusion: a theory-free world of data-driven claims in local contexts with little relationship to wider structural forces (Thomas and James 2006). Instead, TESTA practice mirrors *constructivist grounded theory*, the contemporary revisionist approach, in its emphasis on reflexivity, positioning, and situating research in its historical, social, and situational context (Charmaz 2017, p. 299).

The second is the interpretive or hermeneutic tradition of research, which seeks to read between the lines of social phenomena to make sense of them, treating social encounters as texts to be read and interpreted for meaning. Interpretive research goes back and forth from granular stories to the big picture (Cousin 2009), using some of the tools of ethnography to make sense of data (Geertz 1973; Goodall 2000): observation, reading between the lines for meaning, looking for hidden storylines, cross-referencing with other researchers and critical friends. As in ethnography, the challenge is making the familiar strange with the purpose of perceiving social realities differently. The TESTA audit takes the familiar world of the module seen from the perspective of the lecturer and enables academics to move from part (the module) to the whole (the programme), seen from the perspective of the students. One of the main challenges of interpretive research is that it seeks to provide coherent explanations for phenomena, and in the process, researchers may fail to notice or bring to the surface contradictory interpretations and rival hypotheses. TESTA research wrestles with the challenge of telling a compelling story with a coherent interpretation of students' experiences of assessment and feedback, while attending to alternative readings of the data. The format of the TESTA case study provides scope for contradictory student voices in the analysis of the qualitative data (see Appendix A).

TESTA is a research and change process, so it is unsurprising that the third tradition it draws on is action research (Reason and Bradbury 2006; Wicks and Reason 2009). Reason and Bradbury (2006) describe the purpose of action research as bringing an action orientation to the overly quietist tradition of knowledge generation, in a quest to move from language to action. Action researchers engage with participants in cycles of action and reflection 'to address issues of practical and pressing importance in their lives' (Wicks and Reason 2009, p. 244). The action research tradition spans from appreciative inquiry looking for the positive core within organisations and communities (Bushe 2007; Cooperider et al. 2008) to critical theory and emancipatory forms of action research drawing on the works of Habermas (Kemmis 2001). It is a broad-church approach, represented in TESTA with both the use of positively framed questions to academics and students and critically framed questions about problems in assessment and feedback. Action research is designed to generate 'fresh understandings and new practices' (Cousin 2009, p. 155). It surfaces these through inquiry in a spirit of openness and reflection. Like action research, the aim of

TESTA is to open a 'communicative space' to reach mutual understanding and consensus, through mediating general and specific needs in response to data (Wicks and Reason 2009, p. 245). This plays out especially in relation to staff negotiations about surrendering some modular autonomy for the greater good of the programme, with the practical outcome of creating more connected assessment and feedback for students.

Translating research traditions into TESTA practice

The main question posed here is how researchers in a variety of institutional contexts have translated TESTA methods to achieve a common purpose through a shared methodology and approach. As in any long-running research project, different researchers with multiple subjectivities, backgrounds, and biographies can work together in parallel to achieve a common purpose in a large-scale research project, given the right conditions.

The data on which this book is based comes from 60 programmes of study in 14 universities. There were 12 researchers involved in collecting, analysing, and interpreting the data on these programmes, all of whom were trained in the TESTA methodology, the techniques of data analysis, and qualitative software use. The researchers conducting TESTA came from a variety of different backgrounds, research traditions, and from several countries, including the UK, India, Bangladesh, and China. Against the backdrop of this diversity, the consistent framework of the TESTA methods and the project team's oversight of the process of data collection, interpretation, and analysis have led to a common approach to conducting TESTA, ensuring comparability of data sets.

Members of the TESTA leadership team trained researchers through a combination of workshops and one-to-one mentoring over time. In a few institutions, a cascade method of training occurred. For example, in one, a TESTA leader worked with a UK head of an academic development centre at a large research-intensive university to explain the methods, who subsequently trained two consultants to undertake TESTA on six programmes in her university. In another university, an academic developer sought help and advice from members of the TESTA team in carrying out the methods with two programmes. The TESTA process was slightly more devolved in these two institutions, leading to slight variance in the style of case studies. In one, there was more emphasis on statistical analysis of the Assessment Experience Questionnaire, and a more traditional representation of the focus group data with plenty of interpretive text framing a few thematically analysed quotations. In the other, there was more emphasis on qualitative data and its thematic analysis. In both cases, there is sufficient comparability of data to warrant their inclusion in the data set.

In a further institution, academic developers trained ten graduate interns to work under the supervision of two TESTA researchers to facilitate focus groups and undertake thematic analysis of the data (Jessop et al. 2018). Graduate interns provided an interesting departure from the more usual practice of a professional researcher conducting focus groups. The interns were much closer in experience (and in age) to the students they were leading through their focus group activities. Reading between the lines, the language in these focus groups was more informal than usual, and students' responses were less guarded than in those where there may have been a more starkly perceived power dynamic between researcher and participant.

One reason for the comparability of the TESTA data is the consistency of the three research methods used to gather data: the audit, assessment experience questionnaire, and focus groups. However, over time, the research instruments used in carrying out the methods on TESTA have evolved in response to the dialogic process of feedback, mainly through debriefings with programme teams, conference questions and discussions, and evaluations. The paradox of research methods is that they may be both consistent and yet evolve as questions and insights arise in the analysis, in interaction with user-groups, and through the publication of data and findings. Evolution to refine and improve research instruments is necessary for good research. One example is the revision of the Assessment Experience Questionnaire (Batten et al. 2019; Wu and Jessop 2018). Developments in the AEQ reflect the changing focus from the psychologically based 'approaches to learning' theory to more sociological theories of alienation and engagement (Barnhardt and Ginns 2014; Case 2008; Mann 2001). They incorporate findings from TESTA about formative assessment and integrated assessment design, pursued further in AEQ V5.1, developed at the University of Bristol (see Appendix D).

Aside from training and mentoring researchers in using its research methods, the TESTA website, an Open Educational Resource (OER), acts as a consistent source for conducting the research. It contains clear guides and research instruments for undertaking TESTA, such as a step-by-step guide to auditing a programme, the Assessment Experience Questionnaire, and a common set of focus group questions. In addition, the website contains guides to various aspects of data collection and analysis, case studies, and exemplars of research outcomes.

Ethics

In each of the 14 universities represented in the book, the methodology has undergone scrutiny to ensure that the research conformed to ethical protocols. Depending on different Universities' ethical systems, this scrutiny may have been through a committee or be signed off by the Chair of that committee. Ethical scrutiny affords protection to research participants about the right to withdraw, data confidentiality and anonymity. In practice, this means that students are fully informed of the purpose of the project, their voluntary role as participants, and their consent is recorded in writing. A similar contract about confidentiality, anonymity, the right to withdraw, and data protection was signed by programme directors who participated in semi-structured interviews to evaluate the effectiveness of TESTA as a method. The analysis of TESTA data honours the contract with research participants with all universities and programmes having been anonymised. Ethical data handling also implies that data are analysed in a transparent way, using consistent and trustworthy methods.

As with any large cross-institutional project, the ethical scrutiny entails sharing of each university's data with the project team for the benefit of wider understanding and publication of data beyond single institutions. The protocols of anonymity and confidentiality extend to avoiding identifying universities when citing data, to protect the reputation of a university or a subject discipline at a university, and the research participants.

The sample

This book is based on two sets of data: the first from 14 universities, 12 in the UK and two in India, representing a wide range of disciplines. This data set consists of 60 TESTA programme audits based on two-hour conversations with programme directors about assessment and feedback in the planned curriculum, triangulated with qualitative data from 102 focus groups facilitated with 552 final year undergraduate students. Researchers have triangulated quantitative data from the Assessment Experience Questionnaire (AEQ) representing 2,434 final year undergraduate students on the same 60 programmes with audit and focus group data in TESTA case studies. Students completed AEQ questionnaires at the start of lectures to maximise participation, either paper-based or online. The questionnaire data contributes to the overall interpretation of findings about assessment patterns and is a core part of the TESTA research (Jessop and Maleckar 2016; Jessop et al. 2014a; Wu and Jessop 2018). Researchers recruited participants for focus groups during questionnaire sessions and offered a small financial compensation for their time.

I have chosen not to emphasise the AEQ data in the book for two reasons: the first is that researchers have used different versions of the questionnaire as the project has evolved (Batten et al. 2018; Wu and Jessop 2018); the second is a conscious decision to focus on the qualitative data from students to bring to life their experience of assessment and feedback. Elsewhere, I have published peer-reviewed articles on analysing numerical data from the audit (Jessop and Tomas 2017; Tomas and Jessop 2018) and on drawing statistical inferences from the data (Jessop and Maleckar 2016; Jessop et al. 2014; Wu and Jessop 2018). While the focus of this book is on the qualitative data in the TESTA research sample, there are instances where it cross-references to numerical findings from the audit and statistical findings from the AEQ to support the case being made.

The second data set consists of semi-structured interviews with programme directors at five universities in the UK. The purpose of this research was to evaluate the effectiveness of TESTA as a research and change process. Researchers conducted the first phase of interviews with ten participating programme directors during the funded project period (2009–2012). These interviews took place in 2011/12 and reflected on 'before' and 'after' processes, where each programme had undergone TESTA twice: first as a catalyst for change, and second to understand how changes had affected students' experience of assessment and feedback. The second phase of interviews took place in 2020. A senior TESTA researcher conducted semi-structured interviews with six programme directors who had participated in the TESTA process once, that is, without a 'before' and 'after' TESTA process. These interviews were conducted on Zoom during the global pandemic. The purpose of both sets of interviews was to evaluate the effectiveness of TESTA, with the first phase providing accountability to an external funding agency, the Higher Education Academy (HEA), now Advance HE; the second reporting on internal funding for TESTA to the institution concerned.

Qualitative data analysis

All the student focus groups conformed to a similar pattern of themed questions (see Appendix E). TESTA researchers recorded focus group discussions and transcribed them, aside from a minority of cases where there was provision for professional transcription in the budget. The researchers generally used Computer-Assisted Qualitative Data Analysis (CAQDA) to assist with the analysis of data. CAQDA is very helpful in organising large data sets, but it can lead to fragmentation and the clerical treatment of coding (Holloway and Jefferson 2013, pp. 63–65). However, in most cases, the act of transcribing brought researchers closer to the whole structure of the conversation, aided by the memory of facilitating the focus group and taking notes. This to some extent mitigated against fragmentation.

In analysing the data, researchers coded the data as a way of getting to grips with it: 'to understand it, to spend time with it, and ultimately to render it into something we can report' (Elliott 2018, p. 2851). TESTA researchers coded data using both the *a priori* codes or prefigured codes which link to the scales on the AEQ and the focus group schedule, and emergent codes in line with a generative grounded theory approach, being open to listening for emergent ideas related to students' experience of assessment and feedback. They distilled themes from the codes using a recursive process of surveying the data, coding, and categorising the codes into broader bundles of meaning, using the techniques of grounded theory. They recorded the frequencies of codes across transcripts from each programme to illustrate the weight of discussion in focus groups. At times, the codes reflected commonly used phrases by students, for example, primary education students described the difference in tone between lecturer feedback with their ideal of giving encouraging and developmental feedback to schoolchildren. This led to coding best practice in feedback as 'two stars and a wish' to reflect the use of this phrase by students. Similarly, students often referenced marker variation and inconsistency of practice, which were coded using students' own words.

Researchers used a similar approach to transcribing, analysing, and coding interview data in semi-structured interviews with programme directors. The main difference was the depth and single voice of each semi-structured interview compared to the discursive group conversations within focus groups. In the analysis of student focus groups and programme leader interviews, researchers complemented technical and systematic coding with the ethnographic and intuitive eye of reading between the lines of the text, while seeking not to distort its shape. An awareness that 'participants construct stories that support their interpretation of themselves' (Bell 2002, p. 209) was part of a wider understanding that personal stories take place in a social context (Clandinin 2006). The second set of evaluation interviews about TESTA took place during the global pandemic with the result that all the interviews were recorded on Zoom, making it challenging to do the ethnographic work of interpreting cues of gesture, hesitation, and body language in an interview setting.

Representing qualitative data

Representing qualitative data presents researchers with choices about how best to honour the voices of participants, exercise fidelity, and bring participant viewpoints and stories to life. The creative representation of qualitative data is the subject of debate about the format of texts which tell a compelling story, invite confirmation and contestation, yet remain faithful to the findings (Becker 2007; Goodall 2000; Richardson 1990, 2000; Sword 2009, 2013).

Conventional education and social science texts privilege interpretation in the representation of research findings and use respondent quotations sparingly to illustrate themes and issues arising from the data. Richardson's provocative confession that she had yawned her way through 30 years of reading social science texts, often on riveting topics, first arrested my interest when I was writing my PhD (Richardson 1994). It was the spur for my decision to write up some of the interview data as poetry (Jessop 1997; Jessop and Penny 1999). This decision was not purely stylistic: it was an attempt to use a different format to bring the stories and voices of research participants to life. In outlining the risks of experimental texts, Richardson describes how conventional writing formats hold extraordinary symbolic power over how texts are written, which texts are worthy of publication, and what value is assigned to them:

> Each of these conventions favours – creates and sustains – a particular vision of what constitutes knowledge. The conventions hold tremendous material and symbolic power over social scientists. Using them increases the

probability of one's work being accepted into "core" social science journals, but they are not prima facie evidence of greater- or lesser-truth value or significance than social science writing using other conventions.

(Richardson 2000, p. 928)

As Appendix A shows, the first two sections of the TESTA case study contain numerical data in tables from the audit and Assessment Experience Questionnaire, and textual data about the programme audit. The third section represents thematically analysed focus group data in a narrative format using authorial headlines followed by illustrative student quotations. The headlines form a narrative thread which is populated by student quotations under each sub-heading. This format privileges student voice data over authorial interpretation. The effect is to strengthen academics' engagement with student voice data, which is often the strongest impetus for action on broader themes raised in the TESTA data. Interviews with Programme Leaders to evaluate the TESTA process confirmed that the words of students had often given them the authority and impetus to act on the data. This approach resonates with the view that student voice is a vital component in shaping students' learning and assessment, and influential for academics (Buckley 2018).

TESTA case studies privilege student voice, with all the vibrance and emotional freight of students' words about their programme at the front and centre of the narrative. In similar vein to the feminist arguments about the need for emotion to be allowed into the academy in the anthropological work of Ruth Behar (1997), the case studies allow emotion into the discussion through the words of students in the thematically analysed qualitative data. The programme debriefing invites readers, the academics teaching the students, to engage with the TESTA case study as a programme team. Academics laugh, they gasp in indignation, they smile at the warmth of student praise, and they wave their hands in protestation at misunderstandings, as they pick their way through the story of the themed qualitative data. The impact of privileging student voice within a creative format is to enliven the discussion, and to deepen readers' appreciation of issues being raised in the research data. Evaluation interviews with Programme Directors point to moments in the debriefing and in reflecting on students' words afterwards that are the catalysts for change.

A brief synopsis

This chapter outlines the challenges of analysing data from a large, complex, distributed education project, led by the author. It examines notions of positionality for the qualitative researcher and argues that all research involves human choice and is therefore positioned. The chapter gives a transparent account of the traditions on which TESTA research stands, and describes who undertook the research in different universities, and how comparability of research data and methods has been achieved. The chapter describes the sample, ethics, and data collection approaches, and indicates authorial choice about which data to privilege in the book. The final sections examine how qualitative data is analysed and represented in fresh and vibrant ways to capture the imagination of readers, and to spur on changes in practice.

References

Barnhardt, B., and P. Ginns. 2014. An alienation-based framework for student experience in higher education: New interpretations of past observations in student learning theory. *Higher Education* 68: 789–805.

Batten, J., T. Jessop, and P. Birch. 2019. Doing what it says on the tin? A psychometric evaluation of the assessment experience questionnaire. *Assessment & Evaluation in Higher Education* 44 (2): 309–320, DOI: 10.1080/02602938.2018.1499867

Becker, H. 2007. *Writing for Social Scientists.* Chicago. University of Chicago Press.

Behar, R. 1997. *The Vulnerable Observer: Anthropology that Breaks your Heart.* Boston. Beacon Press.

Bell, J. S. 2002. Narrative inquiry: More than just telling stories. *TESOL Quarterly* 36 (2): 207–213. https://doi.org/10.2307/3588331

Buckley, A. 2018. The ideology of student engagement research. *Teaching in Higher Education* 23 (6): 718–732, DOI: 10.1080/13562517.2017.1414789

Bushe, G. 2007. Appreciative inquiry is not (just) about the positive. *OD Practitioner* 39 (4): 30–35.

Case, J. M. 2008. Alienation and engagement: Development of an alternative theoretical framework for understanding student learning. *Higher Education* 55: 789–805.

Charmaz, K. 2017. Constructivist grounded theory. *The Journal of Positive Psychology* 12 (3): 299–300, DOI: 10.1080/17439760.2016.1262612

Clandinin, J. D. 2006. Narrative inquiry: A methodology for studying lived experience. *Research Studies in Music Education* 27: 44–55.

Cooperider, D., D. Whitney, and J. Stavros. 2008. *Appreciative Inquiry Handbook: For Leaders of Change.* Brunswick, OH. Crown Custom Publishing.

Cousin, G. 2009. *Researching Learning in Higher Education.* Abingdon. Routledge.

Dean, J., P. Furness, D. Verrier, H. Lennon, C. Bennett, and S. Spencer 2018. Desert island data: An investigation into researcher positionality. *Qualitative Research* 18 (3): 273–289. https://doi.org/10.1177/1468794117714612

Denzin, N. K., & Y.S. Lincoln (Eds.). 1994. *Handbook of qualitative research.* Thousand Oaks, California. Sage Publications.

Diversi, M. 1998. Glimpses of street life: Represented experience through short stories. *Qualitative Inquiry* 4 (2): 131–147.

Elliott, V. 2018. Thinking about the coding process in qualitative data analysis. *The Qualitative Report* 23 (11): 2850–2861. https://doi.org/10.46743/2160-3715/2018.3560

Geertz, C. 1973. *The Interpretation of Cultures.* New York. NY. Basic books.

Gibbs, G., and H. Dunbar-Goddet 2009. Characterising programme-level assessment environments that support learning. *Assessment & Evaluation in Higher Education* 34 (4): 481–489.

Glaser, B. G., and A. L. Strauss 1967. *The Discovery of Grounded Theory: Strategies for Qualitative Research.* New York, NY. Aldine.

Goodall, H. L. 2000. *Writing the New Ethnography.* London. AltaMira Press.

Holloway, W., and T. Jefferson 2013. *Doing Qualitative Research Differently: A Psychosocial Approach.* London. Sage.

Jessop, T. 1997. '*Towards a grounded theory of teacher development: a study of the narratives of rural primary teachers in Kwazulu-Natal*'. Unpublished PhD Thesis. University of Southampton.

Jessop, T. 2016. Seven years and still no itch – Why TESTA keeps going. *Educational Developments* 17 (3): 5–8.

Jessop, T. 2017. 'Inspiring transformation through TESTA's programme approach', In D. Carless, S. Bridges, C. Ka Yuk Chan, and R. Glofcheski. (Eds) *Scaling Up Assessment for Learning in Higher Education.* Singapore. Springer.

Jessop, T. 2019. 'Changing the narrative: A programme approach to assessment through TESTA. Chapter 3' (pp. 36–49). In C. Bryan and K. Clegg. (Eds) *Innovative Assessment in Higher Education.* Abingdon. Routledge.

Jessop, T., Y. El Hakim, and G. Gibbs. 2011. Research inspiring change. *Educational Developments* 12 (4): 12–16.

Jessop, T., Y. El Hakim, and G. Gibbs. 2014a. The whole is greater than the sum of its parts: A large-scale study of Students' learning in response to different programme assessment patterns. *Assessment & Evaluation in Higher Education* 39 (1): 73–88.

Jessop, T., Y. El Hakim, and G. Gibbs. 2014b. TESTA in 2014: A way of thinking about assessment and feedback. *Educational Developments* 14 (3): 21–24.

Jessop, T., and B. Maleckar. 2016. The influence of disciplinary assessment patterns on student learning: A comparative study. *Studies in Higher Education* 41 (4): 696–711, DOI: 10.1080/03075079.2014.943170.

Jessop, T., and A. J. Penny. 1999. A story behind a story: Developing strategies for making sense of teacher narratives. *International Journal of Social Research Methodology* 2 (3): 213–230, DOI: 10.1080/136455799295023

Jessop, T., C. Saunders, and C. Pontin. 2018. The challenges of academic development as a first graduate job: 'am i doing it right?. *International Journal for Academic Development* 24 (4): 317–329, DOI: 10.1080/1360144X.2018.1555758

Jessop, T., and C. Tomas. 2017. The implications of programme assessment patterns for student learning. *Assessment & Evaluation in Higher Education* 42 (6): 990–999, DOI: 10.1080/02602938.2016.1217501

Jones, E. B., and J. M. Bartunek. 2021. Too close or optimally positioned? The value of personally relevant research. *Academy of Management Perspectives* 35, 335–346. https://doi.org/10.5465/amp.2018.0009

Kemmis, S. 2001. Exploring the relevance of critical theory for action research: Emancipatory action research in the footsteps of Jürgen Habermas. In P. Reason and H. Bradbury. (Eds) *Handbook of Action Research: Participative Inquiry and Practice* (pp. 91–102). London: SAGE.

Kreber, C. (Ed). 2010. *The University and Its Disciplines: Teaching and Learning Within and Beyond Disciplinary Boundaries.* Abingdon. Routledge Taylor and Frances.

Lincoln, Y., and E. Guba 1985. *Naturalistic Inquiry.* Newbury Park, CA. Sage.

Mann, S. J. 2001. Alternative perspectives on the student experience: Alienation and engagement. *Studies in Higher Education* 26 (1): 7–19.

Palmer, P. 1993. *To Know as We Are Known: Education as a Spiritual Journey*. San Francisco, CA. Harper One.

Polanyi, M. 1966. *The Tacit Dimension*. Chicago, IL. University of Chicago Press.

Reason, P., and H. Bradbury. (Eds). 2006. *Handbook of Action Research*. London. Sage.

Richardson, L. 1990. *Writing Strategies: Reaching Diverse Audiences* Vol. 21. Thousand Oaks, CA. Sage.

Richardson, L. (1994). Writing: A method of inquiry. In N. K. Denzin & Y. S. Lincoln (Eds.), *Handbook of qualitative research* (pp. 516–529). Thousand Oaks, CA: Sage.

Richardson, L. 2000. 'Writing: A method of inquiry' Chapter 36 (pp. 923–948). In N. K. Denzin and Y. S. Lincoln. (Eds) *Handbook of Qualitative Research*. Second Edition. Thousand Oaks, CA. Sage.

Shulman, L. S. 2005. Signature pedagogies in the professions. *Daedalus* 134 (3): 52–59. http://www.jstor.org/stable/20027998

Strauss, A. 1987. *Qualitative Analysis for Social Scientists*. Cambridge. Cambridge University Press.

Sword, H. 2009. Writing higher education differently: A manifesto on style. *Studies in Higher Education* 34 (3): 319–336.

Sword, H. 2013. *Stylish Academic Writing*. Cambridge. MA. Harvard University Press.

Thomas, G., and D. James 2006. Reinventing grounded theory: Some questions about theory, ground and discovery. *British Educational Research Journal*, 32: 767–795. https://doi.org/10.1080/01411920600989412

Tomas, C. & T. Jessop 2019. Struggling and juggling: a comparison of student assessment loads across research and teaching-intensive universities. *Assessment & Evaluation in Higher Education*. 44:1, 1–10, DOI: 10.1080/02602938.2018.1463355

Wicks, P. G., and P. Reason. 2009. Initiating action research: Challenges and paradoxes of opening communicative space. *Action Research* 7 (3): 243–262. https://doi.org/10.1177/1476750309336715

Wu, Q., and T. Jessop. 2018. Formative assessment: Missing in action in both research-intensive and teaching focused universities? *Assessment and Evaluation in Higher Education* 43 (7): 1019–1031, DOI: 10.1080/02602938.2018.1426097

Chapter 2

The TESTA method

Tools, techniques, and approaches

Introduction

Transforming the Experience of Students through Assessment (TESTA) is a research process designed to provide an in-depth perspective of students' overall experience of assessment and feedback on a programme of study. Its purpose is to make visible programme assessment patterns through research data, and to use that evidence as the catalyst for change. TESTA consists of three research methods: an audit, the Assessment Experience Questionnaire, and focus groups with students. Together, these methods provide insights into the programme assessment environment seen through student eyes. They chart the typical student experience over the course of a modular degree from a programme perspective. Discussion of the TESTA case study with the programme team is a key moment in the process. It provides impetus for change, enabling individual academics to see how single modular decisions impact students' experience in the round.

This chapter explains how TESTA is implemented, providing an overview of the methods, tools, and techniques used in both the research and change process. It traces the origins of TESTA, its spread and sustained use, and the evolution of its methods, tools, and change approaches. Chapter 1 is the companion methodology chapter which provides a wide-ranging discussion of TESTA's rationale, the research traditions that inform it, and ethical decisions about sampling, analysis, and representation of data. This chapter focuses on *how* TESTA is undertaken and *what* it is, in contrast to the more philosophical *why* questions in the previous chapter.

The origins of TESTA

An early version of TESTA was piloted by academic developers at Oxford University. It characterised features of assessment on nine different programmes at three different types of university, distinguishing patterns by discipline and institutional type (Gibbs and Dunbar-Goddet 2009). Its theoretical foundations came from cross-disciplinary research examining common conditions in

DOI: 10.4324/9780429347962-4

assessment and feedback which help students to learn (Gibbs and Simpson 2004). It used an audit method, a questionnaire, and focus groups to triangulate data. The study identified common patterns of assessment and feedback and established a framework for categorising features of assessment experienced by students in bands: high, medium, or low volumes of summative and formative assessment, feedback, varieties of assessment, and examinations. Findings demonstrated more variation between different institution types than within them, raising questions about whether quality assurance systems, disciplinary traditions, and individual academics conformed to tacit institutional assessment cultures. Subsequent studies on assessment cultures within disciplines and institutions have shown that they are highly context-dependent, reflecting tensions between fear, compliance, assessment for accountability, and assessment for student learning (Harrison et al. 2017; Simper et al. 2022).

TESTA was one of two projects on programme assessment funded by the UK Higher Education Academy as a National Teaching Fellowship Project in 2009 for three years. In parallel, Programme Assessment Strategies (PASS), led by Peter Hartley and Ruth Whitfield at the University of Bradford, investigated the presence of programme-focused assessment (PFA) in UK degree programmes, defining it and developing a bank of examples, case studies, and tools to encourage and support programme leaders in the development of PFA (Hartley and Whitfield 2011; Whitfield and Hartley 2017, 2018). Both TESTA and PASS sought to overcome some of the disadvantages of modularity; both grappled with the challenge of encouraging programme approaches to assessment. Their methods varied, with PASS taking a more conceptual approach, and TESTA an empirical one. Both outlasted their funding periods and have continued to be used in universities.

TESTA adopted research methods used in an earlier study by Gibbs and Dunbar-Goddet (2009) and went on to incorporate a theory and process of change. TESTA was originally led by the University of Winchester, a small university specialising in Arts, Education, and Social Sciences, in partnership with Bath Spa, Chichester, and Worcester. These institutions had similar origins and institutional cultures, with strengths in education, social science, and creative disciplines. Seven programmes were earmarked for TESTA research. They spanned the humanities, creative subjects, and professional programmes. The project team undertook TESTA twice on these seven programmes, with the expectation that the baseline established before the research would change. This was measured two to three years after the original research was undertaken by a repeated TESTA research process. In addition, qualitative interviews with programme directors were conducted, which showed promising signs of change: programmatic shifts to rebalancing formative and summative assessment loads, sequencing varieties of assessment, and the introduction of more dialogic approaches to feedback. Further evaluation has identified a consistent pattern of change that occurs during the TESTA process, which Hopwood-Stephens (2022) has characterised as a movement from *conversation* to *realisation* leading to actions which bring about *simplification*.

The spread of TESTA

Since the conclusion of the funded period (2012), TESTA has continued to be widely used as a research and change process, mainly in UK universities (more than 40 universities[1]) but also in universities in Australia,[2] India,[3] and Ireland.[4] Reach and spread is one indicator of the value of TESTA's methods; another is the knowledge and understanding of programme approaches to assessment and feedback it has generated. TESTA has been influential as a method and approach for understanding assessment and feedback, reflected in the range and number of publications it has generated, including peer-reviewed articles, chapters, and 'grey' publications (circa 30). TESTA project leaders have regularly delivered keynotes, workshops, and invited talks on TESTA in the UK, South Africa, Ireland, and Australia. Most recently, the University of Nottingham led an online conference on Programme Assessment, with TESTA as one of its key inspirations. The conference attracted more than 500 delegates from across Europe, evidence of the sector's continuing interest in programme approaches to assessment.

Educational methods spread and gain credence because they respond to a demand in a particular community, especially when they are perceived to offer robust solutions. The internal reach of TESTA to 157 programmes at the University of Greenwich demonstrated both the power of the methodology and the importance of clear, principled, and well-resourced institutional approaches over a sustained duration of time (Walker et al. 2019). TESTA@ Greenwich invested in research and project staff and student change agents to lead TESTA, permeated the process with the principles of confidentiality and neutrality, and balanced these with accountability and impact (Ibid, p. 429). Integration into quality assurance processes was a key dimension of their work, with recommendations to teams being non-binding, but requiring reflection in the process of curriculum review. 'Top ten challenge' check lists, derived from their TESTA data, gave further institutional impetus to change.

More generally, TESTA's sustained usefulness can be attributed to its ethos and effectiveness as a research approach: its identification of challenges, focus on students' experience, respect for disciplinary practice, and participatory approach (Jessop 2016). It remains valuable and widely used in response to the need to approach assessment and feedback from a programme perspective partly because the challenge of embedding formative assessment and feedback remains, and partly because curriculum design still often occurs in piecemeal modular style. TESTA has remained useful because tools and methods have evolved to take account of experience and theoretical developments about assessment and feedback.

Further, TESTA methods relate strongly to the idea of an 'assessment culture' (Simper et al. 2022) which positions assessment within a wider set of structures, systems, and relationships. It investigates how the broader learning environment influences student learning from assessment and feedback. TESTA repositions the debate about how students learn as wider than whether students take a deep or surface approach to learning, to one that is about fostering student engagement, ownership, and agency in their learning.

It emphasises the value of active, interactive, risk-taking approaches to learning through formative assessment. It invites more dialogic and conversational approaches to feedback and internalising standards. TESTA research is based on the hypothesis that these approaches work best when they are designed across whole degree programmes in a systematic way.

TESTA's research methods

TESTA is a mixed-methods approach that uses qualitative and quantitative methods to build up a picture of assessment and feedback on a programme of study. Its three distinct methods enable researchers to triangulate data, increasing the validity of findings and enhancing understanding of patterns of assessment and feedback which influence student learning. The audit offers a programme director's perception of the planned curriculum, and the Assessment Experience Questionnaire provides statistical insights into students' perspectives of learning from assessment and feedback, both of which are challenged or confirmed by students' qualitative insights in focus groups. On its own, each method gives a limited view of programme assessment patterns, but together they provide a fuller picture of students' experience of assessment and feedback across the whole programme.

Method #1: the TESTA audit

The purpose of the audit is to elicit an accurate picture of assessment and feedback in the planned curriculum (Jessop et al. 2014; Jessop 2019). The planned curriculum is the approved and documented account of assessment and feedback, often relating modules to the programme in a formal outline. In the TESTA audit, researchers engage the programme director (and sometimes members of the team) in a conversation about features of assessment and feedback on individual modules, building up to a full programme picture. They place the programme in the wider context of staff-to-student ratios, the student demography, entry tariffs, and the kinds of careers students pursue as graduates. The outcome of the conversation is captured through visual representation on flipcharts, spelling out assessment requirements in each year of study, module by module.

The audit collects hard count data from each module on features of assessment in a question-and-answer discussion that identifies:

- How many summative assessments on this module (summative assessment measures student achievement with a grade, and counts towards the degree).
- How many formative assessments on this module (defined as *not* counting towards the degree, eliciting feedback (peer, generic, teacher feedback), *all* students expected to do it).
- How many varieties of assessment.

- The proportion of the summative assessment by examination.
- How many words of written feedback a student can typically expect to receive (sampled, collected, and counted post-audit).

The audit normally takes between 90 and 120 minutes to undertake. It challenges the programme leader and the team to look beyond the module and consider how assessment tasks across all the modules may be influencing student learning on the programme. It raises questions about the extent of programmatic oversight over assessment, repetition of methods, the balance of formative and summative assessment, and the sequencing and integration of creative varieties of assessment. It also invites reflection on the overall student experience of studying concurrent modules across the programme, and whether the assessment supports their progress and learning. Translating the written documents into a visual representation, seen by programme directors, can be a powerful experience of seeing beyond the module for the first time, as this comment from an interview with a participating programme director illustrates:

> I realised what they were saying was 'That's only two assessments per module'. And I was like 'Ah, but that's the point. This is a programmatic thing and you're used to thinking about a module. That was surprising I must say. For me that gobsmacked me and made me want to change things…
> (Interview with Arts, Programme Director, 2011)

The audit prompts discussion about formative assessment. Within TESTA, we describe formative assessment as a defined activity which all students undertake, does not count towards the degree, and always elicits feedback, whether from the teacher, peers, or in the form of generic feedback discussed in class. Discussion uncovers varying perceptions and definitions of formative assessment. Some regard it as integral to teaching and therefore see no need for defined formative assessment tasks; others regard summative as effectively formative, aligning with the concept of *learning-oriented* assessment, arguing that assessment design and feedback are the keys to student learning, whether formative or summative (Carless 2007). Many academics are wary of the expectation that all students should undertake it. They make the case that, at best, students might dash it off, and, at worst, not do it at all, as there is no consequence. Summative assessment acts as a 'pedagogy of control' ensuring that students put in the necessary effort (Harland et al. 2015; Wass et al. 2015). Workload concerns also arise in relation to increasing formative assessment and feedback. The principle of rebalancing formative and summative assessment is central to ensuring staff and student workloads are contained. Reducing summative assessment to make space for more formative assessment is essential to effective programme design, so that *what counts* does not compete with *what does not count*, avoiding a competition between summative and formative assessment in an 'assessment arms race' (Harland et al. 2015).

The audit questions the virtue of using different varieties of assessment in a random sequence and underlines the importance of a programmatic overview. On the one hand, variety of assessment is stimulating for students; on the other it may lead to a lack of mastery and confusion about standards. The assumption that variety is an unalloyed good is challenged by considerations about how students internalise standards and make sense of feedback when the process of assessment changes in a random sequence. Students find it difficult to understand the goals and standards of new kinds of assessment when there is not a clear sequence across the programme. This can be an even more acute problem in the absence of formative 'dry runs' designed to help students grasp the requirements of new assessment types.

Volumes of written feedback are collected and calculated outside the audit conversation. These measure the typical number of words of written feedback a student encounters for summative assessment over the course of a degree. TESTA does not collect data on the volume of written *formative* feedback because there is not a standardised repository or way of finding this data. There are disciplinary differences in the amount of summative feedback students typically receive, with 'soft' arts and humanities' disciplines providing more written feedback, and more objective subjects with 'right' and 'wrong' answers being more minimalist (Jessop and Maleckar 2016).

Method #2: Assessment Experience Questionnaire (AEQ)

The Assessment Experience Questionnaire (AEQ) is TESTA's quantitative measure for helping researchers to understand students' experience of assessment across a programme. The AEQ provides statistical data to triangulate with the audit and focus group data, strengthening the validity of the research. The AEQ has undergone development over time in response to questions about whether all the items and scales work equally well and align with the latest theoretical developments in assessment and feedback. As a result, TESTA researchers have together refined the constructs and items in the AEQ over time.

The AEQ 3.3 (Appendix B) was designed to reflect a set of conditions which help students to learn from assessment (Gibbs and Simpson 2004). In developing AEQ 3.3., some scales drew on 'approaches to learning' theory, with its emphasis on deep and surface approaches to learning. Borrowed items and sub-scales from the Approaches to Study Inventory (ASI) and the Course Experience Questionnaire (CEQ) were validated in large-scale testing (Meyer and Parsons 1989; Wilson et al. 1997). Overall, AEQ 3.3 contained nine sub-scales and 28 items. Students were asked to assess the extent to which they agreed with each item on a five-point Likert scale, ranging from Strongly Disagree (1) to Strongly Agree (5). The questionnaire, usually administered to final year students, emphasised that they should consider their whole programme experience, looking back over their degrees. The original sub-scales were: Quantity of Effort; Coverage of Syllabus; Quantity and Quality of Feedback; Use of Feedback; Appropriate Assessment; Clear Goals and Standards; Surface Approach; Deep Approach; and Learning from the Examination.

Deep and surface approaches to learning formed the main theoretical construct underpinning AEQ 3.3. The theory is based on research that identified two distinct approaches that students take to their learning. Students taking a *deep approach* look for meaning, make connections between prior learning and new knowledge, see connections between modules, and can relate theory to practice. In contrast, students taking a *surface approach* tend to memorise facts in isolation, focus on information and rote learning, and struggle to see connections between related concepts (Marton and Saljo 1976). The two scales on the AEQ about deep and surface learning have created ambiguity for TESTA researchers interpreting the scores alongside the audit and focus groups. Often surface and deep scores on a programme are both high and low, which may evidence the influence of the assessment context and students' responses to that, but also introduces interpretive challenges of the 'what is going on here' variety.

The 'coverage of syllabus' scale has been challenging for other reasons. It implies a didactic and content-driven approach to learning static bodies of knowledge. It seems passive and descriptive in its orientation and suggests that students meet the requirements of traditional examinations by proving they have covered everything, without necessarily having understood it. It has a ring of the secondary school about it, which contrasts to the open and choice-laden curriculum of many subjects at university. There are disciplinary differences: some subjects require all students to have a firm grasp of specific content and concepts such as the anatomy of a horse's head for vets or quantum theories for physicists. Other disciplines have more freedom. The items in the scale probe at whether students are being strategic in their learning, using 'cue-conscious' and 'cue-seeking' behaviours to 'spot' what might come up in the examinations (Miller and Parlett 1974). Like 'approaches to learning' theories, AEQ items which test for strategic learning behaviours are designed to tell us more about the students' 'disposition to learn' (Naidoo and Jamieson 2005, p. 278) than about the assessment patterns on a degree programme.

Revisions to the AEQ 3.3 have balanced evaluation of the psychometric properties of AEQ 3.3 with updating it to reflect theoretical developments in the field and findings from TESTA (Batten et al. 2019; Wu and Jessop 2018). They also reflect a shift from the psychological foundations of deep and surface learning theory to the more sociological orientation of alienation and engagement theories (Barnhardt and Ginns 2014; Case 2008; Mann 2001). AEQ 4.0 (Appendix C) trialled a five-factor questionnaire with a separate scale on formative assessment, and removed deep, surface, and appropriate assessment scales to a scale which seeks to identify the extent to which assessment influences student agency through authentic tasks requiring problem-solving, evaluation, and critique. The five scales on the revised AEQ 4.0 are: How students learn;

Formative assessment; Internalisation of standards; Student Effort; and Quality of Feedback.

Further revision of AEQ 4.0 was based on a statistical and theoretical analysis of student data on a range of programmes and drew on insights from colleagues using TESTA in the medical school at University College Dublin. The main refinement was the addition of a scale to measure students' perceptions of how they draw on learning across their modules in relation to the assessment. The 'Integrated Assessment Design' scale seeks to elicit student perspectives on how connected learning is across a programme. AEQ 5.1 (Appendix D) was piloted to ensure its robustness and to reflect further theoretical developments. The ongoing development of the AEQ seeks to ensure that findings from TESTA research are incorporated in the questionnaire, while remaining consistent to the literature and core principles of TESTA.

Method #3: TESTA focus groups

TESTA triangulates the numerical and statistical data from the audit and AEQ using focus groups with final year students. Focus groups originated as a method in market research to test consumer opinion. They have been widely used in political campaigning and have gained credibility as a method in social science research (Morgan 1997). The value of focus groups is that they bring many voices into a discussion, revealing different sides of an issue and bringing out the reasoning behind contrasting viewpoints. As social research, they are also a form of social learning for the participants, for example in TESTA focus groups, students sharpen their thinking and revise their ideas about assessment in conversation with other students with contrasting viewpoints.

Specifically, the focus group explores students' experiences of assessment and feedback in more depth than questionnaires allow, probing and interpreting statistical responses from a wider sample of students in the AEQ. The focus group is facilitated by a researcher external to the programme, who leads the discussion using broad themes linked to the questions explored through the AEQ and audit. A good focus group consists of between four and eight participants and takes an hour to conduct. With the consent of students, the recording is transcribed, either manually or using software to enable systematic analysis of the data.

Like the AEQ, the themes discussed in TESTA focus groups have evolved over time. The opening question is broad and easy to answer: 'Tell me how you are assessed on your programme'. The intention is to get all participants speaking and adding their thoughts and ideas early in the focus group, as a simple icebreaker. Questions for discussion explore students' perceptions of feedback, how they internalise standards, their experience of formative assessment and feedback, when and how assessment develops their capacity to problem-solve, apply their learning, and connect it across modules. Importantly, the TESTA focus group seeks to elicit different and contrasting perceptions and probes students' experience and conceptions of assessment and feedback across the programme as a whole.

The completed focus group data are thematically analysed using qualitative software. The analysis highlights unexpected and surprising themes that have come up in the discussion, and those identified as themes in the AEQ and audit. It is both an emergent way of getting to grips with the data and listening to students' stories, and one which relates focus group data to a predetermined process of thematic analysis (Elliott 2018). Chapter 1 provides a full explanation of TESTA's data analysis process.

Representing TESTA findings in a case study

The TESTA case study brings together data from the three methods. It highlights aspects of assessment and feedback across the programme and within modules that engage students and help them to learn; it underscores aspects that students find problematic. It is crafted to tell a story which is robust, creative, and speaks to the minds and hearts of the readers about the student experience of assessment and feedback. The case study format is used to represent the data as a strategy to deepen teachers' understanding of the bounded system of their programme (Stake 1995; 1978; Yazan 2015). It is a device used flexibly to encapsulate the features of each programme, and to provide an explanation that resonates and develops empathy and understanding with the reader (Stake 1978). On the one hand, it is a systematic text, taking the reader through quantitative and qualitative elements of the data; on the other, it engages with the readers in a way that constructs meaning through surfacing problems that they recognise. In line with Stake's epistemological positioning of case study, it is a constructivist text (Stake 1995; Yazan 2015). It shows how data from different methods interact, confirming and contradicting each other, illustrating key themes, and illuminating ambiguities which might need further exploration. The TESTA case study represents the research, as well as being integral to the change process.

Within the case study, researchers benchmark the bounded system of the individual programme with wider data from similar programmes in other universities. Based on the audit data, the researcher sets out propositions which predict what learning might be like for students on the programme, given identified features of the planned curriculum. For example, a ratio of high summative to low formative is likely to have a negative impact on students' ability to internalise standards in the AEQ and focus groups. The second layer of the case study analyses data from the AEQ and draws inferences about the assessment environment from the triangulated audit and AEQ findings. For example, if there is a large variety of assessments in the audit and students score low on internalising standards on the AEQ, this may indicate that high varieties of assessment are causing confusion about expectations. This is something to explore in focus groups. Comparing audit and AEQ findings often exposes contradictions and provides a trail of clues for the researcher, so for example, if students encounter high volumes of feedback and yet score low on the feedback scale, then the facilitator would pursue a line of questioning to disentangle the contradiction.

The TESTA case study seeks to engage readers with students' perceptions of assessment and feedback in a vital way. For this reason, it sets out the focus group data in a way which privileges student voice over authorial interpretation. Thematically analysed data are represented through a succession of narrative headlines which act as topic sentences for student quotations which follow in clustered themes. This form of creative analytic practice helps to bring the voices of students alive in the discussion meeting (Richardson 2000). The result is something which resonates and lives on in the minds and hearts of the programme team, providing an impetus for reflection and change. The aim of the case study is to tell a story from the focus group data, with all its twists and turns, which the programme team recognise and evokes a sense of empathy in them, without shying away from any problems raised:

> The student data is a hard-hitting mix of personal, funny, poignant, critical, and quite revealing tales of their journeys through the minefield of assessment.
> (Jessop 2016, p. 6)

The final section of the case study 'Interpreting the data' takes a more directive approach, bringing together the evidence, academic development expertise, and assessment principles and tactics from the literature. It poses three or four thematic questions, effectively 'what is going on here?' and sets out actions and options for programme teams to pursue once the debriefing is over, and for teams to discuss on their own. Appendix A contains an anonymised example of a case study.

Planning a productive conversation over TESTA: the debriefing

The case study evokes a lively response from programme team members at the debriefing. In general, TESTA facilitators discuss the case study with the programme director in advance of the debriefing, but reserve sharing it with the team until the discussion to prompt a more productive and spontaneous conversation. This enables the TESTA facilitator to set the tone for the debriefing as a developmental event, with the case study providing external and independent analysis of the programme's assessment and feedback patterns. The discussion is an interaction between the evidence in the TESTA case study and staff perceptions of assessment and feedback, often from the perspective of their individual experience on single modules. The relationship between modular assessment and feedback practices and the programme reality is central to the discussion, and a key task of the facilitator is to highlight programmatic patterns and prompt thinking beyond the module. Staff on the programme have an insider view, from which they recognise data which resonates with their experience and intuition; alternatively, they are able to explain data that has arisen in a context which may be invisible to the researchers and/or students. The facilitators encourage members of the programme team to bring their perspectives into the discussion (Jessop 2016; Jessop et al. 2011).

In some universities, TESTA is an academic-to-academic conversation over the data, and in others students participate in helping to shape the findings from a student perspective (McKenna 2015). There are benefits to both approaches. A staff-only debriefing can give more freedom to participants to make educationally principled assessment and feedback decisions in response to student evidence. Having students in the room may prevent some of the more robust conversations over difficult issues from occurring. On the other hand, a debriefing with students in the room can give more texture to student comments and shape the discussion from a stronger student experience perspective, leading to new insights for staff. Whatever approach is taken, the purpose of the debriefing is to identify the challenges, discuss ideas to improve assessment and feedback, and agree actions to take.

In practice, the debriefing begins with the programme team's impressions of what is going well, and not so well in assessment and feedback. These positives and negatives about the programme collected at the start are shared, and programme teams conduct a quick and impressionistic thematic analysis of their perceptions in the live setting. This activity performs several functions: it builds ownerships and respects the viewpoints of the programme team; it sets the scene as a dialogue of staff and student perceptions, and it enables the facilitators and programme team to cross-reference from staff perceptions to student comments. It provides a useful sense-check of what members of the team expect their students to be saying about the assessment environment. Most significantly, it gives the academic team agency and ownership over the process. They are not simply the recipients of a report, but participants shaping the conversation.

The typical debriefing consists of the facilitator highlighting points in the written report from the audit and AEQ, suggesting how these might affect students' learning behaviours. There is always the need to answer questions, clarify methods and meaning, and field comments and critique. One of our strong steers in this first part of the debriefing is to reinforce that all three methods work together, as each single method does not tell you enough about the assessment environment. The 'aha' moments occur as all the methods begin to tell a compelling story and the various elements come together. The challenge for the facilitator is to welcome questions and comments in the first sections and yet to see the discussion through to the end.

The power of student comments in the final section of the case study usually brings a transformative shift in the tone of the debriefing. The participants read and digest each themed section in a period of silence, although the period of quiet does not last for long! Participants comment, exclaim, and laugh in recognition as they read through each themed section of student quotations. Miller and Parlett (1974, p. 12) describe this as 'phenomenon recognition', where participants recognise what is being described, finding parallels in their own experience. The discussion following each headline and themed section contextualises student comments, enabling participants to express frustration and perplexity, highlight aspects that resonate, question the veracity of perceptions, and probe how widespread students' particular experiences are across the programme. There is normally some distancing from negative practices: 'I don't do that on my module…'. Participants also begin to share innovative modular practices which could have wider application across the programme. This is when and how the case study starts to generate a programme-wide conversation about best practice.

The debriefing is not the 'final word'. It is an open process of discussion, contestation, and contextualisation. TESTA facilitators seek to combine a mix of humility and authority in sharing the findings: humility because the research is conducted by outsiders, often from different disciplines than the programme being discussed; authority, because the evidence ranges across the whole programme, uses robust methods, and points to areas where assessment and feedback can be improved. The authority of the facilitator is to be found in linking the evidence and discussion with proven tactics, educational principles, and problem-solving ideas from colleagues in the room, and from the literature, often drawing on practices from other TESTA programmes.

The evidence has its own dynamic once shared and discussed, and teams decide on, and design strategic interventions based on the evidence. Throughout the process, the TESTA facilitator will guide and steer, support and give advice, emphasise key points, and ask questions to cross-check and facilitate decisions about potential enhancements. Often facilitators identify priorities arising from the debriefing that the team seemed most keen to address and send these to the programme director as an *aide memoire*. They meet with the programme director a few weeks after the debriefing to discuss next steps and provide support for changes.

TESTA's change process: making change stick

Evidence about students' experience of assessment and feedback leads into a dialogue with programme teams about enhancing practice across the whole programme. This is the start of an educational change process, discussed more fully in Chapter 8. The programme director's role in the change process is central, exerting influence through 'informal leadership' with many responsibilities and very little hierarchical or positional power to effect change (Lawrence et al. 2022, p. 4). Programme directors do not have line management responsibilities for the colleagues in their team so rely on leading through influencing others for the set time in which they are in the role. They are often called upon to enact unpopular decisions by senior managers without much support or any levers of change (Moore 2022). Improving metrics from national surveys about teaching, learning, and assessment such as the National Student Survey in the UK usually fall within their remit with the assumption that they have the scholarly background in education to bring about the right changes (Henri 2022).

Interviews with programme directors who have participated in TESTA indicate that the conversations, evidence, and scholarship within the process provide useful nudges towards whole programme solutions. The process offers an externally facilitated opportunity for teams to collaborate in a problem-solving activity which generates and shares many good ideas from within the team, prompted by discussions about robust and independent data. The TESTA process supports 'enabling leadership' for programme directors characterised by 'fostering connections across the team', 'using creative approaches', and 'developing collective commitment about the way ahead' (Parkin 2022, p. 106). However, making programmatic and principled assessment and feedback decisions is contingent on the relationship between programme directors and TESTA facilitators, in particular calling on the programme director's ability to straddle the roles of trusting and validating the process while navigating the scepticism of their colleagues. The TESTA change process has been characterised as a *conversation*, which leads to a *realisation* that prompts *simplification* of assessment patterns (Hopwood-Stephens 2022). The *conversation* begins with the programme director in the audit and culminates with the debriefing meeting where commitment to action is determined by the programme director. Programme directors are central actors in the process.

Interviews with programme directors indicate that conversations can be uncomfortable, nudging teams to confront challenging evidence, which then become the source of change:

> It also allows us to have the conversation with colleagues who are burying their heads in the sand about things or slightly disregarding it all or weren't necessarily that aware of what other colleagues were already doing.
> (Programme Director, Creative Industries, 2020)

Realisation occurs from seeing beyond the myopic field of vision of the module to the whole programme, for example, seeing how much summative assessment there is when modular assessment is aggregated, and realising that students are juggling concurrent modules and making strategic choices about whether to complete formative assessment based on competing demands. Evidence about programme patterns of assessment and feedback gives impetus to changing those patterns, as illustrated here:

> TESTA certainly gave us that focus, maybe a bit of rhetorical ammunition that we needed as well to really push things through at that moment. Things were changing but certainly in terms of the look at formative and how many assessments we were getting the students to do, these conversations were really useful for honing things.
> (Programme Director, Arts, 2020)

Programmes have adopted different approaches to ensure that *realisation* translates into action, often leading to the *simplification* of assessment patterns across whole programmes. This may involve mapping and sequencing formative and summative assessment, and varieties of assessment on whole programmes to reflect students' experience of learning.

Integrating TESTA into cyclical review processes is an integrated approach to bringing about consistent simplification. Linking quality assurance and enhancement processes in this way embeds TESTA into normal periodic review processes and helps all programmes to reflect on patterns of assessment and feedback in programmatic ways. This approach often requires institutional support and buy-in for TESTA which can facilitate more agile changes, for example 'fast tracking' processes of approval, often considered one of the key barriers to changing assessment (Simper et al. 2022). Programme directors see virtue in this institutional backing, as illustrated in this comment:

> My strategy was to implement change little by little, demonstrate results and then within my term as programme director, manage to change everything so when TESTA came along I jumped at the opportunity because I thought this is an excellent chance to get an external view on everything and then also get a bit of an impulse to change things faster and the institutional backing to do that as well.
>
> (Programme Director, Engineering, 2020)

As universities have invested in TESTA, and the stakes have become higher to improve metrics and student experience, so managerial agendas have become more ascendant, with a positive initiative coming to be perceived as a managerial punishment rather than a developmental process (Cunningham and Wilder 2020). That is why it is important to keep the focus on enhancement and to work in trusting and supportive relationships with programme directors, often drawing in academic development institutes to help consolidate scholarly approaches to changes (Ibid, 2020). The balance in enabling leadership is between fostering creativity and collaboration among the programme team, and developing a collective commitment to action, which may involve some modular sacrifices. TESTA@Greenwich supported programme directors through a reflective and structured approach to integrating TESTA improvements in quality assurance using self-reflection through a checklist which proved powerful and effective (Walker et al. 2019). Whatever the approach taken, bringing about programme-wide changes to assessment and feedback requires persuasive leadership and influencing skills with members of programme teams and strong collaboration with programme directors.

A brief synopsis

This chapter has reflected on the origins and spread of TESTA. It has outlined each of the three research methods used in TESTA, and their relationship with one another in drawing a compelling and comprehensive picture of students' experience of assessment and feedback on a programme of study. The final section of the chapter has explored how the case study frames conversations that lead programme teams to adopt evidence-informed changes. It has emphasised the central role of the programme director in navigating these changes.

Notes

1 Aberdeen; Bath Spa University; Birmingham; Brighton; Bristol; Brunel University; Cardiff; Chichester; Christchurch Canterbury; Dundee; Durham; Edge Hill; Edinburgh; Edinburgh Napier; Exeter; Glasgow; Greenwich; Imperial College; Liverpool; London Metropolitan; Exeter; Imperial College; Keele; Kent; Liverpool; Liverpool John Moores; London South Bank University; Loughborough; Nottingham; Oxford Brookes; Portsmouth; Queen Mary University London; Robert Gordon; Roehampton; Sheffield Hallam University; Solent; Southampton; St Andrews; Strathclyde; Swansea; University College London; University of the West of Scotland; Winchester; Worcester; York.
2 University of New South Wales, Australia.
3 Lady Irwin College, University of Delhi; Saurashtra University, Rajkot, Gujarat.
4 Trinity College Dublin; University College Dublin; Dublin University of Technology.

References

Barnhardt, B. and P. Ginns 2014. An alienation-based framework for student experience in higher education: new interpretations of past observations in student learning theory. *Higher Education* 68: 789–805.
Batten, J., T. Jessop, and P. Birch. 2019. Doing what it says on the tin? A psychometric evaluation of the assessment experience questionnaire. *Assessment & Evaluation in Higher Education* 44 (2): 309–320, DOI: 10.1080/02602938.2018.1499867
Carless, D. 2007. Learning-oriented assessment: Conceptual bases and practical implications. *Innovations in Education and Teaching International* 44 (1): 57–66, DOI: 10.1080/14703290601081332
Case, J. M. 2008. Alienation and engagement: Development of an alternative theoretical framework for understanding student learning. *Higher Education* 55: 789–805.
Cunningham, C., and K. Wilder 2020. Programme Leaders as invisible super-heroes of Teaching and learning. QAA Enhancement Themes Collaborative Cluster on Programme Leadership. Available from https://www.enhancementthemes.ac.uk/docs/ethemes/evidence-forenhancement/programme-leaders-as-invisible-superheroes-of-learningand-teaching.pdf?sfvrsn=e862c381_8. Accessed 15 January 2023.
Elliott, V. 2018. Thinking about the Coding Process in Qualitative Data Analysis. *The Qualitative Report* 23(11), 2850–2861. https://doi.org/10.46743/2160-3715/2018.3560
Gibbs, G., and H. Dunbar-Goddet 2009. Characterising programme-level assessment environments that support learning. *Assessment & Evaluation in Higher Education* 34 (4): 481–489.
Gibbs, G., and C. Simpson 2004. 'Conditions under which assessment supports students' learning. *Learning and Teaching in Higher Education* 1: 3–31.

Harland, T. A. McLean, R. Wass, E. Miller & K. Nui Sim 2015. 'An assessment arms race and its fallout: high-stakes grading and the case for slow scholarship', *Assessment & Evaluation in Higher Education* DOI: 10.1080/02602938.2014.931927

Harrison, C. J., K. D. Könings, L. W. T. Schuwirth, V. Wass, and C. P. M. van der Vleuten. 2017. Changing the culture of assessment: The dominance of the summative assessment paradigm. *BMC Medical Education* 17(73): 1–14. https://doi.org/10.1186/s12909-017-0912-5

Hartley, P., and R. Whitfield. 2011. The case for programme-focused assessment. *SEDA Educational Developments* 12 (4): 8–12.

Henri, D. 2022. Case study 8: Coordinating programme design through 'Assessment therapy' (pp. 170–173). In J. Lawrence, S. Morón-García, and R. Senior. (Eds) *Supporting Course and Programme Leaders in Higher Education*. Abingdon. SEDA Series, Routledge.

Hopwood-Stephens, I. 2022. What is TESTA? Presentation to Quality Assurance Agency (QAA) Conference, 11 May 2022.

Jessop, T. 2016. Seven years and still no itch: Why TESTA keeps going. *SEDA Educational Developments*. 17 (3): 5–8.

Jessop, T. 2019. Changing the narrative: A programme approach to assessment through TESTA. Chapter 3, pp. 36–49. In Bryan, C. and K. Clegg. *Innovative Assessment in Higher Education*. Abingdon. Routledge.

Jessop, T., Y. El Hakim, and G. Gibbs 2014. The whole is greater than the sum of its parts: A large-scale study of Students' learning in response to different programme assessment patterns. *Assessment & Evaluation in Higher Education* 39 (1): 73–88, DOI: 10.1080/02602938.2013.792108.

Jessop, T., Y. El Hakim, and G. Gibbs. 2011. Research Inspiring Change. *Educational Developments*. 12(4): 12–16.

Jessop, T., and B. Maleckar 2016. The influence of disciplinary assessment patterns on student learning: A comparative study. *Studies in Higher Education* 41 (4): 696–711, DOI: 10.1080/03075079.2014.943170.

Lawrence, J., S. Morón-García, and R. Senior (Eds). 2022. *Supporting Course and Programme Leaders in Higher Education*. Abingdon. SEDA Series, Routledge.

Mann, S. J. 2001. Alternative perspectives on the student experience: Alienation and engagement. *Studies in Higher Education* 26 (1): 7–19.

Marton, F., and R. Saljo 1976. Qualitative differences in learning:1 – Outcomes and process. *British Journal of Educational Psychology* 46 (1): 4–11.

McKenna, D. 2015. TESTA@Greenwich – Engaging students in assessment and feedback. *Compass: Journal of Learning and Teaching* 6 (10): 1–3.

Meyer, J. H. F., and P. Parsons 1989. Approaches to studying and course perceptions using the Lancaster inventory – a comparative study. *Studies in Higher Education* 14 (2): 137–153.

Miller, C., and M. Parlett 1974. *Up to the Mark: A Study of the Examination Game*. London. SRHE.

Moore, S. 2022. Empowering programme leaders: Developing relational academic leadership (pp. 124–135). In J. Lawrence, S. Morón-García, and R. Senior (Eds) *Supporting Course and Programme Leaders in Higher Education*. Abingdon. SEDA Series, Routledge.

Morgan, D. L. 1997. *Focus Groups as Qualitative Research*. Thousand Oaks, CA. Sage.

Naidoo, R., and I. Jamieson. 2005. Empowering participants or corroding learning? Towards a research agenda on the impact of student consumerism in higher education. *Journal of Education Policy* 20 (3): 267–281, DOI: 10.1080/02680930500108585

Parkin, D. 2022. Programme leaders as educational and academic leaders: A question of influence – Relationships, behaviour, and commitment (pp. 95–108). In J. Lawrence, S. Morón-García, and R. Senior (Eds) *Supporting Course and Programme Leaders in Higher Education*. Abingdon. SEDA Series, Routledge.

Richardson, L. 2000. 'Writing: A method of inquiry' Chapter 36 (pp. 923–948). In N. K. Denzin and Y. S. Lincoln. (Eds) *Handbook of Qualitative Research*. Second Edition. Thousand Oaks, CA. Sage.

Simper, N., K. Mårtensson, A. Berry, and N. Maynard 2022. Assessment cultures in higher education: Reducing barriers and enabling change. *Assessment & Evaluation in Higher Education* 47 (7): 1016–1029, DOI: 10.1080/02602938.2021.1983770

Stake, R. E. 1995. *The Art of Case Study Research*. Thousand Oaks, CA. SAGE Publications.

Stake, R. E. 1978. The case study method in social inquiry. *Educational Researcher* 7(2): 5–8. https://doi.org/10.2307/1174340

Walker, S., E. Salines, A. Abdillahi, S. Mason, A. Jadav, and C. Molesworth. 2019. Identifying and resolving key institutional challenges in feedback and assessment: A case study for implementing change. *Higher Education Pedagogies* 4 (1): 422–434, DOI: 10.1080/23752696.2019.1649513

Wass, R., T. Harland, A. McLean, E. Miller, and K. N. Sim 2015. Will press lever for food: Behavioural conditioning of students through frequent high-stakes assessment. *Higher Education Research and Development* 34 (6): 1324–1326.

Whitfield, R., and P. Hartley 2017. Whatever happened to programme assessment strategies? *Educational Developments* 18: 1.

Whitfield, R., and P. Hartley. 2018. Assessment strategy: Enhancement of student learning through a programme focus (Chapter 16, 239–255). In A. Diver. (Ed) 2018. *Employability via Higher Education: Sustainability as Scholarship*. Cham, Switzerland. Springer Nature.

Wilson, K. L., A. Lizzio, and P. Ramsden 1997. The development, validation and application of the course experience questionnaire. *Studies in Higher Education* 22 (1): 33–53, DOI: 10.1080/03075079712331381121

Wu, Q., and T. Jessop. 2018. Formative assessment: Missing in action in both research-intensive and teaching focused universities? *Assessment & Evaluation in Higher Education* 43 (7): 1019–1031, DOI: 10.1080/02602938.2018.1426097

Yazan, B. 2015. Three approaches to case study methods in education: Yin, Merriam, and stake. *The Qualitative Report* 20 (2): 134–152. Retrieved from http://nsuworks.nova.edu/tqr/vol20/iss2/12

Part II

Alienation and engagement

Chapter 3

Alienation in assessment

Opening Pandora's box

Introduction

The 'tragic gap' between dreams and reality is expressed in the space between students' hopes about their university education and their disappointment with it (Palmer 2009). Dashed educational expectations are felt most acutely in assessment, which is why it is often the locus of mistrust, frustration, and discontent. In the National Student Survey (NSS), the largest public survey of students across the UK, students persistently rate their assessment and feedback experience at least ten percentage points lower than any other scores about teaching and learning at university (Buckley 2021; Williams and Kane 2009). A wider analysis of ten countries' national surveys about students' educational experience at university demonstrated that the measures themselves were conceptually outdated. They reinscribed students' negative views of feedback by diminishing their agency and making them passive recipients (Winstone et al. 2022). While surveys designed to make institutions accountable give an indication that there may be something wrong, they do not explain what the problems are, or point to solutions.

Alienation theory brings fresh insights into why students struggle to learn from assessment and feedback. This chapter charts a brief history of the theory, from its origins in the industrial revolution to its psychological and philosophical manifestations. It identifies the key features of alienation and interprets them in the higher education context. Typically, universities establish the type, timing, and nature of assessment, contributing to students' sense of not being in control of their learning. Marketised higher education has exacerbated student perceptions that they are passive in their education, expected to replicate ideas rather than understand, evaluate, and suggest alternative interpretations. Examinations tame the imagination by demanding conformity to standard answers – while they test knowledge and understanding they can undermine ingenuity and innovation. The meaning of higher education has changed in an era of marketisation with the demand for value for money emphasising its utilitarian purpose: the discourse of employability, when interpreted bluntly, has supplanted more philosophical ideas about the idea of the university. This

DOI: 10.4324/9780429347962-6

further alienates students. As participation has widened, so has the potential increased for students to find themselves outsiders, lost in a large intellectual complex. Students display the signs of a lack of 'sense of belonging', or in the language of alienation theory, social isolation. This is part of the wider social context for 21st-century students living in a digital age, with the threat of climate change, and the rise in mental illness among young people. Shifting from alienation to engagement, this chapter advances an alternative approach to engage students in their learning, using the more contextual approach of 'Transforming the Experience of Students through Assessment' (TESTA).

Alienation theory provides a context-rich way of thinking which helps to explain students' dissatisfaction with assessment and feedback from a socio-logical perspective. As a theory applied from sociology, philosophy, and psy-chology, it has gained some purchase as a way of thinking about students' educational experience in higher education (Barnhardt and Ginns 2014; Case 2008; Mann 2001). More recent work has drawn on ideas about relational pedagogies, authenticity, and the experience of 'mattering' to understand stu-dents' feelings of isolation and alienation in higher education (Bovill 2020; Gravett and Winstone 2022). The history and background of alienation the-ory provides a wider sociological context for engaging with and applying stu-dents' experience of assessment and feedback to the theory. This represents an alternative perspective to the more psychological 'approaches to learning' theory. The central argument in this chapter is that identifying structural and socio-cultural causes of alienation is a powerful starting point for fostering agency and engagement in students' learning.

What is alienation?

Alienation as a bridging concept between structure and meaning

Alienation has its theoretical roots in Marxist analyses of the workplace at the time of industrialisation. Its sociological origin as a critique of capitalism in the context of production and workers' alienation from the means of production has translated into psychological theories about meaning, isolation, and estrange-ment (Schacht 1970). It has been described usefully as a 'bridging concept' between social conditions and individual responses, where human experience is mediated by structure and agency (Yuill 2011, p. 106). For Marx, alienation was mainly evident in the structures and institutions of labour, civil society, and property. However, in observing the nature of work in industrialising society, he identified a connection between production and the self-realisation of the hu-man person (Schacht 1970). This implied that self-realisation and even freedom and creativity were thwarted when labour became an acquisitive activity with the sole purpose being 'merely the increase of wealth' (Schacht 1970, p. 79).

In Marxian terms, alienation occurs when labourers have no choice over what they produce, when creativity is suppressed, and when the products of labour are part of a wage labour system, as was the case in the emerging industrial society in which he was writing. For Marx, labour played a central role in providing meaning and purpose for human beings, to the degree that he described it *as* a person's life, 'for what is life but activity' (Schacht 1970, p. 100). A person is dehumanised when labour is directed by another person, and it becomes wage labour. While Marx came to reject the term alienation as 'philosophical nonsense', his subsequent writing is shot through with ideas which would widely be regarded as expressions of alienation (Williamson and Cullingford 1997).

Alienation has resonance in thinking about assessment and feedback because it encompasses ideas about people being the objects of a system, lacking agency, removed from the fruits of their labour, and denied the potential of creativity (Barnardt and Ginns 2014; Case 2008; Mann 2001). This is the structural condition of oppression which Marx wrote about in relation to the capitalist economy. Sociological depictions of alienation focus on a process of being subjected to a system or structure, with feelings of powerlessness and meaninglessness ensuing. In a university experience marked by alienation, these feelings chip away at students' enthusiasm and leave them jaded. Marx recognised the interplay between alienation as a sociological process and the psychological state it induced.

Defining alienation in psycho-social terms

Alienation as a concept is well-rehearsed in psychoanalysis, mainly through the prolific writings of psychologist Erich Fromm, whom Schacht (1970) describes as using the term 'so freely and loosely that the results are much more confusing than illuminating' (p. 139). In their exploration of the uses and misuses of the term, Williamson and Cullingford (1997) caution about the dangers of using alienation loosely as a 'catch-all term or buzzword'. They recognise that it is a powerful and alluring metaphor which 'strikes a chord with lay people' yet is inherently ambiguous and elusive. Rae (2010) challenges this perspective, citing Feuerlicht, who asserts that the ambiguity of the concept is its greatest quality:

> After all, some of the most powerful words, words that have aroused and impassioned millions of people, words that language and perhaps even science can hardly do without are equally difficult to define. Consider, for example, "freedom" and "love".
>
> (Feuerlicht, 1978, p. 17 in Rae 2010)

Seeman (1959) is helpful in clarifying the definition through articulating psycho-social categories of alienation. As a social psychologist, he was well-placed to develop empirical categories of alienation which straddle the psychological and social. These categories draw on Marx and provide a wide-ranging interpretation of the human condition of alienation, giving impetus to analytical and experimental research about alienation in the decades that followed. His thesis drew on the idea that social conditions produced different variants of alienation, which have behavioural consequences. His categories of powerlessness, meaninglessness, normlessness, estrangement, and social isolation are particularly pertinent in higher education.

Powerlessness describes the gap between a person's expectancy and reality. It is when a person is powerless to realise their dreams because they cannot control the outcomes of their actions. Diverging from Marx, Seeman does not focus on the social order, nor does he invite moral-ethical discussion about the conditions which give rise to powerlessness. He frames it as psycho-social, as the interplay between a person and social conditions, going beyond Marx's original workplace context of powerlessness. Seeman's focus is on expectancies about control and freedom rather than the social order, with some recognition that the social order influences a person's capacity to fulfil expectations. Power is found in the 'sensed ability to control outcomes' (Seeman 1959, p. 786). The inability to control outcomes is linked to the kinds of helplessness that seed anxiety, depression, and mental ill-health (Seeman 1983). He argues that these are not only psychological but often a response to bureaucratic, political, and economic deprivation. However, 'system blame' can spawn a different kind of powerlessness by removing personal agency.

Meaninglessness refers to a person's inability to make sense of events and their resulting struggle to make appropriate choices between alternatives using insight and intelligence. In Seeman's view, meaninglessness is about finding events in society incomprehensible, not understanding their dynamics, and being unable to predict the future. Lack of understanding contributes to low confidence in decision-making. Meaninglessness occurs in intimate microrelations as well within wider social relations (Seeman 1983). It inhabits conditions of uncertainty and ambiguity, and echoes features of powerlessness. It occurs when it is hard to define expectations, and there is a gap between a person's ideals and their realisation. In summary, meaninglessness leads to the inability of a person to make sense of conditions, to take surefooted and morally cogent decisions, and to predict the outcomes of those decisions.

Normlessness is when social rules governing individual behaviour do not seem to exist. Achieving goals is then down to chance, with the expectation that actors will use socially unapproved behaviours to reach desired ends. Breaking the rules works, which is why Seeman described the flipside of this kind of alienation as innovation. However, the loss of commonly held standards breeds individualism and may develop instrumental and manipulative attitudes to achieving goals. In a context where the rules no longer function reliably, mistrust flourishes.

Isolation or social isolation is a symptom of alienation characterised by a person's detachment from societal norms to the extent that they assign low value to things typically regarded as high value in society. In line with Seeman's overarching alienation narrative about expectations, isolation is not simply loneliness or aloneness but a form of rebellion against cultural norms.

Alienation is also manifest in self-estrangement, when a person fails to find fulfilment from an activity for its own sake, echoing Marx's depiction of wage labour as a form of dehumanising slavery. Self-estrangement separates a person from their creative instincts. Rewards lie outside the activity, so self-estrangement is marked by a loss of pride in work and a lack of intrinsic satisfaction. It generates instrumental behaviours. An aspect of self-estrangement is the failure to recognise true human capability.

The waxing and waning of alienation

Alienation pre-dates Marxism. It is a powerful idea in the Judeo-Christian tradition, dating back with its original conception dating back to the story of Adam and Eve's fall in the Garden of Eden. Reformation theologians, Calvin and Luther, describe human beings' estrangement from God, true self, and one another in ways which resemble Parker Palmer's depiction of the tragic gap between expectation and reality, captured in T S Eliot's famous lines from his poem, The Hollow Men: 'Between the idea and the reality...falls the shadow' (Eliot 2002).

The modern expression of alienation is often linked to industrialisation and the social and material conditions of separation it created. In the realm of ideas, alienation was given prominence by the enlightenment and the shifts in conception about what it meant to be human that it heralded (Rae 2010). Following the Scientific Revolution in the 16th and 17th century, the age of enlightenment was a period of questioning the authority of tradition, church, and monarchy, placing more emphasis on individuals and human reasoning. Ideas about freedom, reflexivity, creativity, and freedom from subordination to external constraints led to more emphasis on both the rational and emotional life of humans. Together these new possibilities within enlightenment thinking gave alienation greater prominence in a philosophical and existential sense. It brought implicit feelings of self-estrangement into public discourse: 'the subject-centred nature of modern thought allowed the constitutive link between the notion of alienation and the self that had always been implicit to become explicit' (Rae 2010, p. 26).

Freedom and protest gave prominence to alienation as a concept in the 1960s and 70s, reflecting challenges to traditional and authoritarian values (Rae 2010; Yuill 2011). The *zeitgeist* of this era, with its mix of protest, challenge to orthodoxy, and unprecedented freedom, was reflected in the 'flower-power' movement, Parisian students at the barricades, anti-Vietnam war protests, and the Civil Rights movement in America. Social psychologist Melvin Seeman prefigured these developments in categorising new ways of understanding alienation in the 1950s, breaking free from blue-collar definitions of Marxism. His empirical categories of alienation had resonance with the times to the extent that he declared alienation a core part of sociology, a declaration which he recanted in 1983, observing that 'the idea of alienation has had its day' (Seeman 1975, p. 172). Even after he had read the last rites over it, Seeman continued to believe that alienation was leading a 'lively underground life' although the label had all but disappeared from the lexicon of published authors (Ibid, p. 172).

A combination of factors led to the waning of alienation as a theory reverenced by sociologists and the cultural intelligentsia. These included the collapse of communism in Eastern Europe, aligned with the waning of the original Marxist vision of workers taking ownership of the means of production. Alienation in the workplace had been solidly a blue-collar phenomenon, until the rise of the knowledge economy and service industries in the 1980s with attendant shifts from heavy manufacturing to light industry. William Blake's 'dark Satanic mills' had been replaced by the 'bright Satanic offices' of the 20th and 21th century (Baldry et al. 1998). Postmodernism with its rejection of grand narratives in favour of more relativistic perceptions of power made alienation theory appear a blunt instrument, caught in a dualistic time warp.

The case for reclaiming the more subtle shades of alienation theory is worth making, to understand how it might occur in more insidious ways in 21th-century society. The rise in a mental illness among young people could be interpreted through the lens of alienation, using Seeman's categories, and may be the result of hidden continuities of alienation, beyond the 'zero-sum' game and binaries of its Marxist incarnation, as argued here:

> Just because the theory has fallen from grace does not entail that somehow society no longer presents problems of meaning, self-realization and social isolation for the people who live in and create that society. Indeed, given the current social trends of increasing individualization, the reconfiguration of the workplace, the deepening commodification of many aspects of life, and increasing inequality, it is perhaps now timely to remember what alienation theory can offer as a means to both describe and explain the emotional, individual and social landscapes of this phase of modernity.
>
> (Yuill 2011, p. 115)

Applying theories of alienation to student learning

Theories of alienation offer a new vocabulary for understanding how students learn, widening the discussion beyond dominant psychological models of learning. They place an emphasis on encouraging agency and engagement in the design of learning within its wider structural context. They also reclaim ideas about authenticity, belonging, and the pedagogic relationship in students' experience of higher education (Bovill 2020; Gravett and Winstone 2022). Traditionally, studies of alienation in education have focused on the adolescent experience, particularly looking at deviance such as truancy, anti-social behaviour, and illegal drug use (Williamson and Cullingford 1997). Recent conceptual studies on the student experience have given impetus to using alienation as an analytical framework for understanding student learning and engagement

(Barnhardt and Ginns 2014; Case 2008; Mann 2001). These studies prompt a more holistic interpretation of student learning than psychological approaches, bringing the influence of context to the fore and privileging approaches that foster students' sense of agency, belonging, and intellectual growth.

Mann (2001) examines students' experiences of alienation related to identity formation and their loss of student agency. Her analysis uses Marxist perspectives to critique the narrowing purposes of higher education in its role as a servant of the economy and the world of work. This impedes students' sense of 'becoming' and compromises their intellectual and personal development through the dominance of instrumental and utilitarian values. The teaching context promotes compliance over creativity, denying students the opportunity to be playful, experimental, and original in their learning. Students are often expected to be passive listeners and consumers of expert ideas and theories, rather than producers and co-producers of emergent and novel ideas. At the time when Mann was writing (2001), she observed that there were limited opportunities for students to apply the knowledge they had learnt. More recent developments in authentic learning and assessment have opened opportunities for applied learning and agency, often linked to digital practices (Lombardi 2007; Villarroel et al. 2018; Wakefield et al. 2022).

In the assessment context, alienation is evident when teaching and institutional requirements dominate, requiring students to work at the behest of others to deliver answers to questions which originate elsewhere. Students' lack of ownership and autonomy over the process of assessment is manifest in the timing, type, and conditions for undertaking assessment, contributing to feelings of powerlessness (Seeman 1959). The products of student work do not 'belong' to the student and are part of a mark-awarding transaction, becoming part of a 'system of exchange'. Certain assessment practices, particularly examinations and reflections, domesticate students' imagination. Mann (2001) depicts an alienating continuum from examinations exerting power over students to the confessional genres of learning journals and reflections forcing a kind of docility in a climate of surveillance. These assessment practices mirror Marxist definitions of alienation within labour conditions where factory workers implement others' ideas and are a paid a wage for their efforts.

Mann's analysis goes further. In broad terms, academic discourse shapes identity formation and positions students as types rather than individuals: a first-year student, a consumer, a widening participation student, a minority ethnic student, a mature student, an international student, for example. Categories and labels 'other' students, with the result that they experience the alienation of being outsiders (Halabi 2022). Students from diverse backgrounds feel like outsiders, 'strangers in a foreign land', crossing the border into higher education (Mann 2001, p. 11). Feelings of dislocation ensue for students who feel ill at ease because they have limited knowledge of the language, conventions, and culture of higher education. Students are unclear about the norms, leading to alienation as a form of normlessness (Seeman 1959). Mann's depictions of alienation paint higher education as a field of narrowing possibility, instead of expanding horizons.

Case (2008) contextualises the discussion of alienation in post-apartheid South Africa with its radical transformation of the demography of students. Theories of alienation provide insights into students' entry into higher education, fitting in, and staying in the higher education community. Using Mann's conceptualisation, Case proposes alienation as a productive alternative to the dominant 'approaches to learning' theory, while recognising some common ground. There is a resemblance between surface approaches to learning and alienation in that both are characterised by an instrumental and disconnected focus on concepts in isolation from one another. There are further overlaps between the kinds of approaches which students take to their learning ('deep' or 'surface') and whether they survive or thrive in higher education, or in Case's terms, 'fit in'.

The distinguishing feature of alienation theory is that it provides a wider canvas for understanding how students learn than the mainly cognitive focus of 'approaches to learning' theory. This means that entry into higher education is not simply about grades and cognitive markers of success but poses a more philosophical question of students' orientation to higher education, whether that be personal, vocational, social, or academic (Ibid, p. 329). Similarly, fitting in will be influenced by the wide array of experiences which shape students' lives and have a bearing on how they engage or feel alienated from their studies. Most significantly, as higher education has expanded and diversified in the 20th and 21th century, theories of alienation and engagement invite discussion and action about context, power relations, and historical disadvantage. The question of why students from working-class backgrounds perform less well than those from middle-class backgrounds is one which refuses to be addressed by labels about deep and surface learning. Alienation enables in-depth analysis of social issues and is a prompt to universities to think more radically about interventions to address persistent inequalities (Case 2008, p. 330).

Barnhardt and Ginns (2014) problematise the use of alienation as a macro-theory for understanding teaching at the micro-level. In bridging the gap between 'approaches to learning' as a macro-theory and students' learning experience at the micro-level, they propose mapping between Seeman's categories of alienation and the Australian Course Experience Questionnaire (CEQ), a survey grounded in approaches to learning theory. The factors they map across to are: 'Appropriate Assessment' (assessment which leads to growth in personal understanding rather simply requiring than factual recall), where low scores represent self-estrangement and learner dependence; 'Clear Goals and Standards', where low scores reflect a psychological state of meaninglessness; and 'Independent Learning', where low scores reflect passive learning behaviours, or student agency when positive. Their article brings data about students' approaches to learning to the discussion about alienation, turning abstract and theoretical ideas into concrete, empirical findings. While the use of data develops links between theory and evidence, the mapping is complex, and relies solely on quantitative data to explore the impact of context on student learning.

Mapping alienation theory to assessment and feedback

In Table 3.1, I have mapped Seeman's psycho-social categories of alienation to assessment and feedback practices, drawing on analyses in the literature discussed in the chapter. The mapping identifies what alienation looks like in assessment and feedback. It suggests how to turn alienation into engagement, foreshadowing Section 3 of the book, which examines the interaction between analysis and practice. Working with TESTA programme teams has generated many of these concrete and principled approaches to address alienation and to foster student agency and engagement.

The contrasting model of 'approaches to learning' theory

Theories of alienation and engagement provide new ways of analysing and addressing the challenges of assessment and feedback. They offer a rival perspective to 'approaches to learning' theory, the dominant means of understanding student learning for 40 years of Scholarship of Teaching and Learning (SOTL).

Approaches to learning theory arose out of a study conducted at Gothenburg University by education psychologists. The findings showed that students took two distinct methods in how they approached reading a 1,500-word essay. One group of students displayed an approach which was subsequently called a 'deep approach', the other displayed a 'surface approach'. Reading for understanding, making connections, and finding personal meaning in a text characterised the deep approach; in contrast, students taking a surface approach tended to focus on rote learning, factual recall, reproduction, and task completion (Marton and Saljo 1976).

Research on approaches to learning has formed the basis for large-scale surveys on how students learn, transforming what originated as a small-scale qualitative study occurring in context into influential national surveys. The Approaches to Study Inventory (ASI) measured the extent to which students were taking a deep or surface approach to learning (Meyer and Parsons 1989). The ASI developed a further 'approach' to learning, termed the 'strategic' approach to learning, where students combined deep and surface approaches out of a motivation to be as tactical as possible: how and where to expend effort for the highest gain; and when to be minimalist because assessment 'doesn't count' or appears not to add tangible gains. Deep, surface, and strategic learning have a firm hold in the lexicon of higher education.

Approaches to learning theory is the orthodoxy underpinning national benchmarking surveys, university teaching rankings, and institutional performance management. The Course Experience Questionnaire (CEQ) was

Table 3.1 Mapping alienation theory

Seeman: five categories of alienation	What this form of alienation looks like in assessment and feedback	Turning alienation into engagement: suggested approaches
Powerlessness arises in the gap between expectation and the outcome. Powerlessness is characterised by low control and feelings of helplessness.	a. Students expect time and space to explore and go into depth, but they are overwhelmed with the volume of assessment and fullness of the curriculum. b. Students expect to engage with each other and their teachers, but they are kept at arm's length and their experience feels passive. c. Students lack ownership over assessment processes; they have little freedom and control over assessment questions, timing, and types of assessment.	a. Reduce summative assessment; embed formative tasks and feedback to engage students more in exploring concepts and theories. Be more selective and reduce curriculum content. b. Build active and peer learning strategies into teaching and assessment processes, especially through peer review and authentic tasks for a real audience. c. Involve students in co-creating criteria, designing MCQs for use with other students, learning to pose questions, and contributing ideas about appropriate assessment types.
Meaninglessness is the inability to comprehend events, to predict outcomes and make informed decisions. Meaninglessness is characterised by uncertainty and ambiguity. **Normlessness** is the absence of socially approved behaviours, with social rules being questioned. Breaking the rules is seen both as rebellion and innovation. It is hard to determine personal goals in the absence of shared rules.	a. Students perceive marking, feedback, and standards to be variable; they do not trust feedback enough to act on it. b. Students are uncertain about goals and standards. c. Students find assessment fragmented, displaying little coherence across degree programmes. a. Shared rules for assessment and maintaining academic integrity are invisible, inconsistently applied, and make little sense to students. b. Assessment norms, such as referencing, and the disciplinary discourse are not made explicit; students struggle to navigate assessments successfully. c. Students do not understand what analysis, critique, and good academic practice look like, so they 'rebel' and invent new practices.	a. Programme teams calibrate standards and agree consistent feedback; they build trust through audio, screencast, and dialogic feedback. b. Involve students in mock-marking, peer review, and discussing a range of exemplars to internalise standards. c. Plan and map assessment across programme as a team and invite students to draw links across the big picture; establish a shared purpose and rhythm of assessments. a. Programmes and departments interpret rules in consistent ways across modules; students contribute to thinking through fair approaches to assessment. b. Teachers spend class time engaging students in activities which familiarise, shape, and challenge assessment norms and invite students to reflect on disciplinary ways of thinking. These are shared and honed at the programme level. c. Students discuss, see, and critique examples, and are taught how to write, problem-solve, and think in their disciplines.

(Continued)

Table 3.1 (Continued)

Seeman: five categories of alienation	What this form of alienation looks like in assessment and feedback	Turning alienation into engagement: suggested approaches
Social isolation is detachment from societal norms; a misalignment between things valued by a person and by society, rebellion against social values.	a. Assessment criteria and learning outcomes drive a conservative and risk-averse approach; students must conform to approaches for which they do not see the value. b. Mass assessment modes reduce personal connection and feel industrial; they divide rather than integrate concepts. c. Students are mainly asked to reproduce knowledge, concepts, and theory, and they learn things in isolation from big questions in society.	a. Use Barnett and Coate's 'knowing, acting and being' curriculum model (2005) to devise holistic criteria and learning outcomes; enable students to pursue lines of inquiry which have meaning to them. b. Incorporate case studies, scenarios, and problems requiring students to connect their learning and development to prior learning and experience. c. Ensure assessment responds to and generates ideas and questions of relevance to students and society.
Self-estrangement is the inability to find fulfilment in activities for their own sake, loss of pride in work, lack of satisfaction	a. Assessment rewards compliance over creativity; students are passive and become adept at implementing others' ideas. b. Students are unable to process critique and reject it, partly for emotional reasons; they take criticism personally. c. Students feel that feedback is generic, impersonal, and does not speak to them as individuals.	a. Devise assessments which challenge students to inquire, bring novel interpretations, and cross discipline-boundaries. Reward thinking outside-the-box. b. Lecturers share their own approaches to dealing with criticism; formative and peer feedback are diffused through the curriculum; students develop their capacity to make use of feedback. c. Personalise formative feedback, be conversational in annotations, use audio, screencast, and live marking; avoid cut and paste generic feedback. Inject your personality into feedback while balancing the needs for standards and criteria.

developed in Australia by one of the originators of the ASI, as a performance indicator of student learning (Wilson et al. 1997). This is now used as a national benchmarking tool for all Australian universities. The CEQ became the basis for the UK's National Student Survey (NSS) which has been used since 2005 to measure students' perceptions of their studies within their subject fields. The NSS is used to rank universities, to performance-manage academics, and as the main underpinning metric for the Teaching Excellence Framework (TEF) in the UK. Both the CEQ and the NSS are underpinned conceptually by approaches to learning theory.

Critiques of 'approaches to learning' theory

'Approaches to learning' theory persists as a dominant way of understanding how students learn in higher education. As a heuristic, it has helped the higher education community to think about student learning, and 'given us a language through which we can exchange ideas and dilemmas' (Shulman 2002, p. 42). However, since it has gained the status of orthodoxy, the theory has become normal. Like any dogma, it has lost some of its playful and creative spirit as widespread acceptance of a theory closes the door on different perspectives. Theories like Bloom's taxonomy, constructive alignment, and approaches to learning 'are powerful…as long as we don't take them too seriously, as long as we don't transform mnemonic into dogma or heuristic into orthodoxy' (Ibid, p. 42).

While 'approaches to learning' theory has given the sector a useful vocabulary for talking about teaching and learning, been a catalyst for action, and focused attention on teaching and assessment design, a handful of scholars have questioned its dominance (Haggis 2003; Howie and Bagnall 2013; Malcolm and Zukas 2001; Webb 1997). As the 'big answer' to all the questions about how students learn, they argue that it is underdeveloped, simplistic, and open to semantic slippage (Howie and Bagnall 2013); it over-emphasises cognitive psychology at the expense of the social and structural context (Malcolm and Zukas 2001); and it underplays students' agency (Haggis 2003). It is also out of step with more holistic, affective, and relational theories of how students learn (Beard et al. 2007; Bovill 2020; Cavanagh 2016; Quinlan 2016a)

Scholars have critiqued the over-reliance of approaches to learning theory on cognitive psychology, the least visible and most individual aspect of student learning. Case (2008) and Barnhardt and Ginns (2014) identify the limitations of isolating students' learning from the wider structural and social conditions in which they are learning. Context influences students' engagement, sense of agency, and learning, whether within university structures or through the influence of wider social factors. In its original form, approaches to learning theory did recognise the interaction between the innate learning behaviours of individual learners and the university environment in which students were learning. However, the theory begs questions about whether deep and surface theories are about innate learning and study behaviours or about the power of the learning environment to trigger these behaviours. It also sets up a binary between deep and surface learning which has inadvertently led to a diminished view of the role memory plays in students' learning, particularly in some disciplines and cultural contexts (Kember 2016).

One of the limitations of adopting a psychological theory of student learning is what it leaves out. Higher education encompasses developing the life of the mind but extends further and deeper than expanding the mind. Recent research argues for an episteme which recognises that learning involves emotions, intuition, and interaction between the head and the heart (Behar 1997; Cavanagh 2016; Palmer 1993; Quinlan 2016a). A more relational epistemology which engages with the emotions and the intellect sparks curiosity, develops ethical judgement, and helps students to have a personal stake in their learning (Bovill 2020; Palmer 1993; Quinlan 2016b). This aligns with curriculum theories and educational practices which give prominence to the process of 'becoming' through approaches which focus on the moral, ethical, and intellectual development of students (Barnett and Coate 2005).

A key implication of approaches to learning theory is that students' learning behaviours can be controlled through changing the learning environment, using different teaching techniques, and altering our assessment regimes. Techniques and principled educational changes are helpful to nudge learning behaviours. However, the values and intentions that underpin their use are more significant than the techniques themselves. Values such as trust, responsiveness, listening, and an ethic of participation enable student agency, and are expressed in relational teaching techniques and assessment tactics (Bovill 2020; Brookfield 2015). Student agency and engagement are about respecting and valuing what each student brings to their learning engagement. They call for a more relational approach to teaching and assessment which acknowledges the complexity of the binary categorisation of deep and surface learning, as argued by Haggis (2003):

> One of the fundamental problems with the view of learning that the model presents is that it removes the individual learner from the richness and complexity of his/her multiple contexts. It also constructs 'the learner' as a being…passively amenable to reconstruction as a 'deep' learner through a new set of moulding processes that take place within the university. The learner, in this model, is a human being without agency.
>
> (Haggis 2003, p. 98)

TESTA's stance: from 'approaches to learning' to alienation and engagement

Chapter 2 explains how the tools and techniques of TESTA began within the 'approaches to learning' tradition and have relied on some aspects of the model to understand students' learning behaviours. However, over time, the student data from focus groups demonstrated more contextual and structural realities influencing students' learning, engagement, and agency. These stretched beyond the constructs of 'approaches to learning' and foregrounded the impact of modular degree structures in a mass higher education system on students' learning, compounded by the influence of marketisation. TESTA findings have pushed the boundaries of 'approaches to learning' theory and led to an exploration of the value of alternative theories of alienation and engagement to analyse students' experience of assessment and feedback more holistically. As Shulman observes, an educated person is 'someone whose commitments always leave open a window for sceptical scrutiny, for imagining how it might be otherwise' (Shulman 2002, p. 41). As the work on TESTA has developed and grown, so 'imagining how it might be otherwise' has been central to evolving insights of the value of a different kind of theoretical framework, in the light of the data.

Many dimensions of alienation appear in TESTA evidence: the erosion of pedagogic relationships in consumer-driven higher education; the positioning of students as objects rather than subjects in assessment and feedback (Jessop and Tomas 2017); students as outsiders to the discourse of assessment and feedback, leading to confusion about expectations (Jessop et al. 2014; O'Donovan et al. 2008); students denied the opportunity to be creative, original, or autonomous in completing assessment tasks to meet narrowly focused criteria and outcomes (Erikson and Erikson 2019; Havnes and Prøitz 2016); loss of ownership over the products of assessment; privatisation of assessment leading to lack of learning from others; artificiality of assessment types, especially examinations (Gibbs and Simpson 2004); and impersonal, anonymised feedback which fails to draw students into a dialogue (Nicol 2010; Pitt and Winstone 2018). Students in focus groups often describe their experience in terms that suggest the affective dimensions of learning have been ignored (Beard et al. 2007). It is for these reasons that TESTA has adopted alienation and engagement theories to understand students' assessment experience in the wider context.

A brief synopsis

Alienation theory provides a sociological approach to understanding how students learn from their assessment, expanding on psychological theories of learning and contextualising them. This chapter provides a brief history of alienation theory and sets out five categories of alienation: powerlessness, normlessness, meaninglessness, social isolation, and self-estrangement. It maps these categories to assessment and feedback in higher education and proposes strategies for turning alienation into engagement. Further, it outlines the history and limits of the more dominant psychological approach to understanding how students learn, known as 'approaches to learning theory'. It shows how 'Transforming the Experience of Students through Assessment' (TESTA) had its foundations in deep and surface approaches to learning. In taking a programme approach to assessment and feedback, and in recognition of wider contextual influences on students' learning behaviours, it has found more explanatory power in alienation and engagement theories.

References

Baldry, C., P. Bain, and P. Taylor. 1998. 'Bright satanic offices': Intensification, control and team Taylorism. Chapter 9, pp 163–183. In Thompson, P. and Warhurst, C. (Eds), *Workplaces of the Future*. Basingstoke. Palgrave.

Barnett, R., and K. Coate. 2005. *Engaging the Curriculum in Higher Education*. Maidenhead. SRHE and Open University Press.

Barnhardt, B., and P. Ginns. 2014. An alienation-based framework for student experience in higher education: New interpretations of past observations in student learning theory. *Higher Education* 68: 789–805.

Beard, C., S. Clegg, and K. Smith 2007. Acknowledging the affective in higher education. *British Educational Research Journal* 33 (2): 235–252.

Behar, R. 1997. *The Vulnerable Observer: Anthropology That Breaks Your Heart*. Boston. Beacon Press.

Bovill, C. 2020. *Co-Creating Learning and Teaching: Towards Relational Pedagogy in Higher Education*. St Albans. Critical Publishing.

Brookfield, S. 2015. *The Skillful Teacher*. San Francisco, CA. Wiley and Sons.

Buckley, A. 2021. Crisis? What crisis? Interpreting student feedback on assessment. *Assessment & Evaluation in Higher Education* 46 (7): 1008–1019, DOI: 10.1080/02602938.2020.1846015

Case, J. M. 2008. Alienation and engagement: Development of an alternative theoretical framework for understanding student learning. *Higher Education* 55: 789–805.

Cavanagh, S. R. 2016. *The Spark of Learning: Energizing the College Classroom With the Science of Emotion*. Morgantown. West Virginia University Press.

Eliot, T. S. 2002. *Collected Poems 1909–1962*. London. Faber and Faber.

Erikson, M. G., and M. Erikson 2019. Learning outcomes and critical thinking – Good intentions in conflict. *Studies in Higher Education* 44 (12): 2293–2303, DOI: 10.1080/03075079.2018.148681

Feuerlicht, I. 1978. *Alienation: From the Past to the Future*. Westport, CT. Greenwood Press.

Gibbs, G., and C. Simpson 2004. 'Conditions under which assessment supports Students' learning. *Learning and Teaching in Higher Education* 1 (1): 3–31.

Gravett, K., and N. E. Winstone 2022. Making connections: Authenticity and alienation within students' relationships in higher education. *Higher Education Research & Development* 41 (2): 360–374, DOI: 10.1080/07294360.2020.1842335

Haggis, T. 2003. Constructing images of ourselves? A critical investigation into 'Approaches to Learning' research in higher education. *British Educational Research Journal* 29 (1): 89–104.

Halabi, R. 2022. Palestinian Students in an Israeli-Hebrew university: Obstacles and challenges. *High Education*. https://doi.org/10.1007/s10734-022-00920-x

Havnes, A., and T. S. Prøitz. 2016. Why use learning outcomes in higher education? Exploring the grounds for academic resistance and reclaiming the value of unexpected learning. *Educational Assessment, Evaluation and Accountability.* 28:205–223, DOI: 10.1007/s11092-016-9243-z

Howie, P., and R. Bagnall. 2013. A critique of the deep and surface approaches to learning model. *Teaching in Higher Education* 18 (4): 389–400, DOI: 10.1080/13562517.2012.733689

Jessop, T., Y. El Hakim, and G. Gibbs 2014. The whole is greater than the sum of its parts: A large-scale study of Students' learning in response to different programme assessment patterns. *Assessment & Evaluation in Higher Education* 39 (1): 73–88, DOI: 10.1080/02602938.2013.792108.

Jessop, T., and C. Tomas. 2017. The implications of programme assessment patterns for student learning. *Assessment & Evaluation in Higher Education* 42 (6): 990–999, DOI: 10.1080/02602938.2016.1217501

Kember, D. 2016. Understanding and teaching the Chinese learner: Resolving the paradox of the Chinese learner. In R. King and A. Bernardo (Eds). *The Psychology of Asian Learners.* Springer. Singapore. https://doi.org/10.1007/978-981-287-576-1_11

Lombardi, M. 2007. 'Authentic Learning for the 21st Century: An Overview', *Educause Learning Initiative Paper 1.* Available at: http://www.lmi.ub.edu/cursos/s21/REPOSITORIO/documents/Lombardi_2007_Authentic_learning.pdf Accessed 4 January 2022.

Malcolm, J., and M. Zukas. 2001. Bridging pedagogic gaps: Conceptual discontinuities in higher education. *Teaching in Higher Education* 6 (1): 33–42, DOI: 10.1080/13562510020029581

Mann, S. J. 2001. Alternative perspectives on the student experience: Alienation and engagement. *Studies in Higher Education* 26 (1): 7–19.

Marton, F., and R. Saljo. 1976. On qualitative differences in learning:1 – Outcomes and process. *British Journal of Educational Psychology* 46 (1): 4–11.

Meyer, J. H. F., and P. Parsons. 1989. Approaches to studying and course perceptions using the Lancaster inventory—A comparative study. *Studies in Higher Education* 14 (2): 137–153, DOI: 10.1080/03075078912331377456

Nicol, D. J. 2010. From monologue to dialogue: Improving written feedback processes in mass higher education. *Assessment & Evaluation in Higher Education* 35 (5): 501–517.

O'Donovan, B., M. Price, and C. Rust. 2008. Developing student understanding of assessment standards: A nested hierarchy of approaches. *Teaching in Higher Education* 13 (2): 205–217, DOI: 10.1080/13562510801923344

Palmer, P. 1993. *To Know as We Are Known: Education as a Spiritual Journey.* San Francisco, CA. Harper One.

Palmer, P. 2009. *A Hidden Wholeness: The Journey Towards an Undivided Life.* San Francisco, CA. Jossey-Bass.

Pitt, E., and N. Winstone. 2018. The impact of anonymous marking on students' perceptions of fairness, feedback and relationships with lecturers. *Assessment & Evaluation in Higher Education* 43 (7): 1183–1193, DOI: 10.1080/02602938.2018.1437594

Quinlan, K. M. 2016a. How emotion matters in four key relationships in teaching and learning in higher education. *College Teaching* 64 (3): 101–111, DOI: 10.1080/87567555.2015.1088818

Quinlan, K. M. 2016b. Developing student character through disciplinary curricula: An Analysis of UK QAA subject benchmark statements. *Studies in Higher Education* 41 (6): 1041–1054, DOI: 10.1080/03075079.2014.966069

Rae, G. 2010. Alienation, authenticity and the self. *History of the Human Sciences* 23 (4): 21–36.

Schacht, R. 1970. *Alienation*. Garden City. Doubleday.

Seeman, M. 1959. On the meaning of alienation. *American Sociological Review* 24 (6): 783–791.

Seeman, M. 1975. Alienation studies. *Annual Review of Sociology*. Chapter 2. 91–123.

Seeman, M. 1983. Alienation motifs in contemporary theorizing: The hidden continuity of the classic themes. *Social Psychology Quarterly* 46 (3): 171–184.

Shulman, L. S. 2002. Making differences: A table of learning. *Change: The Magazine of Higher Learning* 34 (6): 36–44, DOI: 10.1080/00091380209605567

Villarroel, V., S. Bloxham, D. Bruna, C. Bruna, and C. Herrera-Seda. 2018. Authentic assessment: Creating a blueprint for course design. *Assessment & Evaluation in Higher Education* 43 (5): 840–854, DOI: 10.1080/02602938.2017.1412396

Wakefield, A., R. Pike, and S. Amici-Dargan. 2022. Learner-generated podcasts: An authentic and enjoyable assessment for students working in pairs. *Assessment & Evaluation in Higher Education*. 1–18. DOI: 10.1080/02602938.2022.2152426

Webb, G. 1997. Deconstructing deep and surface: Towards a critique of phenomenography. *Higher Education* 33 (2): 195–212.

Williams, J., and D. Kane 2009. Assessment and feedback: Institutional experiences of student feedback, 1996 to 2007. *Higher Education Quarterly* 63 (3): 264–286, DOI: 10.1111/j.1468-2273.2009.00430.x

Williamson, I., and C. Cullingford. 1997. The uses and misuses of 'Alienation' in the social sciences and education. *British Journal of Educational Studies* 45 (3): 263–275, DOI: 10.1111/1467-8527.00051

Wilson, K. L., A. Lizzio, and P. Ramsden 1997. The development, validation and application of the course experience questionnaire. *Studies in Higher Education* 22 (1): 33–53, DOI: 10.1080/03075079712331381121

Winstone, N. E., R. Ajjawi, K. Dirkx, and D. Boud. 2022. Measuring what matters: The positioning of students in feedback processes within national student satisfaction surveys. *Studies in Higher Education* 47 (7): 1524–1536, DOI: 10.1080/03075079.2021.1916909

Yuill, C. 2011. Forgetting and remembering alienation theory. *History of the Human Sciences* 24 (2): 103–119.

Chapter 4

The wider context of alienation in higher education

Introduction

Frustrations with feedback and disaffection with assessment persist despite more than 40 years of research based on psychological theories of learning. This chapter reframes the debate. It proposes a new way of 'seeing' the problem of assessment and feedback, which is more sociological in its orientation. It examines the influence of factors beyond the classroom and exam hall on students' experience of assessment. How does marketisation shape students' ideas about learning, grades, and the pedagogic relationship? In what ways has mass higher education contributed to students' feeling that they are part of an industrial process rather than personally involved in exploring and shaping ideas? Why do students describe fast and fragmented learning as they juggle assessment deadlines on multiple modules? And in what ways are metrics preventing risk-taking and innovation, and encouraging traditional and 'safe' assessment practices? The interaction between macro-level developments and students' micro-level experience of assessment and feedback poses sociological and philosophical questions about alienation, agency, and the purpose of higher education.

For students, alienation in assessment and feedback is characterised by a sense that assessment is 'done' to them, and that they have very little ownership or control over the process and outcome. They may be overwhelmed by the volume of assessment, confused by expectations, and lack joy in their accomplishments. In a mass higher education system, students may also feel unknown and anonymous, and unable to forge relationships with their tutors and peers in ways which strengthen their sense of academic purpose and belonging (Gravett and Winstone 2022; Quinlan 2016). While these features of alienation affect individual students in different ways, wider social and political movements have a pervasive influence on the student experience of alienation in higher education. This chapter explores these macro-level developments and their influence at micro-level (Barnhardt and Ginns 2014). It examines the intersection between political, social, and economic trends, and student alienation and engagement in assessment and feedback. Four trends are outlined

DOI: 10.4324/9780429347962-7

in the chapter: *mass higher education*, *modularity*, *marketisation*, and *metrics*. The analysis draws on the theory of alienation outlined in Chapter 3 and anticipates practice-based chapters based on TESTA evidence in Section 3.

The shape of global higher education has changed significantly in recent decades, with expansion of student numbers linked to widening participation (Burridge 2010; Marginson 2016; Trow 2005); the growth in popularity of modular degrees in the UK, Europe, and African countries (Dejene 2019; French 2015; Rich and Scott 1997); and the marketisation of higher education, shifting the cost of studying for a degree from the state to students (Brown 2015; Bunce et al. 2017; Naidoo and Jamieson 2005; Nixon et al. 2018). An audit culture has accompanied these trends, measuring educational quality through proxies of student satisfaction and contributing to competitive global university rankings (Buckley 2021; Spence 2019; Winstone et al. 2022). These macro-level developments are a global phenomenon, acting in relationship to one another, yet varying in their extent and character in different higher education systems.

TESTA evidence links to the wider literature in demonstrating the impact of modularity on students' learning, the effects of mass higher education on students' perceptions of assessment and feedback, and the imprint of the discourse and realities of marketisation on their 'disposition to learn' (Naidoo and Jamieson 2005, p. 278). Performance measures constrain academics to design assessment and feedback in ways that conform to metrics, which, when focused on student satisfaction, may be designed in response to asking the wrong questions (Spence 2019; Winstone et al. 2022).

Depictions of student alienation and engagement

How is alienation expressed in practice? Analysing student alienation at local level in relation to trends at macro-level is challenging (Barnhardt and Ginns 2014). It requires exercising the 'sociological imagination' to understand the relationship between the personal and the political (Wright Mills 1959). It means pursuing themes from the literature and evidence about students' qualitative experience of assessment and feedback to 'an enormous sea of serious social issues' (Behar 1997, p. 14). Linking between the wider context and student alienation reframes the problem as a more sociological one, from seeing students' disaffection as an individual phenomenon to analysing the relationship between student agency and engagement, and structural conditions. This section seeks to bring depictions of alienation at the local level to life using the licence of creative analytical practice (Richardson 2000).

Alienation is the first-generation student who does not know the hidden linguistic codes to write an academic essay, feels the pain of under-confidence, and experiences the reality of being an outsider (Mann 2005). Alienation occurs when assessment tasks curtail sparks of originality and ownership, and leave students bored and disengaged (Sharp et al. 2017). It is students juggling heavy assessment loads that prevent deep and meaningful engagement (Tomas & Jessop 2018). It is assessment *done to* students, rewarding passivity and docility (Mann 2001). It is continuous assessment every week, which provides a repetitive and formulaic experience of the chemistry experiment (Adams 2020). It is not being known, being in receipt of generic cut and paste feedback that is impersonal and devoid of relationship (Pitt and Winstone 2018). It is one-off feedback that does not influence reflection and action (Boud and Molloy 2013). It is being an outsider and not experiencing a sense of belonging or developing an authentic voice as one learns (Gravett and Winstone 2022).

Alienation has many dimensions: some relate to assessment structures; others to socio-economic and political factors; and yet others to the philosophical process of intellectual growth within higher education (Barnett 2022). Modules designed in isolation fragment learning and prevent feedback from feeding forward (Jessop and Tomas 2017); multiple assessments compete for students' attention working against 'slow' learning (Harland et al. 2015); large classes diminish learning gain (Gibbs 2010); criteria mask the complex judgements involved in marking (Bloxham et al. 2016; Shay 2005); and paying fees for higher education changes the tone of the educational relationship, leading to instrumental learning orientations among students, not least because students are busy with part-time work (Nixon et al. 2018; Bunce et al. 2017). However, certain forms of alienation in higher education are an integral part of student's intellectual and personal development. Weighing different perspectives that challenge taken for granted assumptions is discomforting for students, as is exposure to ambiguity, conflicting perspectives, and the unsettling nature of higher education (Barnett 2022; Baxter Magolda 2001; Perry 1981). These aspects of higher education can be alienating. Indeed some students may choose not to engage and embrace the right to experience alienation (Macfarlane 2016; Mann 2001; Zepke 2014).

In contrast to alienation, student engagement offers a language and practice of hope. Engagement is defined as students' 'cognitive investment in, active participation in, and emotional commitment to their learning' (Zepke and Leach 2010, p. 168). It suggests a wholehearted approach to assessment, an 'ontological engagement' where a student tackles a task with 'enthusiasm, élan, and imagination', becoming one with it (Barnett and Coate 2005, p. 139). Engagement involves the development of personal and academic virtues such as a love of learning, intellectual curiosity, and persistence (Quinlan 2016). Agency is closely associated with the concept of engagement. It refers to a person's capacity to make choices in purposeful and autonomous ways (Nieminen et al. 2022). On an individual basis, agency requires persistence, self-efficacy, and self-regulation (Stenalt and Lassesen 2022). However, these individual characteristics cannot be separated from the wider socio-cultural and learning environments in which agency is exercised, where freedom to act may be constrained or enabled by structural factors. The ecosystem in which assessment and feedback plays out may constrain or enable individuals' capacity to act

(Nieminen et al. 2022). Wider socio-cultural factors influence students' capacities to take action, make choices, develop ownership, and persist – it is to these factors that the chapter turns.

From micro to macro: the big picture of alienation

This section examines major shifts to higher education over the last half century: mass higher education, modularisation, marketisation, and the introduction of often public (and competitive) measures of performance and student satisfaction. Analysing the interaction between these *macro-level factors* and student alienation and engagement is a means of joining the private worlds of students with the public discourse and realities of studying in higher education in the 21st century.

Factor #1: mass higher education

Higher education has grown from an elite to a mass system across the world. In Europe, the USA, and high-income countries, increased rates of participation occurred in the decades after the Second World War (UNESCO 2017). Between 2000 and 2014, rates of participation in higher education almost doubled from 19% to 34% across the world among the members of the population in the school-leaving age bracket (typically 18–23). While there are huge disparities globally in participation rates, women and men now attend Bachelors' and Masters' programmes at the same rate. The dramatic expansion of higher education has been marked by a wider range of institutions of higher learning, a more diverse demographic of students, changing modes of delivery, and diverse and sometimes conflicting interests between the state, the economy, industry, and even universities themselves (Willetts 2017).

Changes from an elite system to a mass higher education system are associated with political imperatives to build a skilled and specialised workforce for the economy (Dearing 1997; Department for Education 2021; Kvale 2007). In theory, the expansion of higher education to develop a highly skilled workforce should diminish the role of examinations in the selection and control of students, initiating approaches to assessment which enable lifelong learning: assessment *for* learning, innovation in assessment, and a focus on feedback for development. In reality, socio-political changes to expand higher education have set up a 'field of contradictions' for assessment in higher education (Kvale 2007, p. 57). Mass higher education requires efficient approaches to assessment, such as examinations and multiple-choice quizzes, with minimalist, impersonal, or standardised feedback, often causing students to focus more on grades than feedback. In contrast, the relatively small numbers of students in elite systems in the past allowed for closer relationships between students and their teachers, with formative feedback shaping the minds, academic skills, and even the characters of students (Quinlan 2016). However, reflecting further on the 'field of contradictions' should prevent a romanticised view of elite higher education as a golden age. In elite systems, traditional examinations were the most common form of assessment, and their authoritarian, selective, secretive, and anxiety-provoking tendencies brought their own forms of alienation to student learning.

Modular programmes are a feature of mass higher education (Trow 2005). Their flexibility enables a diverse range of students to participate in higher education, who may not otherwise be able to sustain full-time commitments (French 2015). However, the short duration of modules can prevent slow and developmental learning. Relationships between teachers and students are often more distant and impersonal given the number of students, the duration of modules, and the need to be more cost-effective in mass modular systems. In mass systems, large class sizes have more impact on assessment than on teaching:

> As class sizes have increased there have been some economies of scale in teaching (simply by packing more students into classrooms), but economies of scale are difficult to achieve for assessment: most assessment costs go up in direct proportion to the number of students.
>
> (Gibbs and Simpson 2004, p. 10)

Factor #2: modularisation

Modules are small units of learning in a programme of study, that need not be sequential, and for which students accumulate credits leading to the award of a degree. They tend to be short in duration and may align with semesters. Modules represent a content-based division, whereas semesters are the temporal-division of the academic year into two halves (French 2015). Modular degrees are the alternative to traditional year-long linear degrees, which encourage slower forms of developmental learning. Modules have been a common feature of degrees in the United States for more than a century; they have been used in smaller higher education systems such as Sweden, Scotland, New Zealand, and Ireland (French 2015; Hennessy et al. 2010); since the 1980s, modules have become common in UK degrees. They are also increasingly used in African countries (Dejene 2019).

The reason for the widespread development of modular degrees is complex. Modularisation offers faster and cheaper ways to educate growing numbers of more diverse students. It is part and parcel of the mass production of higher education (French 2015; Hennessy et al. 2010). It facilitates international student mobility as part of 'study abroad' opportunities in which students accumulate credits towards the final award. Modularity is also closely linked to more defined approaches to curriculum design that measure and evaluate the achievement of learning outcomes through equivalent sized units of study (Ibid 2010). In principle, modularity offers opportunity for more interdisciplinary study (French 2015).

The emphasis of modular degrees on offering students choice and flexibility overlaps with marketisation. Students can choose modules based on the kinds of assessment they want to undertake; they can exercise their agency in deciding the options they are interested in studying. Similarly, markets provide customers with choices, enabling them to select products which they perceive to have value. The comparison falls short here as the student 'consumer' is also shaping and participating in the 'product' and growing and developing in relation to the process they are undertaking. Students need to make informed choices, and to connect their learning to construct meaningful degrees. The most common criticism of modularity is that it leads to students undertaking incoherent and fragmented degrees (French 2015). The 'deconstruction of the subject' that modularity pre-empts can lead to students not having a foundational grasp of disciplinary knowledge (Bridges 2000, p. 42).

Modules are shorter in duration than traditional linear degrees. Their duration has an impact on how students learn. It leads to intensive approaches to learning, often squeezing out formative assessment and feedback, and fragmenting student learning (Wu and Jessop 2018). It prevents students from engaging in the slow work of integrating concepts over time (Gibbs 2019; Harland et al. 2015):

> These new identities and rationalities assumed by students have the potential to transform learning into a process of picking up, digesting and reproducing what students perceive of as an unconnected series of short, neatly packaged bytes of information. Under these conditions, the student disposition generated may have negative ramifications for the development of higher order skills and more importantly, the dispositions and attitudes required for autonomous, lifelong learning.
>
> (Naidoo and Jamieson 2005, p. 273)

Assessment and feedback are profoundly affected by modularity. In modular degrees, students undertake more assessment to measure each credit-bearing small unit and need to manage their summative assessment loads across several concurrent modules (Tomas and Jessop 2018). On most modules, there is often more than one summative assessment in the aspiration to avoid a single high-stakes summative assessment. This leads to an 'assessment arms race' across modules with formative assessment competing with summative assessment for student time and attention (Harland et al. 2015). Both high summative and low formative assessment loads work against students' 'disposition to learn', discouraging playfulness and risk-taking, and leading to alienation. Students make choices about which assessments they want to avoid (e.g. examinations, presentations, group work) and some may strategically select relatively easy modules to get better grades. This devalues their overall achievement of graduate qualities, undermining the purpose of studying for a higher education degree. The self-assembly of modular degrees may lead to the whole being less than the sum of its parts. Similarly, teachers on different modules may have little understanding of what students are learning elsewhere on their degree and how their module fits into the broader picture of students' learning journey. Assessment across the programme may be varied and randomly sequenced, leaving students unable to internalise standards or act on their feedback. Problems emerge when the feedback from the first assignment in a module comes close to the end of the module, allowing little time for students to benefit from advice before the final assessment, as confirmed by TESTA evidence (see Chapter 6).

Factor #3: marketisation

Marketisation is linked to the rapid expansion of global higher education. It is largely a consequence of the state's inability to fund mass higher education, which shifts the burden of cost from the public purse to students. Marketisation has been defined as 'the attempt to put the provision of higher education on a market basis, where the supply and demand of student education, academic research and other university activities are balanced through the price mechanism' (Brown 2015, p. 5). However, the price mechanism operates only in a limited fashion, mainly in higher education systems that consist of many private universities, such as in the US. It is applied to international and postgraduate students in many countries, although to a lesser extent in the US (Slaughter and Cantwell 2012). Irrespective of the price mechanism, the higher education market is an economic exchange between fee-paying students and universities.

Paying for a university education has introduced the concept of 'students-as-consumers' into higher education discourse (Bunce et al. 2017; Molesworth et al. 2009; Naidoo and Jamieson 2005; Nixon et al. 2018; Tomlinson 2017). While the student-as-consumer metaphor is dominant in higher education (Macfarlane 2020, p. 542), little is known about its everyday impact on students' academic experience especially in countries outside the global north (Brooks et al., 2021, p. 125). UK-based research has shown that students who view themselves as consumers are likely to perform less well academically than those who do not (Bunce et al. 2017). The impact of marketisation on students' identities varies. Some scholars argue that there has been a sea-change in how students see themselves as consumers and its effect on their academic behaviours and expectations (Molesworth et al. 2009; Naidoo and Jamieson 2005; Nixon et al. 2018). Others argue that students have resisted taking on the identity of being a consumer and continue to engage in university life in similar ways as they did prior to marketisation (Macfarlane 2020; Tomlinson 2017).

In the UK, the regulatory environment reflects the shift to a consumer orientation which plays out in student behaviours. Since 2015, students and universities have been included under the UK's Consumer Rights Act (2015). The Office for Students (OfS) regulates higher education including student access, experience, and outcomes, and acts as the guardian of 'students as consumers' for all students in registered providers of higher education in the UK. Tomlinson (2017) notes that the Office of the Independent Adjudicator (OIA) recorded 'higher levels of complaint and "service" dissatisfaction amongst students in recent years, which appear to be reinforced by new fee structures' (Ibid, p. 455). The market dictates that students have more information at their disposal, universities are more publicly accountable for the quality of education on offer, and students may be more aware of their rights to educational information and services. In theory, students have more choice, which is central to their exercise of agency. In theory too, 'some degree of competition does increase efficiency, responsiveness and, more arguably, innovation' (Brown 2015, p. 6).

There has been an increase in investment in the professionalisation in teaching and learning, accompanied by the central provision of academic development and learning technology support within many universities. This has led to the growth in the scholarship of teaching and learning encouraged by national and international enhancement networks, communities, and organisations (Knapper 2016). Measures to improve and professionalise teaching relate to the reality that students are paying for a service and reflect the competition between universities to achieve better teaching rankings. Academics with teaching qualifications are consistently rated more highly by students than those who have no qualification (Gibbs 2010). There is also a positive relationship between students' learning and staff engagement in the scholarship of learning and teaching (Brew and Ginns 2008). Notwithstanding these more positive developments, two questions persist: how does marketisation influence the way students interact with their learning? What is the impact of marketisation on students' experience of assessment and feedback?

Section 3 offers granular insights from TESTA research which illustrate the relationship between students' learning experience and the impact of marketisation on them. It shows a mix of transactional consumer views, characteristics of alienation, and ways in which agency and engagement may be realised in a context which positions students in a relationship of exchange.

Factor #4: metrics

Public performance measures of teaching are increasingly used as proxies for the quality of teaching and assessment in marketised, mass higher education systems (Gibbs 2010; Spence 2019; Winstone et al. 2022). They are also used to rank universities and subjects in competitive league tables, and to help students make informed consumer choices about the 'product' they are purchasing, in line with the logic of markets. The nature of measuring teaching quality has changed as higher education has grown. In the UK, it has moved through three stages: from internal institutional scrutiny, such as observation of teaching practice and departmental reviews, to 'collective security', entrusting judgements of quality to peer institutions and academics, under the supervision of the state and quality agencies, to market competition as the key safeguard of quality. The authority of expert academic judgement has been superseded by markets and student satisfaction measures (Brown and Carasso 2013).

Metrics about teaching quality exist to a varying extent across the world, with some measures fuelling competition between universities and others providing information for internal university consumption and enhancement purposes. The emphasis of some metrics is on student engagement, positioning students as producers and agents who are responsible for their learning (Buckley 2014; Kuh 2003.) Engagement metrics illuminate how students learn, integrate concepts, and collaborate with others. They are a good way of understanding how engaged students are in their learning. In general, these are not the metrics that contribute to the competitive ranking of universities. Indeed, these metrics are likely to measure what is valued rather than value what is measured (Winstone and Pitt 2017; Winstone et al. 2022).

In theory, national teaching quality metrics ensure that universities and programmes are publicly accountable to students, taxpayers, regulatory bodies, and the state. They may even be the impetus for universities investing resources to enhance teaching, learning, and assessment. But are they accurate measures of teaching quality? Taking aim at the UK's National Student Survey, Spence (2019) argues that it is a 'low-cost, crude way of measuring teaching quality' (Ibid, p. 770) and 'an intellectual short-cut' to teaching excellence that is likely to disrupt Humboldtian visions of cultivating critical minds with the 'instrumentalism of student satisfaction' (Ibid, p. 762). In their editorial on teaching excellence, Gourlay and Stevenson (2017) highlight the blind spot of relying on survey data as the sole measure of excellence: the context is missing. Teaching quality metrics are silent on some of the strongest indicators of teaching quality, such as class and cohort size, extent of close contact with teachers, the quality of the teachers, and the extent of collaborative learning, all of which relate to the context of learning (Gibbs 2012, pp. 14–15). Yet, in the UK, metrics of student satisfaction influence institutional behaviour to 'an unprecedented extent' while not always being good indicators of educational quality (Gibbs 2010, p. 14).

Questions about the validity of teaching quality metrics are a longstanding concern (Buckley 2021; Gibbs 2012; Surridge 2009). In their analysis of ten national surveys in the UK, Europe, North America, Australia, and East Asia, Winstone et al. (2022) provide a granular critique of feedback questions. Feedback items in national surveys ask questions which reinscribe the agency of teachers (not students), privilege one-way communication, encourage passive recipience by students, and measure frequency as a proxy for quality (Ibid, p. 1531). High scores on questions which are antithetical to educational principles about how students learn from assessment might improve a university's competitive ranking, but they are the low road to mediocrity.

The validity of measures relates not only to the items and their relevance to proven factors that influence teaching quality but also to whether the metrics are measuring the same units of study as students experience. Gibbs (2012) identifies that the National Student Survey (NSS) measures students' experience of a programme of study, when in a mass higher education system, many students experience a loose assembly of modules *as* their programme of study, which may have a weak relationship to the NSS subject category. This creates an institutional problem of interpretation, and the challenge of knowing how to act on the data. In some institutions, subjects are being deliberately aligned to NSS categories, which has the ironic effect of providing less student choice (Ibid, p. 9). The expansion of education surveys to include items on students' psychological well-being further dilutes their ability to provide insight on the quality of education. These may be good questions to ask, but they are not measures of educational quality.

Metrics nudge students towards a consumer orientation. Rankings and ratings imply that education is a product that can be measured and evaluated easily, rather than a complex and evolving process which often defies measurement. Studies on the moral and intellectual development of students demonstrate that some ambiguity, discomfort, and alienation are part and parcel of the student journey in higher education (Baxter Magolda 2004; Perry 1981). Barnett (2022) has described teaching as 'setting up educational situations so that students acquire the energies to go on by themselves and become their own agents' (Ibid, p. 111). He uses the metaphor of bungee jumping to depict teaching as a form of provocation where teachers urge students to leap across a chasm and to have courage, knowing that the risk is intentionally limited. He argues that 'student anxiety is part of higher education' (Ibid, p. 113). One of higher education's purposes is to challenge students' commonly accepted assumptions and ways of understanding the world, discomforting them. For these reasons, it may not produce 'satisfaction' in the conventional, customer-oriented sense of the word.

A brief synopsis

This chapter follows on from the theoretical exposition of alienation and its influence on assessment and feedback in Chapter 3. It outlines macro-level socio-economic, political, and cultural influences which pervade higher education systems across the world: mass higher education, modularisation, markets, and metrics. It invites readers to read the rest of the book with the wider view of the context in mind, in particular the chapters in Section 3, which bring students' micro-level experiences to the fore. The intersection between wider influences and students' granular experience is a focal point for understanding alienation and engagement in relation to assessment and feedback.

References

Adams, C. J. 2020. A constructively aligned first-year laboratory course. *Journal of Chemical Education* 97 (7): 1863–1873, DOI: 10.1021/acs.jchemed.0c00166

Barnett, R. 2022. *The Philosophy of Higher Education: A Critical Introduction.* Abingdon. Routledge.

Barnett, R., and K. Coate. 2005. *Engaging the Curriculum in Higher Education.* Maidenhead. Open University Press.

Barnhardt, B., and P. Ginns. 2014. An alienation-based framework for student experience in higher education: New interpretations of past observations in student learning theory. *Higher Education* 68: 789–805.

Baxter Magolda, M. B. 2004. *Making Their Own Way: Narratives for Transforming Higher Education to Promote Self-Development.* Sterling, VA. Stylus Publishing.

Behar, R. 1997. *The Vulnerable Observer: Anthropology That Breaks Your Heart.* Boston. Beacon Press.

Bloxham, S., B. den-Outer, J. Hudson, and M. Price. 2016. Let's stop the pretence of consistent marking: Exploring the multiple limitations of assessment criteria. *Assessment & Evaluation in Higher Education* 41 (3): 466–481, DOI: 10.1080/02602938.2015.1024607

Boud, D., and E. Molloy. 2013. Rethinking models of feedback for learning: The challenge of design. *Assessment & Evaluation in Higher Education* 38 (6): 698–712, DOI: 10.1080/02602938.2012.691462

Brew, A., and P. Ginns. 2008. The relationship between engagement in the scholarship of teaching and learning and students' course experiences. *Assessment & Evaluation in Higher Education* 33 (5): 535–545.

Bridges, D. 2000. Back to The future: The higher education curriculum in The 21st century. *Cambridge Journal of Education* 30 (1): 37–55.

Brooks, R., A. Gupta, S. Jayadeva, and A. Lainio. 2020. Students in marketised higher education landscapes: An introduction. *Sociological Research Online* 2020 26 (1): 125–129.

Brown, R. 2015. The marketisation of higher education: Issues and ironies. *New Vistas* 1 (1): 3–9.

Brown, R., and H. Carasso. 2013. *Everything for Sale? The Marketisation of UK Higher Education.* Abingdon. Routledge.

Buckley, A. 2014. Voice or data? Surveying student engagement in the UK sector. HEIR Annual Conference, Oxford Brookes University, September 2014. Available at: http://www.heirnetwork.org.uk/wp-content/uploads/sites/18/2014/10/Buckley-Keynote.pdf Accessed 24 January 2023.

Buckley, A. 2021. Crisis? What crisis? Interpreting student feedback on assessment. *Assessment & Evaluation in Higher Education* 46 (7): 1008–1019, DOI: 10.1080/02602938.2020.1846015

Bunce, L., A. Baird, and S. E. Jones 2017. The student-as-consumer approach in higher education and its effects on academic performance. *Studies in Higher Education* 42 (11): 1958–1978, DOI: 10.1080/03075079.2015.1127908

Burridge, M. (Ed). 2010. *Martin Trow: Twentieth-Century Higher Education Elite to Mass to Universal.* Baltimore. The Johns Hopkins University Press.

Dearing, R. 1997. *Higher Education in the Learning Society: Report of the National Committee of Inquiry into Higher Education.* London. Her Majesty's Stationary Office.

Dejene, W. 2019. The practice of modularized curriculum in higher education institution: Active learning and continuous assessment in focus, *Cogent Education*, 6 (1), DOI: 10.1080/2331186X.2019.1611052

Department for Education. 2021. *Skills for Jobs: Lifelong Learning for Opportunity and Growth*. London: Department for Education. https://www.gov.uk/government/publications/skills-for-jobs-lifelong-learning-foropportunity-and-growth

French, S. 2015. 'The Benefits and Challenges of Modular Higher Education Curricula'. Issues and Ideas Paper. Melbourne Centre for the Study of Higher Education. University of Melbourne.

Gibbs, G. 2010. 'Dimensions of Quality'. York. Higher Education Academy. Available at: https://www.advance-he.ac.uk/knowledge-hub/dimensions-quality Accessed on 30.03.23

Gibbs, G. 2012. Implications of 'Dimensions of Quality' in a market environment. York. Higher Education Academy. Available at: https://www.advance-he.ac.uk/knowledge-hub/implications-dimensions-quality-market-environment Accessed on 30.03.23

Gibbs, G. 2019. 'How assessment frames learning' (Chapter 2 pp. 22–35). In C. Bryan and K. Clegg. (Eds) *Innovative Assessment in Higher Education: A Handbook for Academic Practitioners*. Abingdon. Routledge.

Gibbs, G., and C. Simpson 2004. 'Conditions under which assessment supports students' learning. *Learning and Teaching in Higher Education* 1: 3–31.

Gourlay, L., and J. Stevenson. 2017. Teaching excellence in higher education: Critical perspectives. *Teaching in Higher Education* 22 (4): 391–395, DOI: 10.1080/13562517.2017.1304632

Gravett, K. & N.E. Winstone 2022. Making connections: authenticity and alienation within students' relationships in higher education, *Higher Education Research & Development*, 41:2, 360–374, DOI: 10.1080/07294360.2020.1842335

Harland, T., A. McLean, R. Wass, E. Miller, and K. Nui Sim. 2015. An assessment arms race and its fallout: High-stakes grading and the case for slow scholarship. *Assessment & Evaluation in Higher Education*, DOI: 10.1080/02602938.2014.931927

Hennessy, E., R. Hernandez, P. Kieran, and H. MacLoughlin. 2010. Teaching and learning across disciplines: Student and staff experiences in a newly modularised system. *Teaching in Higher Education* 15 (6): 675–689, DOI: 10.1080/13562517.2010.507301

Jessop, T., and C. Tomas. 2017. The implications of programme assessment patterns for student learning. *Assessment & Evaluation in Higher Education* 42 (6): 990–999, DOI: 10.1080/02602938.2016.1217501

Knapper, C. 2016. Does educational development matter? *International Journal for Academic Development* 21 (2): 105–115, DOI: 10.1080/1360144X.2016.1170098

Kuh, G. D. 2003. What we're learning about student engagement from NSSE: Benchmarks for effective educational practices. *Change: The Magazine of Higher Learning* 35 (2): 24–32, DOI: 10.1080/00091380309604090.

Kvale, S. 2007. 'Contradictions of assessment for learning in institutions of higher learning'. In D. Boud and N. Falchikov. (Eds) 2007. *Rethinking Assessment in Higher Education*. Abingdon. Routledge Taylor and Francis.

Legislation.gov.uk. 2016. *Consumer Rights Act 2015*. [online] Available at: <http://www.legislation.gov.uk/ukpga/2015/15/part/1/chapter/3> [Accessed 1 March 2023].

Macfarlane, B. 2016. The performative turn in the assessment of student learning: A rights perspective. *Teaching in Higher Education* 21 (7): 839–853, DOI: 10.1080/13562517.2016.1183623

Macfarlane, B. 2020. Myths about students in higher education: Separating fact from folklore. *Oxford Review of Education* 46 (5): 534–548, DOI: 10.1080/03054985.2020.1724086

Mann, S. J. 2001. Alternative perspectives on the student experience: Alienation and engagement. *Studies in Higher Education* 26 (1): 7–19.

Mann, S. J. 2005. Alienation in the learning environment: A failure of community? *Studies in Higher Education* 30 (1): 43–55, DOI: 10.1080/0307507052000307786

Marginson, S. 2016. The worldwide trend to high participation higher education: Dynamics of social stratification in inclusive systems. *Higher Education* 72: 413–434.

Molesworth, M., E. Nixon, and R. Scullion. 2009. Having, being and higher education: The marketisation of the university and the transformation of the student into consumer. *Teaching in Higher Education* 14 (3): 277–287, DOI: 10.1080/13562510902898841

Naidoo, R., and I. Jamieson. 2005. Empowering participants or corroding learning? *Towards a research agenda on the impact of student consumerism in higher education. Journal of Education Policy* 20 (3): 267–281, DOI: 10.1080/02680930500108585

Nieminen, J. H., J. Tai, D. Boud, and M. Henderson. 2022. Student agency in feedback: Beyond the individual. *Assessment & Evaluation in Higher Education* 47 (1): 95–108, DOI: 10.1080/02602938.2021.1887080

Nixon, E., R. Scullion & R. Hearn. 2018. Her majesty the student: marketised higher education and the narcissistic (dis)satisfactions of the student-consumer. *Studies in Higher Education.* 43:6, 927–943, DOI: 10.1080/03075079.2016.1196353

Perry, W. 1981. 'Cognitive and ethical growth: The making of meaning' Chapter 3 (pp. 76–116). In Jossey Bass (Ed.). *The Modern American College.* San Francisco, CA. Jossey-Bass.

Pitt, E., and N. Winstone. 2018. The impact of anonymous marking on students' perceptions of fairness, feedback and relationships with lecturers. *Assessment & Evaluation in Higher Education* 43 (7): 1183–1193, DOI: 10.1080/02602938.2018.1437594

Quinlan, K. M. 2016. Developing student character through disciplinary curricula: An Analysis of UK QAA subject benchmark statements. *Studies in Higher Education* 41 (6): 1041–1054, DOI: 10.1080/03075079.2014.966069

Rich, T., and C. Scott. 1997. Modularization and semesterization: Ringing the changes. *Perspectives, Policy and Practice in Higher Education* 1 (3): 70–76.

Richardson, L. 2000. 'Writing: A method of inquiry' Chapter 36 (pp. 923–948). In N. K. Denzin and Y. S. Lincoln. (Eds) *Handbook of Qualitative Research.* Second Edition. San Francisco, CA. Sage.

Sharp, J. G., B. Hemmings, R. Kay, B. Murphy, and S. Elliott. 2017. Academic boredom among students in higher education: A mixed-methods exploration of characteristics, contributors and consequences. *Journal of Further and Higher Education* 41 (5): 657–677, DOI: 10.1080/0309877X.2016.1159292

Shay, S. 2005. The assessment of complex tasks: a double reading. *Studies in Higher Education.* 30(6), 663–679, DOI: 10.1080/03075070500339988

Slaughter, S., and B. Cantwell. 2012. Transatlantic moves to the market: The United States and The European union. *High Education* 63, 583–606. https://doi.org/10.1007/s10734-011-9460-9

Spence, C. 2019. 'Judgement' versus 'metrics' in higher education management. *High Education* 77, 761–775. https://doi.org/10.1007/s10734-018-0300-z

Stenalt, M. H., and B. Lassesen. 2022. Does student agency benefit student learning? A systematic review of higher education research. *Assessment & Evaluation in Higher Education* 47 (5): 653–669, DOI: 10.1080/02602938.2021.1967874

Surridge, P. 2009. *The National Student Survey Three Years on: What Have We Learned.* York. Higher Education Academy.

Tomas, C., and T. Jessop. 2018. Struggling and juggling: A comparison of student assessment loads across research and teaching-intensive universities. *Assessment & Evaluation in Higher Education* 44 (1): 1–10, DOI: 10.1080/02602938.2018.1463355

Tomlinson, M. 2017. Student perceptions of themselves as 'consumers' of higher education. *British Journal of Sociology of Education.* 38(4), 450–467, DOI: 10.1080/01425692.2015.1113856

Trow, M. A. 2005. Reflections on the Transition from Elite to Mass to Universal Access: Forms and Phases of Higher Education in Modern Societies since WWII. UC Berkeley Working Papers. Available at: https://escholarship.org/uc/item/96p3s213 Accessed on 29.03.2023

UNESCO, 2017. Six ways to ensure higher education leaves no one behind. Policy Paper 30. Paris. April 2017. Published by Global Education Monitoring Report.

Willetts, D. 2017. *A University Education.* Oxford. Oxford University Press.

Winstone, N., and E. Pitt. 2017. Feedback is a two-way street. So why does the NSS only look one way? *Times Higher Education,* Sept 14, 2017. Accessed 26 June 2022. https://www.timeshighereducation.com/opinion/feedback-two-way-street-so-why-does-nss-only-look-one-way

Winstone, N. E., R. Ajjawi, K. Dirkx, and D. Boud 2022. Measuring what matters: The positioning of students in feedback processes within national student satisfaction surveys. *Studies in Higher Education* 47 (7): 1524–1536, DOI: 10.1080/03075079.2021.1916909

Wright Mills, C. 1959. *The Sociological Imagination.* Oxford. Oxford University Press.

Wu, Q. & T. Jessop. 2018. Formative assessment: missing in action in both research-intensive and teaching focused universities? *Assessment & Evaluation in Higher Education,* 43 (7): 1019–1031, DOI: 10.1080/02602938.2018.1426097

Zepke, N. 2014. Student engagement research in higher education: Questioning an academic orthodoxy. *Teaching in Higher Education* 19 (6): 697–708, DOI: 10.1080/13562517.2014.901956

Zepke, N., and L. Leach 2010. Improving student engagement: Ten proposals for action. *Active Learning in Higher Education* 11 (3): 167–177, DOI: 10.1177/1469787410379680

Part III

Engaging assessment and feedback

From analysis to practice

Chapter 5

From alienation to engagement in assessment design

Introduction

Assessment design is complex and challenging. Every single assessment presents a 'wicked problem' (Forsyth 2023), as academics wrestle with tensions between fairness and authenticity, aiming to set tasks which enable students to demonstrate a deep grasp of concepts. As Jones et al. (2021) argue, designing assessment involves tensions for academics which are wider than how reliable, engaging, or pedagogically principled each assessment is, and are linked to the increasing importance of student well-being. Balancing these tensions is difficult at the level of each individual assessment. This is made more challenging in a context where assessment is influenced by wider socio-cultural, economic, and political changes, and has become the focal point of fast-paced discussions about the implications of generative AI (Cotton et al. 2023; Rudolph et al. 2023). As O'Donovan (2018) outlines, assessment is the focus of tensions in higher education:

> Arguably, nowhere are the tensions between a more consumerist student body and a burgeoning managerialism versus the integrity of knowledge and academic standards so intense as in the arena of assessment.
>
> (O'Donovan 2018, p. 13)

At the micro-level, assessment design challenges often fall on individual academics and relate to assessments on 'their' modules of study. An Australian study by Bearman et al. (2017) about teachers' design decisions shows that individuals prioritise certain activities as essential such as aligning teaching and assessment, and are more selective about designing tasks to nurture student agency, for example. It is unsurprising that aligning assessment tasks with teaching and the intended learning outcomes is uppermost in the minds of teachers, given the dominance of constructive alignment as a curriculum model (Biggs and Tang 2011). The focus on aligning assessment to intended learning outcomes at a modular level has had some unwelcome consequences. These include increasing summative assessment at the expense of formative

DOI: 10.4324/9780429347962-9

(Gibbs and Dunbar-Goddet 2009); creating a culture of compliance rather than analytical and critical thinking, and thereby potentially limiting student learning and agency (Havnes and Prøitz 2016); and focusing on measurable markers of learning at the expense of more developmental, longitudinal, and intangible outcomes (Erikson and Erikson 2019). While programme approaches cannot solve all the problems of an outcomes-based model of education, they can lead to a more integrated and developmental approach to assessing outcomes, paradoxically focusing more on the process of learning than on outcomes (Gibbs 2010, 2012; Whitfield and Hartley 2017).

This chapter takes a different starting point from designing individual, modular assessments. Students' experience of assessment needs to be seen from the perspective of the whole programme and the wider ecosystem in which they are learning. This is both challenging and liberating as it calls on a team approach to assessment design. The challenge is to step back to understand the assessment experience of students on modular degrees from a programme perspective. This often entails sacrificing some individual assessment practices for the greater good of the programme. A programme approach liberates teachers and students from placing too high a burden of expectation on each assessment in isolation from the whole. In undertaking TESTA, there are shifts in how academics perceive the connections between modules such as rebalancing formative and summative assessment to encourage more learning from assessment and with that more freedom to experiment; better sequencing of assessment varieties across the programme; attention to the purpose and timing of feedback so that it incorporates more formative and dialogic principles; and more of a focus on assessment as part of the pedagogic relationship (Bovill 2020).

TESTA data provides empirical evidence of programme-wide patterns of assessment and their influence on students' learning. Granular qualitative data from 102 focus groups with 552 students in 14 universities provides a student perspective of how assessment patterns influence their engagement, or contrastingly, lead to alienation. The evidence makes visible programme patterns of assessment; it brings out the implications of modular design on students' experience of assessment and feedback. Based on the evidence, teams develop practical approaches to designing assessment across their whole programme that foster student agency and engagement.

Student engagement and agency

Assessment measures student learning, and it should help students to learn and to develop intellectual and personal skills to become life-long learners. So how do assessment practices engage students and nurture their sense of agency? How do they foster agency and engagement in a wider context that introduces a host of contradictory pressures? According to Kahu (2013), there are different dimensions of engagement which are multi-layered and responsive to the context. The behaviourist dimension involves influencing student behaviours, especially 'time-on-task' and approaches to study. The psychological dimension engages students through their emotions and motivation to study, for example when assessment piques interest, generates enthusiasm, and cultivates a sense of belonging. Cognitive engagement occurs when assessment is designed to call on students' self-efficacy, self-regulation, and engenders the characteristics of deep learning. Structural engagement relates to the design of assessment tasks as a system, in interaction with the curriculum. Structural factors such as the socio-economic, political, and cultural context of higher education also influence students' engagement.

Definitions of agency vary from describing agency as 'the power of the individual to choose what happens next' (Lindgren and McDaniel 2012, p. 344) to a broader definition that it is 'the capability of individual human beings to make choices and act on these choices in a way that makes a difference in their lives' (Martin 2004, p. 135). Social constructivism is the learning theory most likely to promote agency, with its central thesis that students can make meaning in interaction with their environment and in their relationship with others. In social constructivist settings, students are not passive; learning is not 'done' to them. Students are motivated to achieve when they have agency, and they find personal relevance in learning as they have more of a stake in the process and the outcome (Lindgren and McDaniel 2012). Certain types of assessment enable students to choose and determine 'what happens next', reinscribing their sense of agency: problem-based learning, creative and collaborative tasks, research and inquiry-based projects, reflective activities, and choices about areas and questions of study determined by students. When assessment engages students, it stimulates their interest, prompts questions, and fires up their imagination, prompting them to make connections across modules and between concepts on a programme of study, within their disciplines, and beyond the university into the world of work.

Alienating assessment patterns: a systems perspective

Analysis of TESTA audit data from 60 undergraduate degree programmes in 12 UK universities and two Indian universities demonstrates typical patterns of assessment across programmes of study. The programmes in the sample are evenly spread across research-intensive and teaching-focused universities. The audit data examines four features of assessment. These are:

- volume of summative assessment
- volume of formative assessment
- the number of different varieties of assessment
- proportion of assessment by examination

The audit conversation captures the Programme Director's interpretation of the planned curriculum, in a guided conversation. Definitions of summative and formative assessment align closely with Shepard's distinction that summative measures students' achievement by a grade, while 'formative gives qualitative insights about students' understandings and misconceptions to improve

Table 5.1 High, medium, and low interquartile ranges on n=60 programmes

Characteristic	Low	Medium	High
Volume of summative assessments	17—33	33–45 (Median 38)	56–135
Volume of formative assessments	0–4	4–23.5 (Median 8)	24–116
Varieties of assessment	6–11	11–15.5 (Median 12)	16–30
Proportion of Examinations	0–9%	10–31% (Median 21.5%)	31–79%

learning' (Shepard 2005, p. 22). In practical terms, TESTA describes formative assessment as not counting towards the degree, with the expectation that all students undertake it, and it always elicits feedback, whether from teachers, peers or through guided reflection. In general, the purposes of formative assessment are to help students to:

- engage in low-risk tasks that invite playfulness and creativity while learning
- create staging posts to distribute their effort, spending more 'time-on-task'
- practise novel forms of assessment
- engage in drafting and re-drafting processes using feedback
- reflect on and refine their understanding and academic skills
- learn from mistakes or misconceptions.

Varieties of assessment are the different types of assessment that students encounter on a programme, from standard formats like essays and examinations to more novel formats such as podcasts, industry projects, posters, and patchwork portfolio assessments. The proportion of assessment by examination measures the volume of examinations as a percentage of all the summative tasks. This measure masks the weight of examinations in many students' grades. The proportion may be low, but the weighting may be high.

The data is categorised according to low, medium, and high boundaries using interquartile analysis[1], Interquartile ranges and medians are the most accurate measures of representing TESTA audit data.

Interpreting programme assessment patterns from TESTA audit data

Taking the medium category as typical, four features stand out. The first is that the typical volume of summative assessment (33–45) is high compared to the original categorisations of Gibbs and Dunbar-Goddet (2009) which ranged from 15–40. The typical ratio of formative-only assessment is low in comparison too, at 4–23.5 formative assessments, compared to the original sample of 15–40 (Ibid 2009). The typical ratio of formative to summative assessment is 1:5. The overall paucity of formative assessment is illustrated by the median of 8 formative assessments which equates to between two and three formative assessment tasks per year of a three-year undergraduate degree. The third feature is the proportion of examinations. This shows that one in every five assessments is an examination, with a higher proportion of exams in research-intensive universities, and in certain disciplines. It corroborates findings in previous studies (Jessop and Maleckar 2016; Wu and Jessop 2018). The fourth feature is about varieties of assessment and indicates that there are high varieties of assessment, between 11 and 15.5, with a median of 12, compared to the much lower typical range in the earlier study of 4–6 different varieties of assessment. The current median of 12 means that students could encounter a new assessment variety once in every three assessment tasks if varieties were evenly distributed.

TESTA audit data further shows that the system as it stands is focused more on assessment *of* learning, with weak formative assessment, high volumes of summative assessment, one in five closed-book, timed examinations, and high varieties of assessment. There is a mismatch between these patterns of assessment and design principles to foster learning, engagement, and student agency. This is the systemic problem which TESTA seeks to address. The following sections outline the implications of each of these patterns of assessment.

Pattern #1: disproportionate summative assessment

Measuring student achievement dominates in a modular degree system. One of the consequences of modular assessment design is that summative assessment has multiplied (Jessop 2016; Jessop and Tomas 2017; Jessop et al. 2014; Tomas and Jessop 2018; Wu and Jessop 2018). Each module contains at least one, often two, and sometimes more summative assessment points, in recognition of the requirement to measure outcomes at the modular level, and to make modular credits transferable. From a student perspective, assessments seem to be designed in isolation with little cognisance of competing demands across the programme:

> I often feel like the units don't collaborate on when our deadlines are. Like last term, after reading week, I had about six essays due, all in the space of a few weeks … This term and next term, I've got it again – I've got essays and presentations in the same weeks, but nothing this side of term.
>
> (Student, Humanities, 2020)

Teachers often design several modular assessments to enable students to have grades 'in the bank', a practice which is spurred on by the belief that splitting the high stakes summative tasks lowers the risk for students and contributes to better well-being. Ironically, this may not be the case:

> There was the poster submission, thesis, then the poster presentation, then the exam. It was a very stressful time. Motivation was hard to come by.
>
> (Student, Life Sciences, 2011)

It is common in the sciences to design continuous assessment, which leads to students 'banking' small percentages of their grades weekly through completing problem sheets or laboratory reports (Adams 2020). Whatever the reason for multiple summative assessment points, it is rare for the walls of modules to be breached with assessment which spans across modules and draws together threads of learning from several modules. Aside from the final year project which most students undertake, it is unusual for any assessment to synthesise material from several modules or the whole programme, sometimes described as a 'capstone' assessment (PASS 2012). Indeed, assessment on a single module sometimes fails to draw together the conceptual threads from that very module, with some assessments being topic-based. As one student observed in a focus group:

> I attend all my lectures as they cost about £80 a pop, but I only concentrate in the week when the topic of my assessment is being taught
> (Student, Humanities, 2014)

Sadler argues that continuous assessment, the practice of frequent, sometimes weekly, small summative assessments, constitutes 'contamination of the grade' (Ibid 2016, p. 1088) measuring a series of 'non-achievements', as outcomes can only be properly measured at the end of a course of learning. Measuring bite-size outcomes along the way compromises the idea of outcomes and may contribute to an inaccurate overall grade. Certainly, it diminishes opportunities for the iterative process of learning which formative assessment provides, often characterised by 'false starts, errors, bumbling attempts and time spent going up blind alleys' yet leading to deep understanding by the end of a course (Ibid 2016, p. 1088). High volumes of summative assessment also promote grade-orientation and instrumental approaches to learning (Harland et al. 2015; Wass et al. 2015).

The motivation for designing summative assessment can be both to measure achievement and to stimulate student effort. Critics decry frequent high stakes summative assessment when it is used as a 'pedagogy of control' (Harland et al. 2015), a form of behaviourist conditioning to trigger effort (Wass et al. 2015). As a 'pedagogy of control', summative assessment substitutes for genuine formative assessment by incentivising students to notch up grades which measure effort along the way rather than the achievement of outcomes. High summative assessment loads on one module spur on the proliferation of assessment on concurrent modules in a competition for student effort, leading to an 'assessment arms race' (Harland et al. 2015). Students inevitably prioritise assessment that counts when formative and summative assessment compete for student time and effort:

> It's also the kind of balance if you get to a stage where you know you've got all these deadlines coming up. You think I'll prioritise those rather than prioritising things that don't really count.
> (Student, Sciences, 2019)

We spent a solid two weeks doing the one that counted, and then I did the one that didn't count an hour before. I did it an hour before in my bed. Other things are prioritised, you know, cause if I do better in the one that didn't count, it's sort of demotivational. But I think there's always that kind of like in the back of your mind 'Oh well it doesn't count, I'm not going to spend as much time on it'.

(Student, Social Sciences, 2020)

The 'assessment arms race' can also lead to students being overwhelmed by the volume of summative assessment:

S3: Once in the second year we had five – five! – group projects, plus one or two individual ones. All done in the exact same time. And-
I: How did that affect how you studied? How you worked?
S3: You just don't have a life
S4: I nearly quit the course, I couldn't handle it.
S2: I had to completely ignore everything that was exam related until after the hand-ins
S6: I stopped going to lectures and things like that – didn't have time.
S5: I didn't go to lectures. [I was] in the library for hours, just to finish the project.
S7: I think two coursework units per term is manageable. I know a couple [of students] who are doing three and they're barely keeping their heads above water.
S4: I can confirm, I'm one of those people (Students, Engineering, 2019).

The relationship between high cognitive loads and assessment volume is well documented (Tomas and Jessop 2018; Kalyuga 2011; Lizzio et al. 2002; Lizzio and Wilson 2013). Students juggling multiple summative assessment deadlines across parallel modules experience cognitive overload and this impacts the quality of work they can do:

The different modules and different programmes aren't necessarily aware of each other's deadlines, so it gets to a point where, we've had it before like a big report the week after the end of final exams in two weeks or something, and it feels like you're not prioritising the quality of your work at that point, you're just kind of focused on getting over each hurdle.

(Student, Sciences, 2019)

High assessment volumes and concurrent deadlines can be a spur for students making tactical choices and taking intellectual short-cuts which restrict their learning to familiar and easy topics rather than challenging ones:

I'd much rather learn something new, but when I know I'm going to be stressed because I've got all of these three [essays] in the same week. I just need to pick one that can get done easily. That feels quite sad, so I've done two or three things on liminality now. I don't want to do anything more on that, I want to do something new.

(Student, Humanities, 2019)

In a mass higher education system, teachers complain of over-assessment, high marking loads, and feedback wastage where students do not use or act on feedback (Tuck 2012; Winstone et al. 2017). Students describe the impact of high assessment volumes on their approaches to learning, engagement, and well-being in TESTA focus groups:

In weeks 9 to 12 there is hardly anyone in our lectures because we're too stressed. I'd rather use those two hours to get my assignment done.

(Student, Social Science, 2014)

It's been non-stop assignments. I've had to rush every piece of work.

(Focus Group, Humanities, 2012)

Pattern #2: an absence of formative assessment

High assessment loads on modular degrees squeeze out opportunities for formative assessment, the most valuable and effective approach to student learning, engagement, and motivation (Adams 2020; Black and Wiliam 1998; Morris et al. 2021; Nicol and Macfarlane-Dick 2006; Sadler 1989; Weurlander et al. 2012). A recent systematic review of formative assessment and feedback in higher education confirmed previous literature on learning gains, depending on implementation factors (Morris et al. 2021). Black and Wiliam's large-scale meta-analysis of factors that contribute to learning concluded that 'innovations that include strengthening the practice of formative assessment produce significant and often substantial learning gains' (Black and Wiliam 1998, p. 40). Sadler (1989) describes the virtue of formative assessment and feedback as its capacity for 'short-circuiting the randomness and inefficiency of trial and error' learning' (Ibid, p. 120). Formative practices help students to fine-tune their understanding and internalise standards through cycles of reflection on feedback (Nicol and Macfarlane-Dick 2006). Teachers can identify points where students are struggling by how well they manage formative tasks and adapt their teaching responsively (Hattie and Timperley 2007). Well-designed formative assessment is a mechanism to encourage and distribute student effort (Gibbs and Simpson 2004).

The design of formative assessment is integral to its success. When it is focused solely on improving student performance and is heavily dependent on corrective feedback from teachers, it is unlikely to engage students and make them become agents of their own learning. Formative assessment designed as a mechanism to improve grades is based on an instrumental premise

(Pryor and Crossouard 2008, p. 3). As these comments show, it does not fire the imagination, galvanise effort, or encourage wholehearted participation:

> There was a mock exam, we could do over Christmas. I think only 12 people of 180 did it in the first like two weeks or something.
>
> (Student, Science, 2020).

> I'd definitely say that I put more effort into summatives than formatives – especially after the thing last term when I didn't get my formatives back until I'd done my summatives. It's just kind of discouraged me from doing them at all, or doing them to the best of my ability, because I just don't feel like they're that useful.
>
> (Student, Humanities, 2019)

Many students fail to see the worth of formative assessments that replicate traditional summative assessments, regarding them as no different, yet without the benefit of a grade. They also raise false expectations about improvements in performance which may be dashed:

> And sometimes I feel like it's necessary, but just for practice and you get feedback on how to structure your essay, but sometimes it's just like if I don't have time, I don't feel the need to do it. Because if it doesn't count for anything, I might not do it.
>
> (Student, Sciences, 2020)

> I don't know who marks our essays but last term, for a formative essay I went to office hours to speak to the lecturer, and they told me to structure it in a certain way, then someone else marked it and said it was structured wrong.
>
> (Student, Humanities, 2019)

In contrast, formative assessment and feedback that works from within a social constructivist paradigm invite students to shape their learning in more open-ended and exploratory ways (Pryor and Crossouard 2008). Tasks are creative and experimental; they help students make sense of concepts; feedback probes at misconceptions, nudging students to a more holistic understanding. These kinds of formative assessment and feedback help students develop a more sophisticated understanding of concepts and disciplinary skills, and iron out misconceptions:

> Sometimes I struggle to understand the concepts, and so having formative feedback, where they can be like, okay, this is this little bit here is a misunderstanding of the concept, that's so helpful for me.
>
> (Student, Social Sciences, 2020)

Engaging formative assessment helps students 'become' agents of their learning in a discursive relationship of questioning, challenge, and encouragement. Students construct fresh understandings in the context of their subject and revise their work in the light of feedback exchanges. They are not passive error-correctors; they are active meaning-makers:

S1: The lecturer offered to do a small project kind of thing where he would give us a problem [to solve] and in real time he would give us feedback about it. And that was extremely helpful and every single person who attended said it was just the best thing ever.

S3: It was the fact that it was in real time, the lecturer was actively overseeing what we're doing, and saying, "maybe you want to approach it in a different manner, are you sure that this is the right answer, why?" and just pushing us through it.

S3: And... you were able to ask direct questions and get the feedback instantly. I'd say that's probably the only bit of the course that ever ended up making sense to me (Students, Engineering, 2019).

In theory, formative assessment is a powerful means of learning and engagement. In practice, it is difficult to design well in a competitive context which prizes performance and achievement over learning for the longer term. It is often 'poorly understood' and 'weak in practice' (Black and Wiliam 1998, p. 20). Prevailing approaches to formative assessment and feedback often re-inscribe transmission approaches to feedback as 'telling'; they uphold meticulous specifications of criteria and outcomes, and they take on the instrumental values of achieving higher grades (Dann 2014; Sadler 2007; Torrance 2007). Well-designed formative assessment requires tactical skill, conviction about its value, setting expectations early on, and challenging both traditional practices and wider structural factors. So how can teachers emphasise the value of formative assessment in a culture focused on accumulating good grades?

Strategies to disrupt assessment patterns in support of learning

Reducing high volumes of summative and increasing formative assessment and feedback has the potential to strengthen students' engagement and sense of agency in their learning. Programmes undertaking TESTA have adopted various tactics to good effect:

- *Take a programme approach:* agree the balance of summative and formative assessment at a programme level. This may involve sacrificing some modular autonomy for the greater good of the programme.
- *Design engaging and purposeful formative assessment:* students are often quite strategic about their studies. They take calculated decisions about the value of spending time on academic activities in the context of competing agendas

which may include part-time work. Students need to undertake summative assessment tasks to pass their degrees. In contrast, formative assessment requires additional incentives for students to understand the value of engaging in it. In conducting TESTA, teachers repeatedly explain that only the keen, intrinsically motivated, and 'best' students undertake formative tasks unless there is a universal requirement to do it. The following approaches have been proven to encourage wholehearted participation in TESTA programmes.

- **Authentic, public domain tasks** which replicate disciplinary and professional outputs and are presented to an audience (whether in class, industry or on a social media platform). Examples include blogs, podcast interviews, book reviews, presentations, posters, infographics, exhibition plans, a ministerial brief, and debates).
- **Practice runs** which enable students to undertake assessment tasks as a dress rehearsal for the summative assessment, reinscribing that learning is a process and that drafting is the first stage in an iterative process of refining ideas and ironing out misconceptions. Practice runs range from draft essays, to adopting two-stage examinations, where stage one is individual, and stage two is the group completion of an exam. The key to effective practice runs is providing timely developmental feedback, whether from peers or teachers.
- **Collaborative tasks** which motivate students to work on tasks together over time, usually with an audience in mind, building in social learning and team-working habits. Collaborative tasks can take the form of problem-solving, inquiry-based learning, or involve projects with external organisations such as schools, NGOs, community-based organisations, or industry.
- **Research- and inquiry-based tasks** which encourage students to investigate topics relevant to the area of study through empirical or theoretical means. As a formative task, this can be part of a process of refining a research question or proposal and testing its focus and appropriacy.
- **Reflective tasks** which provide students with an opportunity to step back and assess their personal and intellectual growth over time, keeping a record of challenges and progress through the course of their learning.
- **Writing and problem-solving,** creating time and space inside and outside of class for students to wrestle with questions in their discipline on paper in a concentrated and personal way. Enabling students to write and problem-solve in creative and exploratory ways ramps up their engagement.
- **Link formative to summative,** making it clear to students that formative assessment is not 'busy work'. The links may be conceptual or in the mode of assessment, especially if students are encountering a

novel assessment type for the first time. There are two ways to ensure good links between formative and summative: the first is design; the second provision of timely, developmental feedback on which students can act.

- *Design an integrated formative feedback system:* formative assessment is only as good as the feedback which ensues. One-off formative feedback may help students to improve on isolated summative tasks and it may hone students' generic academic skills beyond the module. However, it is the dialogic process of feedback over time which strengthens students' capacity to know how to improve, and to bridge the gap between their current performance and the standard. The following ideas from TESTA and the literature for designing formative feedback have helped students to engage and motivated them to learn.

- **Demonstrate the use of formative feedback** by requiring students to reflect on changes made to a draft in the subsequent draft using tutor feedback. This creates a system of reflecting on feedback across the programme.
- **Use rebuttal of formative feedback** as a practice for students to exercise judgement and agency about accepting, acting on, or rejecting critical feedback with a clear explanation for decisions. This approach, pioneered by Harland et al. (2017) develops students' abilities to evaluate teacher and peer feedback in a systematic way, and show how they will act on aspects of it.
- **Give quick formative feedback to motivate students.** With small classes, it is easier for the teacher to give quick formative feedback, but there are other ways of making feedback more immediate for bigger classes, for example, sampling work and giving generic feedback using anonymised examples, quiz feedback, sharing techniques for giving peer feedback with students and giving opportunities for in-class peer feedback.
- **Digital approaches to formative feedback** including short Zoom office hours providing 'live' feedback to students on formative work while looking at it together. Using various digital tools including quizzes and software to facilitate peer review.
- **Provide more feedback on formative work, less on summative assessment** to reflect the emphasis on helping students to learn. Summative feedback oscillates between being developmental and justifying the grade, partly because of moderation processes and the potential of appeals in a context where the feedback audience includes a variety of stakeholders.

Pattern #3: prevalence of closed-book examinations

Audit data indicates that about one in five assessments is a closed book, timed examination. In research-intensive universities, the proportion of examinations is higher, at almost one in three assessments. Similarly, STEM programmes generally have a higher proportion of examinations. The weighting of examinations (how much they count towards the degree award) is often higher than their proportion. This is not a direct measure in the TESTA audit, but module documents demonstrate their overall impact on students' awards. Examinations are efficient; they prevent plagiarism; they can be standardised across large student populations, and when students have enough time to prepare, they can enable students to integrate their learning (Forsyth 2023). However, they often lead to study behaviours that focus on memorisation rather than meaning; they raise the stakes of assessment; and they can be stress-inducing for students (Jones et al. 2021). Their complex demands are accentuated in professional accreditation examinations which require students to demonstrate both academic and professional proficiency.

Examinations are the archetypal form of discipline and control in assessment types, removing much of students' autonomy and agency, and reinforcing exclusivity (Kvale 2007; Mann 2001; Tai et al. 2022). Their long history, from testing civil servants in the Han dynasty in China through to medieval and modern universities, is one that prioritises selection, competition, conformity, and narrow prescription over the ill-structured problems that will confront graduates in their professions and lives (Kvale 2007). Their focus on memorising content deprives students of control and choice in their learning, and this leads to superficial engagement:

> I find exams easier, but I think I learned less because basically I just memorise what I need to know to practise questions and then regurgitate it in one or two hours and then that's it.
>
> (Student, Science, 2019)

Typically, examinations are written papers, either in the form of multiple-choice questions, short and long answer questions, essays, or complex numerical problems. Oral viva voce examinations are more common in clinical disciplines, the professions, and at the PhD level, and in certain countries. Preparation for most closed-book examinations is often characterised by memorising large quantities of the curriculum which leads students to strategic behaviours, such as 'cramming' and 'spotting' material to get a comparative advantage (Miller and Parlett 1974).

In TESTA focus groups, students are most critical of examinations as an assessment type. Although students do not declare how well they have done (or not) in examinations during focus groups, their views align with Ajjawi's observation that "examinations are by far the largest source of assessment design

critique and anxiety for students [who have failed academic subjects...]"
(Ajjawi et al. 2020). It is an even stronger signal that students view examinations as negatively impacting learning and well-being, regardless of how well they perform in them. Students describe memorising, regurgitating, and forgetting as typical of their experience of examinations:

S7: The thing with exams is that you learn to pass the exam. I've done exams for seven years in a row – you learn to pass the exam. The second you walk out, you forget everything.
I: Does anyone else share this view?
S4: Yeah, one hundred percent.
I: So you learn for the exam and then it's gone?
S4: Yeah.
S5: Forever (Students, Engineering, 2019).

> It's just cramming - I want to leave that behind in secondary school and actually learn to form an argument, not feel like I'm just having to learn a huge amount of information
>
> (Student, Humanities, 2020)

In general, they are critical of the artificiality of exams, and struggle to see the point of them:

> I wouldn't say I learned very much. With exams you were literally wasting four weeks just focusing on one thing, stressing out, ignoring all of your other work because you're revising for this big exam
>
> (Student, Life Science, 2021)

> I don't think exams were helpful at all and it doesn't match the real-world application of the skill because it's pointless.
>
> (Student, Science, 2020)

Ways to enhance student learning and engagement in examinations

Despite critiques of examinations, they are unlikely to disappear, especially in mass higher education systems where they are efficient and relatively cheap to run. They have survived for thousands of years. Proclamations of the 'death of three-hour exams' uttered during the pandemic now seem premature as institutions evaluate the worth of rival methods of assessment (McKie 2021). In the age of generative artificial intelligence and contract cheating, examinations are one of the simplest ways to authenticate learning (Dawson 2021). Professional bodies regard some exams as essential. Given these realities, how can examinations embrace more innovative practices that engage students and reduce the burdens of memorisation and stress? The following ideas used by programmes undertaking TESTA re-imagine closed-book examinations to retain the best elements, while embracing student initiative in authentic learning.

- **Case-based exams** test students' application of knowledge and theory through case studies and scenarios within an exam setting.
- **Two-stage exams** enable students to take the same examination individually, and in the second stage, collaboratively. Students teach and learn from each other by exchanging ideas about questions they have attempted on their own. Students learn and collaborate more, while developing consensus-building skills (Levy et al. 2018).
- **Mini viva voce examinations:** offer students the opportunity to demonstrate their learning through fielding questions in a one-to-one setting with their teacher, usually online to maximise efficiency, and with clear criteria to help build equivalence. These mini orals can also be used to authenticate learning after online open-book papers (Aricò 2021).
- **Integrated and applied exams** adapted from the clinical OSCE (Objective Structured Clinical Examination) in other disciplines which replicate the format of live stations simulating scenarios with oral questions which require students to explain the inner workings of procedures and phenomena.
- **Reducing the number of exams across the programme** to make room for more learning-oriented assessments, such as inquiry-based projects and authentic assessment tasks, and to incorporate more forms of assessment that support student well-being.
- **Reducing memory load and strengthen student preparation** by allowing students to take one page of notes in an in-person examination. In preparing, they will organise, prioritise, and integrate concepts rather than spend most of the time memorising, and in the examination, they will free up room to use their minds on the task at hand.

Pattern#4: random varieties of assessment

In principle, assessment variety is creative and engaging for students, and prompts independent learning, ownership, and agency. Authentic assessment types which require students to apply knowledge and work on real-world projects and ill-defined problems are challenging for students in a positive way (Kvale 2007; Lombardi 2007; Villarroel et al. 2018; Wakefield et al. 2022). Varieties of assessments are often more inclusive, enabling students with diverse needs to demonstrate their learning in different ways (Jones et al. 2021). However, when varieties are designed at the modular level, they can occur randomly, confuse students about requirements, and may be stress-inducing (Ibid 2021). This is compounded in the absence of formative assessment to practice novel varieties of assessment, which enable students to get to grips with expectations using formative feedback.

Assessment patterns are often dominated by repeated occurrences of traditional assessment types, such as essays and exams. Innovative assessments on occasional modules occurring as a one-off are confusing and stressful for students in isolation. Students find it difficult to interpret the assessment task without exemplars or formative practice runs with feedback. They give conflicting messages in TESTA focus groups about the implications of designing assessment without reference to the whole programme, expressing boredom at the repetition of traditional types, and bewilderment at novel and untested types:

> But mainly it's essays. Quite often you do two essays per module. Which is good, but it does get a bit old after a while. We do presentations as well I suppose.
>
> (Student, Arts, 2014)

> P5: Once you've written one critical reflection, you've written them all. It's a bit pointless and tedious after the second one.
>
> P4: After the second one when you've got it down it's a bit like mmm… especially when it's every semester, we normally at least have one or two every semester.
>
> (Students, Social Science, 2015)

> I've never made a blog or read one, and to be told you have to make a blog, I didn't know where to start, and I felt like I wasn't helped out knowing where to start, and I didn't know how to present it. When you look at blogs, they're really informal, but it had to be quite formal because it was being assessed. And it was hard to find the balance.
>
> (Student, Arts, 2014)

How to foster engagement through different varieties of assessment

- **Determine the qualities** the programme seeks to nurture in students with the whole team. Based on these, decide on the bank of assessment varieties most likely to develop these qualities, and weave these through modules and levels in ways that build up students' familiarity, knowledge, and skills in undertaking different assessment types through the programme.

- **Introduce new varieties** from the start of students' degrees to disrupt traditional expectations and ensure that every novel variety has a formative-only practice-run with feedback, for example, students unfamiliar with podcast assessments might need technical skill building, and they may work in pairs on a formative podcast. Following feedback, new pairs might work on more sophisticated questions using the new format (Wakefield et al. 2022).
- **Map and sequence** varieties graphically across the programme so that colleagues and students can see the distribution of different varieties, and cross-reference to students' experience of them.
- **Breach modular walls** by building up varieties in a nested approach across cognate areas, for example, one module might require students to generate research questions, write a research proposal for peer review, and develop a short-annotated bibliography. A follow-up module may use this material to write a literature review and develop a research instrument for collecting data.
- **Design for inclusion** by offering equivalent choices for students to demonstrate their learning where possible.

A brief synopsis

This chapter has examined the challenge and promise of assessment design that fosters student learning, agency, and engagement. The central message of the chapter, demonstrated by TESTA data, is that modular design undermines the role of assessment in fostering learning and engagement. It reinforces a culture of measurement both through high volumes of summative assessment and their over-arching purpose, and it narrows conceptions of the purpose of formative assessment. Students and staff routinely view formative assessment as the means to the end of achieving better grades through practice and corrective feedback, rather than seeing its central and more playful role in inspiring students to engage and shape their own learning. Programme-wide decisions can redress the imbalance and shift the culture of competition and performativity which is threatening student well-being and driving an instrumental approach to learning in higher education. The final sections of the chapter question the role of closed-book, time-restricted examinations as the major element in some degree programmes and propose more authentic alternatives which retain the benefits of time-constrained invigilated assessments. Modular assessment design has prompted many varieties of assessment to flourish. TESTA data indicates that sequencing and planning these at a programme level would yield more benefit for student learning.

Note

1 Interquartile analysis divides numerical data across a range of values into quarters. The first quartile is below 25%, and the top quartile above 75%. The Interquartile Range (IQR) is the middle 50% of data between the first and third quartile, which represents where the bulk of values lie. The median is the middle value in the whole range.

References

Adams, C. J. 2020. A constructively aligned first-year laboratory course. *Journal of Chemical Education* 97 (7): 1863–1873, DOI: 10.1021/acs.jchemed.0c00166

Ajjawi, R., M. Dracup, N. Zacharias, S. Bennett, and D. Boud. 2020. Persisting Students' explanations of and emotional responses to academic failure. *Higher Education Research & Development* 39 (2): 185–199, DOI: 10.1080/07294360.2019.1664999

Aricò, F. R. 2021. 'Evaluative conversations: Unlocking the power of viva voce assessment for undergraduate students' (pp. 47–56). In P. Baughan (Ed). *Assessment and Feedback in a Post-Pandemic Era: A Time for Learning and Inclusion*. York. Advance HE.

Bearman, M., P. Dawson, and S. Bennett, *et al.* 2017. How university teachers design assessments: A cross-disciplinary study. *High Education* 74: 49–64. https://doi.org/10.1007/s10734-016-0027-7

Biggs, J. B., and C. Tang. 2011. *Teaching for Quality Learning at University: What the Student Does.* 4th ed. Maidenhead: Open University Press.

Black, P., and D. Wiliam. 1998. Assessment and classroom learning. *Assessment in Education: Principles, Policy & Practice* 5: 7–74.

Bovill, C. 2020. *Co-creating Learning And Teaching: Towards Relational Pedagogy in Higher Education.* St Albans: Critical Publishing

Cotton, D. R., P. A. Cotton, and J. R. Shipway. 2023. Chatting and cheating. Ensuring academic integrity in the era of ChatGPT. Preprint. https://doi.org/10.35542/osf.io/mrz8h

Dann, R. 2014. Assessment as learning: Blurring the boundaries of assessment and learning for theory, policy and practice. *Assessment in Education: Principles, Policy & Practice* 21 (2): 149–166, DOI: 10.1080/0969594X.2014.898128

Dawson, P. 2021. *Defending Assessment Security in a Digital World.* Abingdon. Routledge.

Erikson, M. G., and M. Erikson 2019. Learning outcomes and critical thinking – Good intentions in conflict. *Studies in Higher Education* 44 (12): 22932303, DOI: 10.1080/03075079.2018.1486813

Forsyth, R. 2023. *Confident Assessment in Higher Education.* London. Sage.

Gibbs, G. 2010. 'Dimensions of Quality'. York. Higher Education Academy. Available at: https://www.advance-he.ac.uk/knowledge-hub/dimensions-quality Accessed on 30.03.23

Gibbs, G. 2012. Implications of 'Dimensions of Quality' in a market environment. York. Higher Education Academy. Available at: https://www.advance-he.ac.uk/knowledge-hub/implications-dimensions-quality-market-environment Accessed on 30.03.23

Gibbs, G., and H. Dunbar-Goddet. 2009. Characterising programme-level assessment environments that support learning. *Assessment & Evaluation in Higher Education* 34 (4): 481–489.

Gibbs, G., and C. Simpson 2004. 'Conditions under which assessment supports students' learning. *Learning and Teaching in Higher Education* 1 (1): 3–31.31.

Harland, T., A. McLean, R. Wass, E. Miller, and K. Nui Sim. 2015. An assessment arms race and its fallout: High stakes grading and the case for slow scholarship. *Assessment & Evaluation in Higher Education*. DOI: 10.1080/02602938.2014.931927

Harland, T., N. Wald, and H. Randhawa. 2017. Student peer review: Enhancing formative feedback with a rebuttal. *Assessment & Evaluation in Higher Education* 42 (5): 801–811, DOI: 10.1080/02602938.2016.1194368

Hattie, J., and H. Timperley. 2007. The power of feedback. *Review of Educational Research* 77 (1): 81–112.

Havnes, A., and T. S. Prøitz. 2016. Why use learning outcomes in higher education? Exploring the grounds for academic resistance and reclaiming the value of unexpected learning. *Educational Assessment, Evaluation and Accountability* 28: 205–223. https://doi.org/10.1007/s11092-016-9243-z

Jessop, T. 2016. Inspiring transformation through TESTA's programme approach, In D. Carless, S. Bridges, C. Ka Yuk Chan, and R. Glofcheski (Eds). *Scaling up Assessment for Learning in Higher Education*. Singapore. Springer.

Jessop, T., Y. El Hakim, and G. Gibbs 2014. 'The whole is greater than the sum of its parts: A large-scale study of Students' learning in response to different programme assessment patterns. *Assessment & Evaluation in Higher Education* 39 (1): 73–88.

Jessop, T., and B. Maleckar. 2016. The Influence of Disciplinary Assessment Patterns on Student Learning: A Comparative Study. *Studies in Higher Education* 41 (4): 696–711.DOI: 10.1080/03075079.2014.943170.

Jessop, T., and C. Tomas. 2017. The implications of programme assessment patterns for student learning. *Assessment & Evaluation in Higher Education* 42 (6): 990–999, DOI: 10.1080/02602938.2016.1217501

Jones, E., M. Priestley, L. Brewster, S. J. Wilbraham, G. Hughes, and L. Spanner. 2021. Student wellbeing and assessment in higher education: The balancing act. *Assessment & Evaluation in Higher Education* 46 (3): 438–450, DOI: 10.1080/02602938.2020.1782344

Kahu, E. R. 2013. Framing student engagement in higher education. *Studies in Higher Education* 38 (5): 758–773, DOI: 10.1080/03075079.2011.598505

Kalyuga, S. 2011. Cognitive load theory: How many types of load does it really need? *Educational Psychology Review* 23 (1): 1–19, DOI: 10.1007/s10648-010-9150-7

Kvale, S. 2007. 'Contradictions of assessment for learning in institutions of higher learning'. In D. Boud and N. Falchikov (Eds). 2007. *Rethinking Assessment in Higher Education*. Abingdon. Routledge Taylor and Francis.

Levy, D., T. Svoronos, and M. Klinger. 2018. Two-stage examinations: Can examinations be more formative experiences? *Active Learning in Higher Education*, 1–16. https://doi.org/10.1177/1469787418801668

Lindgren, R., and R. McDaniel. 2012. Transforming online learning through narrative and student agency. *Educational Technology & Society* 15 (4): 344–355.

Lizzio, A., and K. Wilson 2013. 'First-year Students' appraisal of assessment tasks: Implications for efficacy, engagement and performance. *Assessment & Evaluation in Higher Education* 38 (4): 389–406, DOI: 10.1080/02602938.2011.637156

Lizzio, A., K. Wilson, and R. Simons. 2002. 'University Students' perceptions of the learning environment and academic outcomes: Implications for theory and practice. *Studies in Higher Education*. 27: 27–51.

Lombardi, M. 2007. 'Authentic Learning for the 21st Century: An Overview', *Educause Learning Initiative Paper 1*. Available at: http://www.lmi.ub.edu/cursos/s21/REPOSITORIO/documents/Lombardi_2007_Authentic_learning.pdf Accessed 4 January 2022.

Mann, S. J. 2001. Alternative perspectives on the student experience: Alienation and engagement. *Studies in Higher Education* 26 (1): 7–19.

Martin, J. 2004. Self-regulated learning, social cognitive theory, and agency. *Educational Psychologist* 39 (2): 135–145, DOI: 10.1207/s15326985ep3902_4

McKie, A. 2021. 'Death of three-hour exam looms as pandemic reshapes assessment'. *Times Higher Education*. 23 June 2023. Available at: https://www.timeshighereducation.com/news/death-three-hour-exam-looms-pandemic-reshapes-assessmen. Accessed 30 January 2023.

Miller, C. M. L., and M. Parlett. 1974. *Up to the Mark: A Study of the Examination Game*. London. Society for Research into Higher Education.

Morris, R., T. Perry, and L. Wardle. 2021. Formative assessment and feedback for learning in higher education: A systematic review. *Review of Education* 9 (3): 1–26. https://doi.org/10.1002/rev3.3292

Nicol, D. J., and D. Macfarlane-Dick. 2006. Formative assessment and self-regulated learning: A model and seven principles of good feedback practice. *Studies in Higher Education* 31 (2): 199–218.

O'Donovan, B. M. 2018. *Assessment matters: a critical appraisal of assessment practice in higher education with a particular focus on enhancing student understanding of standards and criteria*. Unpublished PhD thesis. Oxford Brookes University.

Programme Assessment Strategies (PASS Project) 2012. Available at: https://www.bradford.ac.uk/pass/. Accessed 5 June 2022.

Pryor, J., and B. Crossouard. 2008. A socio-cultural theorisation of formative assessment. *Oxford Review of Education* 34 (1): 1–20, DOI: 10.1080/03054980701476386

Rudolph, J., S. Tan, and S. Tan. 2023. ChatGPT: Bullshit spewer or the end of traditional assessments in higher education. *Journal of Applied Learning & Teaching* 6 (1): 1–23. https://doi.org/10.37074/jalt.2023.6.1.9

Sadler, D. R. 1989. Formative assessment and the design of instructional system. *Instructional Science* 18: 119–144.

Sadler, D. R. 2007. Perils in the meticulous specification of goals and assessment criteria. *Assessment in Education* 14 (3): 387–392, DOI: 10.1080/09695940701592097

Sadler, D. R. 2016. Three in-course assessment reforms to improve higher education learning outcomes. *Assessment & Evaluation in Higher Education* 41 (7): 1081–1099, DOI: 10.1080/02602938.2015.1064858

Shepard, L. 2005. 'Formative Assessment: Caveat Emptor'. ETS Invitational Conference 2005. The Future of Assessment: Shaping Teaching and Learning, New York. Accessed from http://www.cpre.org/ccii/images/stories/ccii_pdfs/shepard%20formative%20assessment%20caveat%20emptor.pdf

Tai, J., P. Mahoney, R. Ajjawi, M. Bearman, J. Dargusch, M. Dracup, and L. Harris. 2022. How are examinations inclusive for students with disabilities in higher education? A sociomaterial analysis. *Assessment & Evaluation in Higher Education*. DOI: 10.1080/02602938.2022.2077910

Tomas, C., and T. Jessop. 2019. Struggling and juggling: A comparison of student assessment loads across research and teaching-intensive universities. *Assessment & Evaluation in Higher Education* 44 (1): 1–10, DOI: 10.1080/02602938.2018.1463355

Torrance, H. 2007. Assessment as learning? How the use of explicit learning objectives, assessment criteria and feedback in post-secondary education and training can come to dominate learning. *Assessment in Education* 14 (3): 281–294, DOI: 10.1080/09695940701591867

Tuck, J. 2012. 'Feedback-giving as social practice: teachers' perspectives on feedback as institutional requirement, work and dialogue. *Teaching in Higher Education* 17 (2): 209–221.

Villarroel, V., S. Bloxham, D. Bruna, C. Bruna, and C. Herrera-Seda. 2018. Authentic assessment: Creating a blueprint for course design. *Assessment & Evaluation in Higher Education* 43 (5): 840–854, DOI: 10.1080/02602938.2017.1412396

Wakefield, A., R. Pike, and S. Amici-Dargan. 2022. Learner-generated podcasts: An authentic and enjoyable assessment for students working in pairs. *Assessment & Evaluation in Higher Education.* 1–18, DOI: 10.1080/02602938.2022.2152426

Wass, R., T. Harland, A. McLean, E. Miller, and K. N. Sim. 2015. 'Will press lever for food': Behavioural conditioning of students through frequent high stakes assessment. *Higher Education Research & Development* 34 (6): 1324–1326, DOI: 10.1080/07294360.2015.1052351

Weurlander, M., M. Söderberg, M. Scheja, H. Hult, and A. Wernerson. 2012. Exploring formative assessment as a tool for learning: students' experiences of different methods of formative assessment. *Assessment & Evaluation in Higher Education* 37 (6): 747–760, DOI: 10.1080/02602938.2011.572153

Whitfield, R. and P. Hartley. 2017. Whatever happened to programme assessment strategies? *SEDA Educational Developments*, 18 (1): 13–18.

Winstone, N., R. Nash, J. Rowntree, and M. Parker. 2017. 'It'd be useful, but i wouldn't use it': Barriers to university students' feedback seeking and recipience. *Studies in Higher Education* 42 (11): 2026–2041.

Wu, Q., and T. Jessop. 2018. Formative assessment: Missing in action in both research-intensive and teaching focused universities? *Assessment and Evaluation in Higher Education* 43 (7): 1019–1031, DOI: 10.1080/02602938.2018.1426097

Chapter 6

From alienation to engagement

Realising the promise of feedback

Introduction

Picture the scene. It is a cold and grey January morning. Assessment enthusiasts from a faculty have assembled in a large, horseshoe-shaped lecture theatre, which smells vaguely of the residue of old chemicals. Thirty conference participants are scattered across the room, sitting on wooden benches, eagerly anticipating a stimulating morning talking about assessment and feedback. Enter stage right, the conference convenor, opening the proceedings with a dramatic statement about the impasse we have reached about feedback. On the screen, he displays a marked cover sheet showing the hand-written scrawl of a conscientious tutor who has carefully identified the virtues of an assignment, and ways to improve it. Then he bends down behind the wooden bench at the front and lifts a plastic basket overflowing with uncollected assignments. Jaded academics smile knowingly. Administrators whose offices are presumably overflowing with plastic baskets of uncollected scripts shuffle hopefully. Job done. Tone for the conference set. It takes no more than 15 seconds, but the message to the audience is unequivocal. Academics are doing their jobs, burning the candle at both ends, while students are not. Many simply do not care enough about feedback to bother to collect it. This mistaken assumption permeates feedback discourse. It obscures the problem of students' apparent disengagement with feedback. It is a story of 'misaligned perceptions of feedback between markers and students' in which 'markers believe that students pay little attention to feedback and that their feedback is highly useful' and 'students view it as inadequate and question its utility' (Medland 2019, p. 7). The wider assessment literature describes student disengagement with feedback as a common problem, exploring reasons for it and ways to encourage students to appreciate and make use of it (Carless and Boud 2018; Price et al. 2010; Winstone and Carless 2020; Winstone et al. 2017).

This chapter analyses the character of the feedback relationship between lecturers and students drawing on evidence in the literature and from TESTA. Programme audit data[1] indicates that students receive a good quantity of feedback. Focus group data illuminates four themes in students' experience of

DOI: 10.4324/9780429347962-10

feedback, providing some explanation for the feedback impasse depicted in the opening scenario. First, the transmission of information and advice dominates higher education feedback practice, positioning students as passive recipients rather than those engaged in a dialogue (Nicol 2010; Winstone and Carless 2020). Students' experience of feedback reinforces the perception that feedback is mainly about 'telling' (Sadler 2010). Second, students find their feedback impersonal in a mass higher education system. They nurture hopes that feedback might be the rare pedagogic moment when they might experience being known by their teachers in an I-thou relationship (Buber 2002). Yet they are often disappointed with the generic, anonymising, and impersonal feedback they receive (Nicol 2010; Pitt and Winstone 2018). Third, on modular degrees, feedback is disconnected, one-off and sporadic, often coming too late to influence students' learning and understanding (Jessop and Tomas 2017). Finally, students describe not trusting the feedback enough to act on it because they perceive variations between markers, and they suspect inconsistencies in feedback, causing them to wonder how transferable from module to module it is (Bloxham et al. 2016).

The metaphor of gift-giving for feedback rituals helps to clarify why feedback leaves many students feeling disappointed. Gift-giving involves students immersing themselves in making their 'gift' for weeks in advance of a deadline. Assessment occupies their deepest thoughts, commands their effort and energy - and then they hand over their gift to their tutors. Their gifts are not opened for a long time, and, when opened, the thank you note feels cursory, impersonal, and technical. Lecturers regard feedback as a rational and intellectual exercise to help students understand the disciplinary discourse. They impart critical advice. Students see critical feedback as a hostile attack on their person. Students' emotional investment in feedback and its relational significance have only recently come to the fore as an influence on their engagement and uptake of feedback (Carless and Boud 2018; Heron et al. 2023; Pitt and Winstone 2018). This comment sums up one student's disappointment in the gift-giving exchange:

> I spent ages planning and I actually quite enjoyed the assignment. Handed it in, got it back, got an average score but the marker had written 'I feel this has been thrown together at the last minute' and I just thought to myself 'I don't know how you can make that judgement on someone's work'.
> (Student, Social Sciences, 2011)

Feedback is a time-consuming activity for academics. Universities invest time and money in feedback processes. How then can its promise for student learning be realised?

The chapter proposes fresh ways to break the cycle of frustration, principally, moving away from feedback as 'telling' (Sadler 2010) and embracing feedback as a sustained dialogue throughout the whole programme. The shift from feedback 'done *to*' students to feedback done *with* and *by* and *for* students is at the heart of reconceptualising feedback as a relationship and a conversation.

Taking a programme approach means stepping back from viewing feedback as a one-off disposable product, an event linked to a single assessment on an individual module, to the long view of feedback as a sequential, iterative, and interactive process over students' entire intellectual journey.

An overview of feedback from TESTA programme audits

TESTA audit data from 60 programmes show how much effort is invested in written feedback. As part of the audit, samples of feedback from across modules and years of a programme are counted and calculated to reflect all the summative feedback that students can typically expect over three years of an undergraduate degree. The calculation includes summary and marginal comments and corrections. Table 6.1 shows the range of written feedback that students typically receive (a) in total, and (b) per task using low, medium, and high categories (Gibbs and Dunbar-Goddet 2009) and interquartile ranges[2].

The interquartile range (values in the two mid-quartiles) reflects a higher volume of feedback than the earlier study (Gibbs and Dunbar-Goddet, 2009) with the typical volume of feedback being 5,000 and 11,500 words over the duration of an undergraduate programme compared to 3,000 to 6,000. The median is also relatively high. Students can expect to receive between 112 and 283 words of feedback on every summative assessment. High volumes of written feedback are indicative of a high investment of time and resources into feedback processes. However, quantity is a limited measure that shows how much effort is going into written feedback but gives no real insight into whether feedback engages students enough to act on it (Price et al. 2010). For this reason, TESTA@Greenwich adapted the methodology to include a detailed analysis of the written feedback examining the balance of praise, criticism and advice given (Walker et al. 2019).

Themes in TESTA focus group data

The following sections present an analysis of TESTA focus group data[3] in the light of wider literature. These themes examine the feedback discourse of 'telling' (Sadler 2010), student expectations of personal feedback in mass

Table 6.1 High, medium, and low interquartile ranges on n=60 programmes

Characteristic	Low	Medium	High
Volume of feedback in words (3 years)	0–5,106	5,106–11,445 (Median 6,339)	11,445–31,582
Volume of feedback words per task	0–112	112–283 (Median 186.5)	283–761

higher education, the problem of one-off feedback across modular degrees, and the question of whether students trust their feedback enough to act on it.

Theme #1: A transmission model of 'telling'

In *The Pedagogy of the Oppressed*, Paulo Freire popularised the idea that education is failing if it operates only as an exercise in transmitting information to students (Freire 1970). Using the metaphor of banking, he depicted the transmission model as a transaction where teachers deposited knowledge into the heads of students, assumed to be empty. The 'banking' model of education reduces the agency of those who learn and implies a one-way transaction. It symbolises an asymmetric power relationship between teachers and students, with students being the passive recipients of education rather than active shapers of it. Reducing the power differential between teachers and students in higher education implies that feedback is a conversation between adults, wrapped in a relationship, where 'they treat you like an adult, like a person rather than just someone they teach' (TESTA focus group, Student, Sociology, 2015).

The alternative to a transmission model is one where students are involved in shaping their learning, in line with social constructivist theories of learning. This is characterised by conceptual shifts from viewing education *as delivery of a product* to seeing it *as a process* in which students actively engage with knowledge in partnership with one another and their teachers (Barr and Tagg 1995; Brookfield 2015; Gibbs 2010). The movement from a transmission model to a social constructivist one has been slow to take hold in assessment and feedback. However, various leading scholars of assessment have challenged feedback as 'consumption' (Higgins et al. 2002), 'telling' (Sadler 2010) and 'monologue' (Nicol 2010), culminating in a new theoretical model developed by Winstone and Carless (2020). Their model proposes reframing feedback from the old transmission paradigm to a new learning-oriented one. Typically, the paradigm shift is from input to interaction; teacher delivery to student action; information to sense-making; cognitivist to social-constructivist (Winstone and Carless 2020, p. 9). This approach positions students as active in their learning rather than passive recipients. The authors of the new model offer useful insights into the persistence of a transmission approach to feedback. One is that external metrics in marketised higher education drive a teacher-centred, input and information-oriented model of feedback. In the UK's National Student Survey (NSS), students rate to what extent they have 'received helpful feedback on my work' and whether 'feedback on my work has been timely' (Ibid, pp. 13–14), reinforcing that they are passive recipients. Analysis of public survey items on teaching and assessment in ten further nations demonstrates a similar adherence to a transmission view of feedback (Winstone et al. 2022). In TESTA data, students are more likely to say that their feedback is a vehicle for telling them about their performance than one which triggers action:

> They tend to talk **at** you instead of talking **to** you. It's not a two-way conversation.
>
> (Student, Health Sciences, 2011)

> How am I going to make that better for the next essay, because I thought I was doing it right? You've told me I've done it wrong but you're not telling me how to do it right.
>
> (Student, Social Sciences, 2019)

> That was the problem. They told me what I was doing wrong, but not how to rectify it.
>
> (Student, Humanities, 2013)

Even in verbal feedback, the face-to-face conversation between students and staff is skewed in the direction of telling, prescription, and advice (Akcan and Tatar 2010; Molloy and Boud 2013). In Molloy's clinical study, feedback exchanges lasted an average of 21 minutes, of which students spoke for a mere two minutes. Lecturers described not having the time to listen and wanted to hurry students along so that they could explain the right and wrong ways of approaching a task (Molloy 2009). This echoes some TESTA data where students welcome oral feedback, but feel that they are imposing on their lecturers:

> Personally, I prefer to speak to them face to face. Stuff gets lost in translation through e-mail or writing. I prefer someone to tell me, even if it's pretty blunt, saying 'You did this, this and this'.
>
> (Student, Humanities, 2010)

> I find it quite intimidating to walk in and get the feedback because firstly you know that they are very busy, that is made quite clear at all times, I think I am safe to say, and so you almost feel as though you are imposing.
>
> (Student, Life Sciences, 2010)

Some students experience more dialogic opportunities to discuss their work with their teachers, while others are hopeful that feedback might be less about talking at them and more about asking the right questions and clarifying meaning:

> What do you mean by this?' is much more understanding rather than prototype... Like it wasn't so much 'this is good or this is bad'. More like 'what do you mean by this?', almost like an interview. At least you got a chance to defend yourself.
>
> (Student, Sciences, 2019)

Maybe a five- or ten-minute interview with each of us with our assessment, just to clarify all the different points. Just ... I don't know if that would take too long, but just to sit down, so you can at least ask questions back.

(Student, Social Sciences, 2019)

Old paradigm approaches tend to focus on addressing the problem using technical-rational tools such as improving rubrics and cover sheets. There is nothing wrong with these in themselves, but effectively they are yet another means of transmitting information to students:

The supervisor would fill out a sheet and sort of tick boxes, which correspond to clarity, organisation and these sorts of things. It's much better to have one to one or one to two feedback about your specific work rather than just sort of ticking a box...

(Student, Sciences, 2019)

In contrast, the new social learning paradigm focuses on relational aspects of feedback and creating opportunities for students to engage in dialogue and interaction (Winstone and Carless 2020). Dialogic feedback enables students to ask questions, reflect on their learning and exercise agency in making sense of, and closing the gap between their work and the expected standards (Sadler 1989). In theory, many academics agree with these principles. In practice, there are challenges. How can dialogue occur in a mass higher education system which resembles the factory rather than the scholarly monastery? How can resistant students who are comfortable with 'receiving' their education be persuaded that feedback might involve action and agency? Transmission model perspectives persist among a proportion of students, many of whom are shaped by their experience as consumers of higher education. Good feedback rests on dialogic foundations and persuading reluctant students of the virtue of learning conversations is challenging. Simple ideas from TESTA programmes illustrate the possibilities of moving from feedback as a one-way monologue to a meaningful dialogue.

Strategies for turning telling into dialogue

a **Students 'speak' first**: turn feedback into a conversation by inviting students to ask for specific feedback on their work at the time of submission. They may ask for feedback on aspects where they feel they have done especially well; or possibly areas where they struggle. These requests for feedback may occur with summative or formative tasks. The key point is that your feedback becomes a response, a reply, in a conversation started by the student. You may go beyond the requested feedback to address other issues, but the activity is good to help students reflect on the strengths and weaknesses of their submission and develops their capacity to judge the quality of their work.

b **Be conversational** in your marginal comments, asking questions and using less formal language. Avoid using phatic symbols like '?', '!!!', or commands like 'explain'. Bean (2011) commends annotations which allow students to hear your reactions such as "Whoa, I'm losing the thread here" instead of peppering essays with exclamation marks or question marks (in student talk = 'angry marks'). Ask questions in your feedback, whether in the annotations or summary feedback. Questioning invites dialogue; telling closes the conversation down.

c **Use rebuttal** as part of the back and forth of the learning conversation: invite students to undertake a task which requires two drafts, for example drafting a grant proposal, and eliciting peer and teacher feedback on the first draft. Then invite students to write rebuttals for each feedback comment, categorising the rationale for accepting, partially accepting, or rejecting the feedback (Harland et al. 2017). Students redraft in the light of their interaction with feedback.

d **Practise dialogic marking**: instead of spending 15 or 20 minutes marking an essay at your desk, mark it live with a student on a digital platform. This is a dialogic approach which enables students to understand your reasoning for judgements. Think beforehand about your marking process and articulate it to yourself or tell a friend or colleague how you go about your marking. Here are some questions to guide the process of preparing to mark 'live'.

- Will you ask the student to read it aloud? Will you read it aloud?
- Will you comment on sentences, paragraphs, or sections?
- Will you initially skim the topic sentences to see if the structure tells a coherent story?
- How will you focus on structure, logical argument, and use of evidence?
- How can you avoid nit-picky comments about grammar, style, and referencing?
- How will you incorporate links to the criteria in the conversation?

Theme #2: impersonal, mass-produced, and missing the relational

Mass higher education has led to changes in the nature of the pedagogic relationship, both in the scale of teaching and assessment, and in the kind of relationship that exists between fee-paying students and their universities in marketised higher education systems. The size of classes has consequences for assessment and feedback. Economies of scale apply to teaching but not to marking and assessment (Gibbs 2010, 2012). Mass higher education is one factor in the introduction of more standardised, efficient, and impersonal marking regimes. Another is marketisation, which has added impetus to greater accountability and transparency, and has led to increased regulatory requirements on universities to evidence value for money (Brown and Carasso, 2013; Corden 2020; Kvale 2007).

Together, mass HE and marketisation have put the spotlight on accountability, generating a paper trail of programme specifications, learning outcomes, marking criteria, and feedback templates (O'Donovan et al. 2008). These symbolise and substantiate a functioning, transparent quality assurance system for current and prospective students, and regulatory bodies. However, the risk of placing too much emphasis on paper-based quality assurance processes is that it erases the traces of human interaction between teacher and student in living feedback conversations. Students on TESTA express disappointment with standardised feedback which may look good as a paper process, but is so formulaic as to say nothing distinctive to them of personal value:

> They give me such general comments. It's like they copy and pasted it. That's probably why I don't use it.
>
> (Student, Social Sciences, 2017)

> I feel very much, when I hand in an essay, I'm being churned through a factory machine. Like they literally have a script and they're copying and pasting stuff that might apply to your essay.
>
> (Student, Humanities, 2020)

Some go further, interpreting mass feedback of this kind as an absence of care:

> Here they say 'Oh yes, I don't know who you are. Got too many to remember, don't really care, I'll mark you on your assignment'.
>
> (Student, Social Sciences, 2010)

> I had feedback this year that was two weeks late because the lecturer hadn't marked it. She didn't even tell us that it would be late.
>
> (Student, Social Sciences, 2017)

The challenge is clear. Students want personal feedback which recognises the particularity of their work, responds to it, and fosters their intellectual development. They also want feedback on time so that it is useful for their next assessment. Students' expectations align with well-researched feedback principles (Gibbs and Simpson 2004; Nicol and Macfarlane-Dick 2006). However, both the principles and expectations are in tension with mass higher education and marketisation. Staff do not have the luxury to personalise feedback for increasing numbers of students from more diverse educational backgrounds. Further, criterion-referenced marking leads to feedback sounding generic and impersonal in tone in what students recognise as 'copy and paste' feedback (Student, Social Sciences 2010) with students receiving similar comments drawn from the vocabulary of criteria. The problem is that students do not trust standardised feedback enough to use it. So how can these tensions between efficiency and standardisation, and personal feedback be resolved?

The tone of standardised feedback tends to be neutral and impersonal. It may also be critical in a way which feels heartless to students yet is likely to be well-intentioned. It is easy to imagine how comments constructed after marking scores of scripts can be read as impersonal, cursory, and even humiliating. Research shows that emotions are significant in learning and that negative emotions often dominate students' engagement with feedback (Carless and Boud 2018; Medland 2019; Molloy et al. 2013). In TESTA data, students speak viscerally about the tone of their feedback, most memorably when a student described receiving a comment which made her feel "like I'd been slapped in the face with a fish" (Student, Social Sciences, 2011). Students describe feeling vulnerable about their work being exposed to critical scrutiny, especially when it is outside a relational context with their teachers. The tone of feedback may often be interpreted as harsh by students, even when the intention is benign.

> I felt that there was a real sense of bitterness in the feedback that I got, to the point where it wasn't objectively telling me what I'd done wrong. It was insulting. They were insinuating that I didn't deserve to be at university, that my work wasn't university level work. It didn't feel professional at all. It was quite shocking.
>
> (Student, Humanities, 2019)

> I don't read feedback because I can't take criticism.
>
> (Student, Media Studies, 2010)

> Having some kind of personalised feedback – "this is what you're doing well, this is what you need to improve upon" – would improve relationships between students and tutors and allow you to feel your work is being appreciated.
>
> (Student, Humanities, 2020)

The antidote to impersonal, mass-produced feedback is personal, individual feedback in the context of a pedagogic relationship. Large programmes undertaking TESTA have shown how this can be done without overloading staff and undermining the standards so intrinsic to quality. Here are some ideas drawn from TESTA programmes about personalising feedback in mass higher education.

Strategies that can help to personalise feedback

a **Design assessment using a programme approach** to reduce summative assessment and integrate cycles of formative assessment as a way of supporting and personalising regular feedback. Integrate formative tasks in class time and engage students in peer feedback, team feedback, and teacher feedback.

b **Use public formative tasks**: invite students to do a short in-class presentation or blog that links to the full summative task and crowd-source peer feedback. Public domain formative tasks raise participation and performance, when linked to a summative task, and with carefully designed peer feedback.

c **Give quick and interactive generic feedback** based on marking a sample of summative assessments, creating a sense of immediacy. Showing students that you are working on their submissions motivates students and triggers reflections about their work while it is fresh in their minds. It is also a reminder to students that you care about their 'gift'. You may want students to jot down what they did best and struggled with in anticipation of your synthesis. This will help to personalise generic feedback.

d **Provide immediate oral feedback on presentations** and other public assessment formats: instinctive reactions and first impressions are useful starting points for thinking through the quality of work. Set the scene that this is quick oral feedback rather than being the 'final word'. You may want to ask students to write down your feedback in bullet points. Getting students to provide a written record and send it to you jogs your memory and tells you whether what the student heard and what you said are aligned!

e **Develop students' maturity in dealing with critical feedback**: all good feedback will have some critique, and students will be at different levels of maturity in their ability to process critical feedback. One approach to helping students process and act on critical feedback is through designing cycles of formative and developmental feedback, some of which enable regular formative peer review. Critical feedback is much more digestible if students have opportunities to act on it before being graded for a final summative assessment.

f **Share your own strategies of dealing with critical feedback**: being vulnerable may help students to understand how to process criticism, and to value it as an academic skill, albeit a discomforting one. Sharing how you have responded to negative peer reviews, even showing students artefacts such as your own writing before and after reviews, can be powerful in helping students to manage their emotional responses to feedback, and get the best from it, even when it stings.

Theme #3: feedback is an episodic, one-off event which students struggle to use

TESTA enables programme teams to see beyond the module to students' overall experience of assessment and feedback on the whole programme, as they juggle assessment demands on concurrent modules. Often, assessment is designed module by module by individual academics or small teams associated with one module. There is very little peripheral vision in the design process to see beyond individual pieces of assessment. When it comes to feedback, markers focus their effort and attention on individual assignments unless there is a designed process to connect assessments across the programme. It is therefore not surprising that students see feedback as a one-off given the context of modular assessment design.

A more sophisticated conception of feedback positions it principally as a curriculum design and teaching challenge focused on ensuring that students are active learners in a process which is designed to enable their participation (Boud and Molloy 2013; Heron et al. 2023; Knight 2000). In contrast to mechanistic and one-off approaches to feedback which accord students 'a lowly status with little volition, limited agency and dependence on teachers or a teaching system' (Boud and Molloy 2013, p. 703), feedback needs to become 'a key curriculum space for communicating, for knowing, for judging, for acting' (Ibid, pp. 706–707). Modular feedback focused on individual assessments limits students' capacity to exercise agency in applying feedback to subsequent tasks. It curtails their learning, reinscribing a passive approach to acting on feedback, as indicated in these focus group comments:

> I don't personally look at it. If it's for the same module, I'll look at the feedback for the one before, but normally it's quite tailored to the essay you've written, not necessarily applicable to anything else.
>
> (Student, Humanities, 2010)

> Sometimes you get given the most feedback when the assignment is done, and you're like, 'Well, what am I supposed to do with that? I know you can still apply it to other things but if I'd known that in a bit more depth, then maybe I could have applied it sooner.
>
> (Student, Life Sciences, 2018)

Students recognise that learning conversations about their work are invitations to more active responses to feedback, which encourage agency and ownership in the feedback process:

> I know it's probably not practical but maybe a face-to-face kind of debrief with the examiner, maybe that would be beneficial, rather than these comments. Maybe to ask, "why did you feel that the sections were inadequate, or badly referenced?"
>
> (Student, Health Sciences, 2019)

The design and timing of feedback, and opportunities to improve students' understanding based on feedback, are pivotal to a well-designed assessment system. For many students, feedback arrives too late for them to act on it, and it is so specific to the assessment and the module that students find little transferable value in the feedback. More tellingly, the timing of formative assessment on one module often competes with a summative deadline on another, acting as a significant disincentive to students' undertaking formative assessment:

If there weren't loads of other assessments, I'd do it.

(Student, Humanities, 2010)

In TESTA data, there is a misperception that formative tasks are mainly about 'time on task' and distributing student effort, with the result that some formative assessment is seen as 'busywork' by students or is poorly connected with teaching and assessment in the wider curriculum. Focusing on formative *tasks* misses the point of formative assessment, which is about helping students become more sophisticated in their thinking through engaging with and acting on formative feedback. Students describe formative feedback sometimes being absent:

The lecturers do formative assessment, but we don't actually get any feedback on that.

(Student, Social Sciences, 2010)

When asked what would help to improve their experience of using feedback, typical student responses include references to formative feedback:

For me it would be being given feedback before an assessment with enough time to improve on it beforehand. So having a pre-feedback session, and then saying this is the feedback, you've got two weeks, you can improve on these things.

(Student, Creative Arts, 2015)

More formative assessment that feeds into our summative assessment at the end of modules would help.

(Student, Social Sciences, 2010)

Formative feedback would be useful – feedback while you're doing the project, not just afterwards.

(Student, Engineering, 2019)

The systems question is how to design feedback in such a way as to foster students' active involvement and nurture their intellectual development across the whole programme. Improving feedback is both a curriculum design question, and a question of purpose. Current feedback practice across programmes begs the question of whether there is a shared purpose informing the practice of feedback between markers and across modules, and within programmes and institutions. What is feedback for? Is it for helping students to polish up the technicalities, or is it about stepping back to see the bigger picture and facilitating higher-order thinking about evidence, method, structure, and argumentation?

TESTA data indicate that much feedback starts from the wrong place, focusing on myopic technicalities rather than the big picture. Students are looking for comments and questions about structure, logic, and the use of evidence and argumentation. They want to improve as academic writers and to learn to think in the disciplinary discourse in ways which enable them to become insiders in their field of study. TESTA shows a dearth of feedback which opens a conversation about how one thinks or writes or composes an elegant proof in the discipline. Instead, students face dead-end comments which are difficult to understand or continue a conversation about. Inscrutable comments subdue students with a level of abstraction on which they are unable to act:

> I find in mine what they write isn't useful because I don't understand what they're talking about. I find it really annoying when they just say something like "needs more analysis" or something like that. Actually, I don't know what that means.
>
> (Student, Sciences, 2020)

> It's more like 'You need to be more analytical', but it doesn't really explain what they mean.
>
> (Student, Social Sciences, 2010)

Comments to 'be more analytical' or 'be more sociological' do not help students to think analytically or sociologically. Ironically, spending in-class time discussing exemplars of more and less analytical work is more likely to help students understand what good analysis looks like while being more effective, less damaging, and cheaper than hours spent writing 'be more analytical' on numerous essays. Some of the best approaches to helping students structure their writing involve formative feedback on drafts, where comments come from the place of encouragement as a writing coach, and students work to improve their drafts based on feedback (Bean 2011). In turn, this practice may enable teachers to offer minimal comments on final drafts and place their effort and energy where it matters most to students.

While highly abstract comments about analysis are inscrutable to students, low-level technical comments do not inspire students to use feedback either. The verdict on technical comments from TESTA data is that they are not useful:

> I've got comments back before marking things like grammar and spelling mistakes and things, and that's just kind of useless to me.
>
> (Student, Arts, 2013)

Realising the promise of feedback 113

I didn't find feedback from my previous essay constructive at all – it was very much nit-picking and saying this is wrong, that's wrong, so I didn't find that very useful.

(Student, Health Sciences, 2019)

Students recognise the value and transferability of comments on structure and argumentation, but they describe these as relatively rare and variably helpful. Some are baffling to students:

I got told that my work wasn't structured very well, I kept going off on tangents in the middle of my essay and I was told I needed to structure it a bit more so it kind of flows, but I was like 'how do I do that?'. Lecturers say this but don't offer ways on how to do it.

(Student, Social Sciences, 2017)

Comments about structure help students enter their discipline's ways of thinking as insiders. The link between a student comprehending complex feedback about structuring an essay, and interactive approaches to feedback is noteworthy:

This year they've really explored different avenues for feedback, where we've had screencast, and audio feedback. You can see tutors interacting with your piece, which is interesting. It really helped me in terms of structure, and also with the method. Some very foundational principles, but it really helped.

(Student, Humanities, 2015)

The most useful is when it's feedback about structuring essays and papers. So, when you get something back that's sort of saying, "oh, you should have mentioned this a bit earlier on in the paper," and it gives it a bit more of a flow, a bit more of a narrative. Because that's one of those things, it is quite hard to sort of work on that yourself, if you don't get feedback.

(Student, Arts, 2013)

Strategies for integrated feedback across the programme

a Design assessment and feedback as a team across the programme. Map, sequence, and design formative assessment and feedback opportunities to support students' capacity to undertake summative assessment as part of a process of learning.

b Ensure that formative assessment does not compete with summative deadlines on concurrent modules by taking a programme approach to designing assessment and feedback. Streamline and sequence varieties of assessment so that feedback feeds forward across similar varieties of assessment.

c Provide formative feedback in time for students to act on it and use combinations of teacher or peer feedback. Link formative tasks and feedback to summative assessments.

d Build in strategies for students to reflect on and use feedback across assessment and modules, potentially asking students to show in reflective writing how they have addressed feedback from a previous or formative submission when they submit the next assignment.

e Spot the mistakes: with technical and grammar mistakes, identify the first few, and ask students to go through the assessment and correct recurrences.

f Focus on 'big picture' feedback about structure, method, use of evidence and logical arguments. Invite students into your disciplinary ways of thinking and writing by demonstrating, discussing, and creating opportunities for students to evaluate anonymous work and its capacity to make disciplinary arguments well. Activities which invite students into the 'secret garden' of discussing standards help to integrate and normalise formative feedback as part of the learning process.

Theme #4: students do not trust the quality of feedback enough to act on it

Perhaps the most disturbing finding from TESTA data is that students are wary of trusting feedback enough to act on it. Variable feedback practices between different lecturers make students sceptical about using feedback. Studies have shown that there are differences between schema- and data-driven markers, with the former more prone to making judgements based on preconceived notions (or schema) than data-driven markers, who tend to be more meticulous and analytical when marking (Batey 2018). Unconscious bias, mood, cognitive load, and even circadian rhythms linked to the time of day when people mark, influence the accuracy of marking. There is evidence in the literature that some markers are stricter than others, with 'hawks' being harsher, marking to the left of the normal distribution curve, while 'doves' are kinder, marking to the right of a curve (Batey 2018, p. 62). In their focus group comments, students echo the idea of hawks and doves:

> There are lecturers who have a reputation for marking harsher than others.
> (Student, Media, 2015)

Whatever the scientific basis for differences in marking, TESTA data repeatedly shows that students perceive inconsistencies and variations between markers that deter them from using feedback. Students have an underlying sense that marking practices are subjective, particularly in disciplines where interpretation is an important element, in contrast to more objective STEM disciplines. Typical comments from focus groups capture these perceptions:

> It can be hard to assess a performance, because everyone has their own opinions and style of theatre they like, and so if a lecturer likes a particular style and you do that one they are going to mark you higher than a different lecturer, so it is quite subjective.
>
> (Student, Creative Arts, 2014)

> There are a lot of discrepancies within the department because it really depends on who's marking it.
>
> (Student, Humanities, 2014)

> I've had a couple of essays where they've literally filled out the rubric and it's very vague ... and then sometimes they've really gone into detail. It's just not constructive, and I feel like there's such a variation of the kind of feedback that you get.
>
> (Student, Humanities, 2020)

Student perceptions of variations in marking practices also link to the volume of written feedback they receive, which is supported by audit data. Audits show a range in volumes of assessment from more than 22,000 words of written feedback over a three-year undergraduate degree to less than 1,000 words. Some of this variation relates to disciplinary differences, with STEM subjects tending to give less written feedback because of the numerical and less discursive nature of assessment tasks (Jessop and Maleckar 2016). However, even within the same disciplines, students report variations in the volume of feedback:

> The quality of feedback varies a lot between tutors but also between modules. I have one piece where there are annotations throughout the essay, and as well as feedback on that particular essay, feedback that I can translate to other assessments, compared to other modules where I've had feedback that's been very minimal. Maybe there's something they could do to level it out a bit more.
>
> (Student, Humanities, 2013)

Variations in the quality and quantity of feedback contribute to students using their feedback less than they might otherwise. This is compounded by the late arrival of feedback:

> With different tutors it varies. With some it's like two months before you get it back. Some you get it back in two weeks.
>
> (Student, Social Sciences, 2010)

I: So how is the timing of feedback?
R1: It's very hit and miss as well.
R5: I would say lacklustre.
R1: It can be really quick, then at other times you could be waiting multiple months.
R2: Depends on the lecturer.

(Students, Computing, 2017)

What I liked is that she gave me the feedback straightway. I did my presentation and then she did it. Some people, four weeks later, will give you feedback on your presentation, and I can barely remember what mood I was in or what I was doing.

(Student, Social Sciences, 2010)

The timing of feedback is critical to students using it, particularly if it is to feedforward into a subsequent assessment. Timing also relates to memory and motivation. Returning to the 'gift' metaphor, feedback which arrives when students remain alive and alert to the gift they have given their tutors is much more likely to be read and used, partly because it signifies the quality of the pedagogic relationship. Students tend to evaluate quick feedback as higher quality than slow feedback, as these comments indicate:

R1: The more quickly they get it the more you generally have written on it.
I: That's interesting. You get more written on it if it's quicker
R1: I've always found people who are prompt they mark properly. People who take ages, they've either got something better in their life, I don't know.

(Students, Social Sciences, 2010)

There's a couple of modules that spring to mind, that we've had things back quickly from, and that's Paediatrics and Anatomy. I think they've been quite on the ball with things, but others have been very slow.

(Student, Health Sciences, 2013)

Strategies to strengthen students' trust in feedback

a Conduct calibration workshops with programme teams at least once a year using anonymised work. Use this as an opportunity to bring tacit criteria to the surface, to critique and refine the agreed criteria, and to discuss priorities in marking. Agree consensus standards and ways of feeding back but leave space for some marker individuality in crafting feedback.

b Discuss and agree acceptable variations (style and personal touches in feedback) and distinguish from unacceptable variations (no annotations, minimal feedback, focusing on referencing and technicalities).

c Mentor Graduate Teaching Assistants and new markers through shadow marking schemes.

d Moderate scripts *before* you mark to calibrate standards.

e Experiment with different modes of feedback to build trust, for example, audio or screencast feedback, and share best practices with the team.

f Reduce the length/scale and volume of summative assessment to ensure quick turnaround times. Economy of word lengths can be more challenging for students. It can also be more authentic, and quicker to mark.

A brief synopsis

This chapter argues for a paradigm shift from feedback as 'telling' to feedback as a learning conversation. Old paradigm feedback is hierarchical, one-directional, and tends to silence recipients. At the heart of the new paradigm is an appreciation for the quality and value of relationships, and with that, an awareness of the personal, emotional, and tender process of learning from wrong turns and failures, in order to come to a deeper understanding. This chapter provides strategies for strengthening relational feedback while recognising the challenges of mass higher education and modules for personalised feedback on which students can act over time. It offers imaginative strategies from TESTA to develop a culture of learning from feedback which liberates more than it overwhelms.

Notes

1 From 60 programmes from 14 universities, mainly in the UK.

2 Interquartile analysis divides numerical data across a range of values into quarters. The first quartile is below 25%, and the top quartile above 75%. The Interquartile Range (IQR) is the middle 50% of data between the first and third quartile, which represents where the bulk of values lie. The median is the middle value in the whole range.

3 552 students from 60 programmes in 102 focus groups, from 14 universities.

References

Akcan, S., and S. Tatar. 2010. An investigation of the nature of feedback given to preservice English teachers during their practice teaching experience. *Teacher Development: An International Journal of Teachers' Professional Development* 14 (2): 153–172.

Barr, R. B., and J. Tagg. 1995. From teaching *to* learning — A new paradigm for undergraduate education. *Change: The Magazine of Higher Learning* 27 (6): 12–26, DOI: 10.1080/00091383.1995.10544672

Batey, J. 2018. *Expectancies, Marking and Feedback in Undergraduate Student Assessment.* Unpublished PhD Thesis. University of Winchester.

Bean, J. 2011. *Engaging Ideas: The Professor's Guide to Integrating Writing, Critical Thinking and Active Learning in the Classroom.* Second Edition. San Francisco, CA. Jossey-Bass.

Bloxham, S., B. den-Outer, J. Hudson, and M. Price. 2016. Let's stop the pretence of consistent marking: Exploring the multiple limitations of assessment criteria. *Assessment & Evaluation in Higher Education* 41 (3): 466–481, DOI: 10.1080/02602938.2015.1024607

Boud, D., and E. Molloy 2013. Rethinking models of feedback for learning: The challenge of design. *Assessment & Evaluation in Higher Education* 38 (6): 698–712.

Brookfield, S. 2015. *The Skillful Teacher.* San Francisco, CA. Wiley and Sons.

Brown, R., and H. Carasso. 2013. *Everything for Sale? The Marketisation of UK Higher Education.* Abingdon. Routledge.

Buber, M. 2002. *Between Man and Man.* Abingdon. Routledge Classics. (First published 1947, Routledge & Kegan Paul).

Carless, D., and D. Boud. 2018. The development of student feedback literacy: Enabling uptake of feedback. *Assessment & Evaluation in Higher Education* 43 (8): 1315–1325, DOI: 10.1080/02602938.2018.1463354

Corden, G. 2020. Value for Money: A Risk, Wrapped in a Mystery, Inside an Enigma. HEPI Blog. Available at: https://www.hepi.ac.uk/2020/11/10/value-for-money-a-risk-wrapped-in-a-mystery-inside-an-enigma/ Accessed 30.03.23

Freire, P. 1970. *Pedagogy of the Oppressed.* London. The Continuum Publishing Company.

Gibbs, G. 2010. *Dimensions of Quality.* York. Higher Education Academy. Available at: https://www.advance-he.ac.uk/knowledge-hub/dimensions-quality Accessed on 30.03.23

Gibbs, G. 2012. *Implications of 'Dimensions of Quality' in a market environment.* York. Higher Education Academy. Available at: https://www.advance-he.ac.uk/knowledge-hub/implications-dimensions-quality-market-environment Accessed on 30.03.23

Gibbs, G., and H. Dunbar-Goddet 2009. Characterising programme-level assessment environments that support learning. *Assessment & Evaluation in Higher Education* 34 (4): 481–489.

Gibbs, G., and C. Simpson 2004. 'Conditions under which assessment supports Students' learning. *Learning and Teaching in Higher Education* 1 (1): 3–31.

Harland, T., N. Wald, and H. Randhawa. 2017. Student peer review: Enhancing formative feedback with a rebuttal. *Assessment & Evaluation in Higher Education* 42 (5): 801–811, DOI: 10.1080/02602938.2016.1194368

Heron, M., E. Medland, N. Winstone, and E. Pitt. 2023. Developing the relational in teacher feedback literacy: Exploring feedback talk. *Assessment & Evaluation in Higher Education* 48 (2): 172–185, DOI: 10.1080/02602938.2021.1932735

Higgins, R., P. Hartley, and A. Skelton. 2002. The conscientious consumer: Reconsidering the role of assessment feedback in student learning. *Studies in Higher Education* 27 (1): 53–64, DOI: 10.1080/03075070120099368

Jessop, T., and B. Maleckar. 2016. The influence of disciplinary assessment patterns on student learning: A comparative study. *Studies in Higher Education* 41 (4): 696–711, DOI: 10.1080/03075079.2014.943170.

Jessop, T., and C. Tomas. 2017. The implications of programme assessment patterns for student learning. *Assessment & Evaluation in Higher Education* 42 (6): 990–999, DOI: 10.1080/02602938.2016.1217501

Knight, P. T. 2000. The value of a programme-wide approach to assessment. *Assessment & Evaluation in Higher Education* 25 (3): 237–251.

Kvale, S. 2007. 'Contradictions of assessment for learning in institutions of higher learning'. In D. Boud and N. Falchikov. (Eds) 2007. *Rethinking Assessment in Higher Education*. Abingdon. Routledge Taylor and Francis.

Medland, E. 2019. "Excited' yet 'Paralysing': The highs and lows of the feedback process. *Educational Developments* 20 (1): 7–10. Available at: https://www.seda.ac.uk/wp-content/uploads/2020/09/publications_267_Educational_Developments_Issue_20.1.pdf Accessed on 30.03.23.

Molloy, E. 2009. Time to pause: Giving and receiving feedback in clinical education (pp. 128–146). In C. Delany and E. Molloy (Eds). *Clinical Education in the Health Professions*. Chatswood, New South Wales. Elsevier.

Molloy, E., F. Borrell-Carrio, and R. Epstein. 2013. The impact of emotions on feedback (pp. 50–71). In D. Boud and E. Molloy (Eds). *Feedback in Higher and Professional Education*. Abingdon. Routledge.

Molloy, E., and D. Boud. 2013. Changing conceptions of feedback (pp. 11–33). In D. Boud and E. Molloy (Eds). *Feedback in Higher and Professional Education*. Abingdon. Routledge.

Nicol, D. J. 2010. From monologue to dialogue: Improving written feedback processes in mass higher education. *Assessment & Evaluation in Higher Education* 35 (5): 501–517.

Nicol, D. J., and D. Macfarlane-Dick. 2006. Formative assessment and self-regulated learning: A model and seven principles of good feedback practice. *Studies in Higher Education* 31 (2): 199–218.

O'Donovan, B., M. Price, and C. Rust. 2008. Developing student understanding of assessment standards: A nested hierarchy of approaches. *Teaching in Higher Education* 13 (2): 205–217, DOI: 10.1080/13562510801923344

Pitt, E., and N. Winstone. 2018. The impact of anonymous marking on students' perceptions of fairness, feedback and relationships with lecturers. *Assessment & Evaluation in Higher Education* 43 (7): 1183–1193, DOI: 10.1080/02602938.2018.1437594

Price, M., K. Handley, J. Millar, and B. O'Donovan. 2010. Feedback: All that effort, but what is the effect? *Assessment & Evaluation in Higher Education* 35 (3): 277–289.

Sadler, D. R. 1989. Formative assessment and the design of instructional system. *Instructional Science* 18: 119–144.

Sadler, D. R. 2010. Beyond feedback: Developing student capability in complex appraisal. *Assessment & Evaluation in Higher Education* 35 (5): 535–550, DOI: 10.1080/0260293090354101

Walker, S., E. Salines, A. Abdillahi, S. Mason, A. Jadav, and C. Molesworth. 2019. Identifying and resolving key institutional challenges in feedback and assessment: A case study for implementing change. *Higher Education Pedagogies* 4 (1): 422–434, DOI: 10.1080/23752696.2019.1649513

Winstone, N. E., R. Ajjawi, K. Dirkx, and D. Boud. 2022. Measuring what matters: The positioning of students in feedback processes within national student satisfaction surveys. *Studies in Higher Education* 47 (7): 1524–1536, DOI: 10.1080/03075079.2021.1916909

Winstone, N., and D. Carless. 2020. *Designing Effective Feedback Processes in Higher Education: A Learning-Focused Approach*. Abingdon. Routledge.

Winstone, N., R. Nash, J. Rowntree, and M. Parker. 2017. 'It'd be useful, but i wouldn't use it': Barriers to university students' feedback seeking and recipience. *Studies in Higher Education* 42 (1): 2026–2041.

Chapter 7

From alienation to engagement

Internalising standards

This chapter examines whether the processes intended to make standards transparent are helping students to make fine judgements about quality. It argues that coming to know what 'good' looks like is a complex and active process. Students need to peep behind the curtains of marking processes and be invited to see and judge varying standards of work for themselves. Currently, the higher education sector relies on transparency and telling students what good looks like, often in the abstract language of criteria, and with a level of certainty that belies practice. Evidence from 'Transforming the Experience of Students through Assessment' (TESTA) shows that students perceive inconsistent standards between markers and are therefore tentative about trusting their judgements and acting on feedback. This prevents feedback from feeding forward. The chapter provides strategies to help students to internalise standards, using practices that encourage student agency and engagement.

Introduction

This chapter sets out the processes that many universities use to explain, justify, and assure standards in a mass higher education system. In a marketised environment, universities are held accountable for fair standards and transparent processes as fee-paying students place a premium on value for money as consumers. With the move from elite to mass higher education over the last decades, the apparatus for setting out and sharing standards has increasingly been based on the transmission of information in writing (O'Donovan 2018; O'Donovan et al. 2008). Processes of accountability and transparency are designed both to provide guidance to students and to meet statutory and regulatory requirements by national governing bodies for higher education. In response, universities have developed elaborate systems to ensure accountability to students and assure fair and comparable standards. Criteria, marking descriptors, double marking, moderation processes and external examining are the mechanisms by which universities seek to provide reassurance of fair, equitable, and objective marking. These practices are also a means to standardise practice across universities so that students have a consistent experience of

DOI: 10.4324/9780429347962-11

assessment and feedback. However, amid these clear expressions of transparency, the complexity of calibrating standards and the messy realities of making judgements can become obscured (Bloxham et al. 2016; Shay 2005). Modular structures can also impede a long view of standards with their staccato approach to packaging learning in isolation from a subject's roots in disciplinary or professional knowledge (Jessop and Tomas 2017). Within this context, how do students come to know what 'good' looks like?

TESTA data provides insights into the student perspective on internalising standards. Despite the elaborate apparatus of criteria, rubrics, and assurances of moderation, students sense the complex hinterland involved in academic judgements about the quality of their work. The vocabulary of criteria affords little recognition of the professional judgement and expertise of markers. Uncertainties about part-time graduate students undertaking marking hovers on the margins of TESTA focus group conversations. Overall, students express concern about inconsistencies in marking, and mixed feelings about the value of criteria. They speak of the gap between the final words of criteria and handbooks, and the messy reality involved in making sense of standards. For many, criteria are inscrutable, and knowing why their work was evaluated as excellent or wanting is a guessing game. Observing, discussing, and evaluating their own, and others' work, occurs only at the edges of their experience, rather than as a central part of it. There is often no space in the curriculum to see and discuss examples of good and indifferent work, and where work is shared, it is often unattainably good, or not discussed. Many students are at a loss about judging the quality of their work and do not know how to 'close the gap' between their performance and the required standard (Nicol and Macfarlane-Dick 2006; Sadler 1989).

Why telling may be good, but not good enough

In the context of mass higher education, marketisation and modularity, the university sector across the world has become more reliant on the transmission of standards in writing and in words than ever before (Bloxham et al. 2016; O'Donovan 2018; O'Donovan et al. 2008). The world in which a few privileged students rubbed shoulders with the same academics over the course of their degrees and picked up standards over time has been supplanted by a very different one. Twenty-first century higher education attracts more and more diverse students, often into large classes, where they encounter many teachers on different modules and a wide variety of assessment types. This complicates coming to know and understand what good looks like, not only for students but also for teachers, many of whom may be part-time academics, PhD students or full-time academics who only teach a few sessions on the module. A shared conception of standards has become more elusive in the context of modular degrees in mass higher education. The shift towards consumer relationships between the student and the 'provider' has elevated written information about assessment almost to the status of small print.

There are two different ways for students to internalise standards. One focuses on telling students what the standards are; the other on inviting students to actively participate in coming to know them. Telling is the dominant discourse, and it is the focus of academic and departmental efforts. In TESTA meeting after TESTA meeting, seasoned teachers speak of their bafflement that students don't understand the assessment expectations, because *they have told them*. And they have! On the first day of modules in many universities across the sector, students are subject to a full rendition of summative assessment, criteria, and expectations, painstakingly telling them how they ought to go about an assignment and what to avoid doing, well in advance of the event, thereby implicitly framing the course as being principally about assessment. Teachers may assume that explaining assessment expectations and pointing them to handbooks or assessment briefs is enough, somehow enabling students to internalise standards. This is a false assumption.

A focus on telling, positioned at the start of modules, highlights the endgame of assessment rather than the process of learning, setting the hares racing in the direction of grades and outcomes from the start. Ironically, it feeds the very attitude that teachers often bemoan, that when the chips are down, students are only interested in their grades. No one would argue with the idea that teachers mention assessment as an important component of a module at the start. It is a question of emphasis, in a culture where outcomes have the potential to dominate in an unhelpful way, epitomised in this focus group comment:

> If someone said: what did you learn on your degree, I'd basically sum it up as saying I learnt what I needed to learn for assignments; I learnt what I learnt because I needed to complete an assignment, rather than I learnt because I was really interested in the whole thing.
>
> (Student, Humanities, 2015)

In a context where learning outcomes are the dominant educational paradigm, it is unsurprising that students are focused on the product of their degrees, rather than the process of learning and exploration in their field of study. This fuels the alienation, lack of ownership and engagement in learning which students describe in TESTA focus groups. It also relates to an 'us-and-them' relationship which is characterised by telling, transmission and passivity (Freire 1970). The rest of the chapter looks at reasons for student alienation in the area of internalising standards, and ways to engage students.

Why telling persists

There are three main reasons for the persistence of telling. The first is that assessment has become part of the technical-rational discourse of accountability and transparency, which enables students and regulatory bodies to hold universities to account for standards, fairness, and the academic rigour of degree awards.

The second is that assessment remains firmly part of the transmission model of education, where knowledge is packaged and 'given' to students, with the expectation that students demonstrate their understanding in response to pre-set questions, rather than developing knowledge in partnership with one another and their teachers. The transmission model represents a worldview defined by received knowledge: in this educational model, there is very little space for students to express their curiosity and imagination in the shaping of assessment questions. The third reason for the persistence of telling is epistemological. In evaluating the quality of student work, a positivist philosophical stance about the nature of knowledge dominates, legitimating knowledge that is rational, externally verifiable, objective, and replicable. This clearly works for subjects governed by the scientific method but does not reflect more intuitive, interpretive, and personal ways of knowing at the heart of subjects characterised by naturalistic and qualitative epistemological paradigms (Lincoln and Guba 1985; Palmer 1993; Palmer et al. 2010; Polanyi 1966). Where knowledge is seen as fixed and certain, then telling follows, which may lead students to formulaic assumptions about standards. The transmission model is a teaching approach which has resonance with a positivist epistemology, with its perception that teaching is information transfer of a fixed set of truths, from expert to novice.

The paradigm of accountability and transparency

The quality of a higher education degree stands or falls on the quality of its assessment. Grades matter and aligning grades with what they signify matters. This means that universities are concerned to demonstrate robust processes so that students and employers can trust that the outcomes of degrees are fair across groups and universities, measuring students' skills and knowledge in ways that are reliable and consistent. That is why accountability and transparency envelop assessment processes. More than this, the paradigm of accountability is meant to reduce arbitrary decision-making about grades in the context of decentralised disciplines in many different institutions. Standards in these highly distributed contexts are developed in collaboration with academics, professional bodies, and external examiners and through the guidance of national quality assurance frameworks. This means that philosophy degrees in Brighton and Bangor can make the claim of being comparable to philosophy degrees in Leeds and Warwick despite differences in size, context, and student intake grades.

The quality assurance apparatus seeks to preserve academic rigour, the robustness of qualifications, and the comparability of degrees. Equally important is the perception and reality of the fairness of grades and awards, and the processes designed to engender a level playing field for students. In the UK, the National Union of Students (NUS, 2008) launched its 'Mark my words, not my name' campaign in 2008 to promote anonymous marking as the means to reduce gender, ethnic and other forms of bias in marking. The NUS Charter on Assessment and Feedback (NUS, 2010) further enshrined anonymous marking as a key principle of fair assessment practices, as did the benchmarking tool which accompanied it. Most UK higher education institutions have adopted anonymous marking, partly in response to NUS campaigning.

There can be absolutely no quibble with the NUS's position on eradicating unconscious bias in marking. Fairness is a cornerstone of quality. However, the belief that anonymous marking eradicates unfairness is mistaken. Some large-scale longitudinal studies have shown no significant differences prior to, and after, anonymous marking was introduced among groups of students who are typically the objects of unconscious bias (Hinton and Higson 2017; Krawczyk 2017). Critics of anonymous marking argue that it is a consequence of an erosion of trust in assessment processes that has negative impacts on personalised, developmental, and dialogic feedback (Pitt and Winstone 2018). Arguably, a transparent process to ensure fairness may be solving a perception problem while simultaneously hampering trust between academics and students and impairing feedback practices.

Transparency is one feature of quality assurance; accountability is another. In many higher education systems, the accountability trail is inscribed in the documents which define a programme of study, from learning outcomes to assessment tasks, criteria and marking descriptors. They constitute what Bloxham et al. (2011) describes as the 'paradigm of accountability', what Shay (2004) calls 'validating practices', and what Orr (2007) critiques as a technical-rational view of curriculum. It is a model of standards explained through criteria, rubrics, the stamp of approval from external examiners, and examination boards. O'Donovan et al. (2008) characterise this explicit model as the dominant logic of mass higher education. It involves telling students about assessment expectations, usually in writing, but sometimes also in person. The explicit model has superseded the 'traditional model' which is the tacit approach of students puzzling out standards by guesswork and trial and error over long periods of time. The explicit model may work better than the traditional approach at helping students to understand 'what good looks like', but it is still inadequate for the task of showing how standards are derived.

Underlying the accountability paradigm is an adherence to a rational planning discourse of curriculum design which works on the assumption that the written outline of a programme mirrors the lived experience of students. The reality is different and far messier. Shay (2004, 2005, 2008) describes marking as a socially situated interpretive act (Shay 2004, p. 307), which is influenced by a marker's disciplinary background, their years of experience, and involvement with students. From her PhD research involving marking practices in two departments, Humanities and Engineering, at the University of Cape Town, she describes the complex process by which staff calibrate standards, over time, through observing how colleagues mark, applying qualities like 'taste', 'intuition' and 'qualitative judgements' in coming to a view about what grade to assign an assessment. Described as 'socialised subjectivity', this process is not about common sense or purely subjective judgements but more about developing a refined sense of making complex judgements through practice over time with colleagues. This raises the dilemma that standards are not fixed and objective, and, indeed, that *your* standards may differ from *my* standards. How then are students to understand complex judgements without deeming them arbitrary or idiosyncratic?

This is where the techno-rationalist perspective makes its appeal to criteria, and to the architecture of quality: moderation, anonymous marking, blind double marking, external examining, and exam boards. Sadler (2009) pokes holes in criteria, describing them as indeterminate and based on the assumption that they represent some externally verifiable markers, when, at best, they are a selection of characteristics, aspired for in an assessment, and expounded by certain academics. Like Bean (2011), Sadler describes the differences between 'analytic' and 'holistic' marking, and the increasing tendency to atomised analytic marking where markers give piecemeal marks for each criterion and add them up. Both Sadler (2009) and Bean (2011) are sceptical about analytical marking, arguing that markers tend to make a rounded judgement and then use analytical categories *post facto*, often to check whether their judgement is accurate. All these technical processes rest on the jealously guarded notion of 'academic judgement' which is the indisputable right of academics to make judgements about the quality of student work - a right considered incontrovertible by virtue of the mantle of being an academic.

For many a student, assessment protocols such as criteria provide some reassurance that marking is robust. However, undergraduate students who have experienced the certainties of analytic marking in the school system where model answers dictate half a point for this, and half a point for that, find the transition to more interpretive and open-ended criteria in higher education unsettling. The implicit interpretation of explicit criteria by markers leads to a sense among students of marker variation and calls into question their usefulness as a shared language for understanding assessment expectations. Students find their trust in criteria slightly misplaced as they often disguise more than they reveal about the complex process of marking, leaving them baffled by the grades they receive. Additionally, they may present false hopes of objectivity about the complex judgements involved in evaluation. Students' disillusionment comes from the spurious sense that criteria give of marking being a science, when any marker who has pored over an essay, mulling on whether it is brilliant or flawed, will know that criteria only go so far in guiding the marker's academic judgement. There is a point in marking where science ends, and the art of judgement begins.

Telling students what 'good' looks like: a transmission approach

Typically, at the start of most modules, teachers walk students through the assessment expectations, telling them what is required and how they should engage, what the criteria are, and how they should prepare. Telling is both a spoken event at the start of modules and written into the documentation. There may be a return to talking about assessment as deadlines come into view, with teachers clarifying and re-telling assessment expectations to their students. The assumption is that telling is good enough and should enable students to get to grips with the tasks at hand. While it is helpful to signpost assessment to students, telling alone will not enable students to internalise standards. It is better than nothing, but not good enough to enable students to know what good looks like.

The problem with telling is that it is an expression of a flawed educational paradigm, which assumes that the main job of a teacher is to transmit information to students. It assumes passive students, who receive knowledge from expert teachers. For students who tune in (or out) of telling, the experience of navigating requirements which have originated from an academic planet in another galaxy is one of powerlessness. Mann (2001) describes students as becoming part of a 'system of exchange' wherein the products they deliver are part of a mark-awarding transaction. Telling is part of a transaction which takes away students' ownership of their assessment.

If the transmission model of telling students the assessment expectations does not help them to become insiders and grasp the standards, what then is the alternative? Socio-constructivist theories of learning argue that students learn from actively engaging in coming to know criteria and standards, through discussion, critique, feedback and applying the criteria to pieces of work (Bloxham et al. 2016; O'Donovan 2018; O'Donovan et al. 2008). Socio-cultural perspectives take this one step further by arguing that standards are continuously developed by academic communities in context (Ajjawi and Bearman 2018). Both approaches regard marking as a complex activity involving socially situated interpretations, during which standards are constructed through discussion and consensus. Inviting students into conversations which enable them to participate in dialogue about the nature of standards, enables them to develop evaluative judgement, defined as the 'capability to make decisions about the quality of work of self and others' (Tai et al. 2018, p. 468).

Telling as a positivist epistemological approach

The long shadow of positivism hangs over assessment. When students ask about the robustness of marking processes, their appeal is to the objectivity of markers. This foundational belief in objectivity is based on a view that there are standards which can be measured: quantifiable, external, and open to scientific scrutiny. The illusion of objectivity is both mistaken and limiting. It is mistaken because there is always interpretation involved in making complex judgements, and it is limiting because some of the most novel, creative, and boundary-breaking achievements defy measurement (Erikson and Erikson 2019). Thinking outside of the box, pursuing inventive lines of inquiry, and being an original thinker: none of these succumb easily to measurement using fixed criteria. Borrowing from Eisner, criteria, like objectives, are "heuristic devices which provide initiating consequences, which become altered, in the flow of instruction" (Eisner 1985, p. 36). In the case of marking and making judgements, criteria are the heuristic devices which enable markers to probe at, discuss and balance the scientific and quantifiable qualities of an assessed task with its artistry. This balancing act challenges assumptions underpinning a positivist framework of knowledge construction which holds that 'knowledge is static, universal and monolithic' (Delandshere 2001, p. 119).

While rationality and the scientific method are central to academic life, there is more to knowing what good looks like than adherence to objective criteria to the exclusion of intuitive and aesthetically pleasing truths. Without these wider approaches to knowing and learning, rational approaches run the risk of being "the thin soup served up when data and logic are the only ingredients" (Palmer et al. 2010, p. 21). Science depends as much on the 'subtle faculties' of 'bodily knowledge, intuition, imagination, and aesthetic sensibility' as on objective data, logic, analysis, and evidence (ibid, p. 21). There are echoes of this in the hard sciences, where mathematicians will glow at an 'elegant' proof, but it is in the Arts that you would expect a strong relationship between truth and beauty as they interweave with argument and critique. The invitation to a wider and more integrated view of education is like being invited to a dinner party where the conversation takes brilliant and unexpected turns, lingering in the imagination and sparking new ideas. Making complex judgements about the quality of students' work should have the quality of savouring and tasting different flavours, bringing together the experience of a connoisseur, albeit with reference points in a recipe. When the recipe dominates and student work is treated with the standardised precision of one who can easily tick off the boxes of a rubric, this denies students and teachers the benefit of academic judgement and expertise.

Knowledge is contestable and 'emphasising uncertainty is a core value' in higher education (Havnes and Prøitz 2016, p. 208). Taking a positivistic approach to marking erases ambiguity and uncertainty, and conflict and dissent, which are at the heart of the process of coming to know what good looks like. It plays to a reductionist perspective of higher education as a form of training in the 'right answers' that there are black-and-white answers to every question, and that the path to truth is formulaic. It constrains students in the early stages of intellectual and moral development to posit dualistic ideas about knowledge which position them as passive recipients of standards defined by experts (Baxter Magolda 2004; O'Donovan 2017; Perry 1981). It offers students a disempowering and alienating experience of assessment which confronts novelty, creativity and an inquiring spirit with settled ideas and received truths about what counts as good work. The goal of higher education is to enable students to wrestle with different perspectives and diverse ways of seeing the world and to develop disciplinary ways of thinking as they come to know how historians, mathematicians or philosophers think, write and act, for example. It is to enable students to develop self-authorship where they become insiders in a discipline (or across disciplines on interdisciplinary programmes) and connect their learning with their own experience. 'Finding your voice' is an integral part of students' intellectual development.

Embracing a heuristic which takes account of interpretation, intuition and subjectivity is not an invitation to an iconoclastic free-for-all in marking, nor a suggestion to jettison rational and evidence-informed judgements. Instead, it is an invitation to question the assumption that marking is a neutral activity, and that anonymous marking removes bias and enables the suspension of subjectivity. There is space for intuition, 'knowing more than we can tell' (Polanyi 1966, p. 4), and for interpretation in applying the criteria. Human beings mark essays, projects, and problem sheets, bringing their judgement, experience, and their personal and social backgrounds to the process of marking - and we should own up to this reality (Batey 2018; Bloxham et al. 2016).

The challenge is that the almost universal trust and allegiance to explicit measures of quality have papered over the cracks in the wall, and it is time to take a long, hard look at those cracks and bring out what lies hidden in the sub-structure of marking. These cracks contain the things that are most difficult to articulate when judging a piece of work, which can subtly influence marker judgements. Feelings and intuition about the value of an assessed task often have no words in the criteria to which we can appeal. They are, however, an indication that marking is both a rational activity and an intuitive one, and we ignore the latter at our peril. The science and art of evaluation need to live together in the same house in the pursuit of fair judgements about the truth and beauty of students' labours.

Indeed, if we allow students to trust in a positivistic view of marking as objective and neutral, we render them a disservice. They may repay us with plenty of written complaints and appeals which probe at the cracks and walls of our flimsy houses. The paradigm of accountability and transparency, a transmission approach to telling students our standards, and positivistic notions of quality, may together create a house in which we would rather not dwell.

Knowing what good looks like: the student perspective

How do students perceive and internalise standards? This section illustrates student perceptions of standards, how they go about internalising them, and what gaps there are in their understanding. It draws on the analysis of TESTA focus group data[1] clustered into five themes. These are: marker variation; mixed feelings about the value of criteria; uncertainty about what good looks like; the value of interactive and dialogic approaches; and internalising standards through formative feedback. The qualitative data illustrates key issues students raise in relation to these themes. Each section concludes with practical and engaging strategies to help address these issues.

Theme #1: marker variation

Students want marking to be fair. The grades they get matter both as an indication of their achievement, and cumulatively, grades make a difference to the kinds of jobs they get. Students want to believe and trust that everything possible has been done to safeguard an even-handed judgement of their assessment efforts. The fairness they seek rests on trusting that marking is consistent, robust, and works to a shared standard. Students are doubtful that fairness is achieved solely through adhering to standards in criteria, rubrics, and moderation alone.

Students identify the variations that exist in marking. Bloxham et al. (2016) and Bean (2011) have shown that markers weight certain criteria as more important than others, and this influences how they assign value, influencing student outcomes. These hidden variations in approach are not always detected through routine procedures such as moderation and double marking. Marking fairly requires surfacing differences honestly and coming to a consensus through the socialisation process of dialogue and through the calibration of marking standards (Shay 2005). Developing shared standards requires talking to each other, revealing doubts and questions, and reaching consensus through conversations about differences of emphasis and interpretation in relation to criteria.

Perceptions of marker variation arise because students do not trust academic judgement and internal and external processes enough to ensure fairness. What they experience feels arbitrary and random and does not satisfactorily explain why judgements have been made. Students are sceptical that there is a shared language and a common approach to marking:

> I just feel like there's no clarity between all the people that mark it, and it's the same with marking different essays. Sometimes the grading can just vary.
>
> (Student, Arts, 2020)

> All the lecturers need to be in one room and talk to each other. I don't think anyone talks to each other. One person says one thing; the other person says something completely different.
>
> (Student, Life Sciences, 2020)

From a student perspective, marking varies across modules, as does assessment guidance, as expressed here:

> It's very dependent on the module and the module lead. There are certain modules where we've had excellent guidance, and so we've been able to focus on learning and focus on areas that are going to come up.
>
> (Student, Health Sciences, 2013)

Students struggle to internalise standards when individual lecturer expectations are ambiguous and varied:

> People have their own way of doing things, so they interpret the very generic and vague marking scheme in their own way. Sometimes you don't really understand what is expected of you, which can be a bit frustrating.
>
> (Student, Humanities, 2020)

Inconsistencies cause confusion, stress, and frustration, leading to perceptions of unfairness:

> The information that we receive is so inconsistent, between lecturers, and it is the most nerve-racking experience, because we're so close, if anything happens now and we trip up, then our whole degree could be jeopardised. It's the inconsistencies. It adds to the stress and adds to our anxiety and frustration. It's been a nightmare.
>
> (Student, Social Work, 2017)

> The way people assess work here isn't fair because there is a severe difference in the level of scrutiny placed by certain people on a document compared with others.
>
> (Student, Humanities, 2010)

Students believe that lecturers' personal preferences dominate, and these are sometimes self-confessed:

> You get lecturers openly saying: 'I'm a tough/generous marker' and I want them to just mark it.
>
> (Student, Social Sciences, 2017)

Like the curate's egg, marking is good in part, with robust processes assuring fairness and consistency in some cases, and subjectivity eroding trust in others:

> In our risk topic, the one lecturer is marking all of them, and then another will look at the grades they gave and re-mark them. I love that they do that because it's actually consistent.
>
> (Student, Social Work, 2017)

> There are certain tutors who really work damn hard to give a fair assessment. There are just the rogue ones.
>
> (Student, Creative Writing, 2010)

> I don't think you're ever going to be able to take subjectivity out of marking. It's going to depend on the lecturer's moods, bias...
>
> (Student, Social Science, 2012)

Programmes undertaking TESTA have sought to address marker variation in different ways. The following actions arose over the course of rolling out TESTA.

Actions to address marker variation

- Calibrate standards in teams by holding a marking calibration exercise using anonymous work. Begin by surfacing what staff are looking for in the pieces of work, rather than assuming that their marking conforms to the criteria. Then align with criteria, potentially asking them to list what they tend to prioritise in marking. Ask them to mark a piece of work in timed conditions and ensure that they commit their decision to the paper that you collect before the discussion commences. The discussion will usually lead to changes in some individual marks, which is part of the point of agreeing on shared standards.
- Familiarise students with marking processes by asking them to review and discuss anonymous work, or to peer review and feedback to peers anonymously. You can begin asking them to free-write reactions and ask a question. Set the tone as positive yet constructively critical. Group discussions about standards can enable students to see that standards do not arise from purely external and objective sources, but also through a contextual socialisation process among markers.

Theme #2: mixed feelings about the value of criteria

Many systems of higher education have signed up to criterion-referenced marking alongside outcomes-based education. This means that students' work is marked against criteria, rather than against each other in a ranking exercise. Unlike the public examination system in the school sector where hundreds of thousands of student grades are adjusted to a normal statistical curve to correct for errors in the standard of papers ('too easy' or 'too difficult'), universities generally have smaller cohort sizes and believe in the intrinsic worth of student answers, marked against criteria. This places a huge weight of expectation on criteria. Pure criterion-referenced marking is something of a fiction though, as markers tend to go back and forth through scripts, essays, and answers to get a feel for the correct ranking of candidates in relation to one another (Bean 2011; Sadler 2009). Explicit criteria call for interpretation and reading between the lines, reflecting the difficulty of attaining shared standards across individual markers whose implicit standards may vary.

Students have quite fuzzy understandings of what criteria are, which may reflect the reality of a patchwork of practices across units, programmes, and departments. In answer to questions about how they use criteria, students mention a raft of assessment artefacts which alternate for criteria in their minds: mark schemes, model answers, grading criteria, handbooks, rubrics, learning outcomes and assessment briefs. The most common conflation is between marking descriptors and criteria. Marking descriptors are generic high-level faculty or university statements about levels of attainment, from first to fail, which often use abstract and language with appropriate modifiers to denote the level of attainment, for example, 'Able to display a command of critical analysis and judgement' for a first-class mark, and 'Deficient under-standing of the issues and concepts taught' for a fail. In contrast, criteria are more specific to programmes, modules, and even assessment tasks, contain-ing more targeted granularity, with the purpose of outlining expectations. These may take the form of rubrics which are presented in a table containing the criteria and may allow the marker to tick areas of achievement against specific boxes.

Students are critical of criteria for being too vague, generic, and abstract to help them understand expectations. These are typical comments:

> Grading criteria are very vague. If you read through them it hardly tells you anything about how to structure it, what elements to incorporate, it just kind of vaguely touches on what they're potentially looking for.
>
> (Student, Humanities, 2020)

> When I read the rubric, it feels so abstract that it's really difficult to actually apply it to the work you're doing.
>
> (Student, Engineering, 2019)

Students' confusion is exacerbated by the language used to describe quite elusive and abstract concepts:

> They mean nothing to me. The language is very complex. It's just elongated sentences and I'm like, I think I fulfilled that but I'm not the one marking it.
>
> (Student, Life Sciences, 2018)

The use of modifiers to depict whether work is excellent, very, good, good, or average, comes in for a particular drubbing:

> It's arbitrary. A 2.1 you have a 'good understanding'. A First is a 'really good understanding'.
>
> (Student, Arts, 2014)

> It would be like 'adequate research done' 'high level of research done' and it's just like I don't know what this means.
>
> (Student, Computing, 2018)

Students recognise that criteria are open to interpretation, and that marking is a complex activity with some 'reading between the lines' between explicit and implicit criteria being necessary:

> When we get the handbook, it's not always clear but sometimes if you read between the lines, you can understand where they are going.
>
> (Student, Social Sciences, 2010)

> With the marking criteria as well, that's again interpreted differently by different lecturers and even sometimes the same lecturer within assignments.
>
> (Student, Science, 2020)

Some students understand less about the complexity of marking and the interpretation involved in weighing up the evidence against the criteria:

> I get the impression that they don't even look at the marking criteria. They read the essay and then they get a general impression then they pluck a mark from the air, whether or not they're impressed by it or not, I don't think they go through everything.
>
> (Student, Humanities, 2011)

> No matter how you want to put it on paper, I do think that an individual lecturer will warm to a certain style of writing, and not warm to another.
>
> (Student, Humanities, 2011)

While some students are critical of the misuses of criteria, others find them useful, especially when seen alongside examples of work:

> Marking criteria help guide you towards what's good.
>
> (Student, Social Sciences, 2010)

> If we saw, for example, a previous assessment that was marked alongside the criteria, so had lines drawn from the criteria to certain aspects of the text, then we'd be able to see what we could do to improve our own parts. And if we knew the marking process, then we'd know how to get those marks in our own pieces.
>
> (Student, Engineering, 2018)

Given that criteria go some way, but not all the way, to helping students internalise standards, what actions can be taken to help students identify the elements of good work? Here are some ideas arising from programmes which have undertaken TESTA.

Actions to familiarise students with criteria

- Invite students to look at the assessment criteria and/or intended learning outcomes, and to write down which criteria play to their strengths, and which are more challenging, and why. Ask students to discuss in pairs. Invite contributions in plenary and discuss any knotty issues that are shared. This is a great activity for familiarising students with the criteria. Do it as an in-class activity.
- Involve students in co-creating criteria. One approach is to give them the existing criteria to discuss in pairs, underlining words they do not understand, and coming up with replacement phrases and words in plain English.
- Give students an anonymised assignment from a previous year and ask them to read it and devise criteria for how they might mark it. Crowdsource the criteria, and then align with the 'real' criteria. Weave student suggestions into new, plain English, student-friendly criteria.

Theme #3: not knowing what good looks like

One of the most crucial skills students should learn at university is the ability to judge the quality of writing, an argument, a performance, an experiment, or a proof, depending on the discipline. This is no simple task, as there are always 'lingering doubts' in any judgement of quality (Nelson 2018, p. 52). However, in some disciplines, making judgements may follow a simpler path than others. Nelson (2018) makes the case that there are three kinds of evaluative judgement: 'hard evaluative judgement' occurs in more objective, convergent disciplines, in the search for truth using empirical evidence, observation, and excellent knowledge of the field (ibid, p. 52). This form of judgement is less fuzzy and interpretive than 'soft evaluative judgement' which determines the value, quality, and importance of ideas, and builds on canonical and cultural perspectives. Finally, there is 'dynamic evaluative judgement', which judges writing, the organisation and communication of persuasive and creative ideas, and aesthetics. Soft and dynamic evaluative judgements tend to be more vexed and open to stylistic, personal, and subjective considerations. However, there is still room for the aesthetic of the elegant proof in 'hard evaluative judgement'. The idea of different shades of judgement is helpful, as is the sense captured by 'soft' and 'dynamic' judgement that standards are not frozen and static. Given that 'what good looks like' may change over time, it is important to develop and fine-tune students' skills of evaluative judgement.

Coming to an understanding of how teachers judge quality in their discipline is an important part of developing evaluative judgement. Sadler argues that to improve learning, students need to 'hold a concept of quality roughly similar to that held by the teacher' (Sadler 1989, p. 121). The implication is that internalising standards entails active strategies to discuss, share, observe and participate in judging quality. It also implies surfacing teacher conceptions of quality that may not be well articulated in explicit criteria.

TESTA focus group data indicate that teachers may not be very good at articulating their implicit theories of quality, or even clarifying what good looks like in explicit terms through criteria and assessment briefs. More tellingly, there is little evidence to suggest that students engage actively with making judgements themselves, seeing and discussing what good looks like, or having experience in the curriculum to develop evaluative judgement. They describe learning by potluck and trial and error, and some are never quite sure why they receive the grade they do. Students describe being in passive receipt of other people's judgements of quality, without understanding why a particular judgement has been made. The metaphors students use to depict their uncertainty about assessment standards are littered with ideas of luck, gambling, and guesswork:

> It feels like no matter how hard you work on an assignment it is always like a guessing game when you submit it.
>
> (Student, Life Sciences, 2017)

> I felt that when I handed all of my essays in after Christmas, it did just feel like a lottery. I didn't know how I was going to do. I couldn't predict.
>
> (Student, Humanities, 2013)

Uncertainty about judging the quality of work leads to questions about the rationale for grades:

> In essays I just don't have a clue, the marks are so volatile for me.
>
> (Student, Social Sciences, 2020)

> I'm clueless as to what is expected of me at uni... my sister has just finished her degree, and she said that at some point you will just learn what they want from you, what they expect to get that grade, to get into the 2.1 and 1st brackets. But I feel very clueless right now.
>
> (Student, Science, 2020)

Students describe a hit-and-miss trajectory towards developing evaluative judgement, which leaves some less clear about standards at the end of their studies than at the beginning:

> I feel that in 3rd year I'm far less confident in myself with writing than I was in my first year. I've completely lost confidence in my essay writing skills because of certain marks and not being sure what to do.
>
> (Student, Humanities, 2013)

In the absence of knowing what lies behind the standards, marking descriptors are meaningless:

> The difference between 'Excellent use' of something rather than 'Good use' of something and it's like, well, how can I judge what is excellent use of something and good use of something?
>
> (Student, Humanities, 2011)

Students feel it would be helpful to see examples of the standards being played out in practice, but some say this is not a regular occurrence:

> I really wish someone would give us some examples of things, like if they say 'You've got to put this, this and this in an essay' then give us an example of one that was good, so that we can actually see.
>
> (Student, Media, 2010)

> There's never been an exemplar essay. I would find that really useful.
>
> (Student, Humanities, 2020)

Different and more sophisticated varieties of assessment such as final year research projects present further challenges in internalising standards:

> A lot of people don't really know how much independent stuff we're meant to be doing. Like, can you get a good mark without coming up with some new theory or something… It's really only this year when you have to come up with things yourself, that there's a bit of, oh, how original or broad does this have to be?
>
> (Student, Arts, 2013)

Many students in TESTA focus groups are unable to judge the quality of their own work and lack confidence in assessing how well they are doing. Developing their evaluative judgement is part of building their ownership of, and trust in, assessment processes, enabling them to be less reliant on external benchmarks and to internalise the standards. Here are some actions that TESTA programmes have taken to help students to achieve this:

Actions to internalise standards

- Anonymise a range of work (good, indifferent, and poor) from previous years' assessments. You can use part or whole assessments, for example, choosing a section. Ask students to read and identify strengths and weaknesses in the exemplars in relation to criteria you have given them and discuss what is good and not so good about the assignment. Students can do this in a group exercise, and you can then summarise the discussion in plenary and draw out key points. You can take this exercise a step further and ask students to rewrite a particularly problematic section to improve it, after the discussion. They could share their improvements in pairs.

- Conduct a mock-marking exercise where you give students anonymous work from a previous year (or you devise an exemplar), and the criteria, and ask them to mark and write feedback individually, and discuss in pairs or groups. In the plenary discussion, you can share the original mark and feedback to compare and discuss why the judgements were made.

Theme #4: standards are best taught, not caught, in interactive and dialogic ways

It is a flawed assumption that students will just pick up how to write or present well, knowing instinctively what good looks like, or learning by trial and error (Sadler 1989). Students describe wanting more explicit and engaging work on academic writing which helps them to discern standards and find their voice and confidence. They want to see and discuss the writing of others, and to learn to discriminate across a range of performances. Students need to be socialised into processes which enable them to evaluate examples in discussion with one another and teachers (Rust et al. 2003). They need to become familiar with the tacit aspects of making judgements which often only become evident through their active engagement in dialogue (Carless et al. 2018).

Students recognise the value of interaction even in the context of telling them about standards:

> We had a session where she talked through how the assessment worked, how we should go about it, and that was maybe, six weeks before we had to hand it in. It was quite dynamic, and you could kind of interact with it, and engage with the topic.
>
> (Student, Sciences, 2020)

In students' minds, writing, engagement and finding an authorial voice are connected. But these are not learnt without an explicit focus on academic writing in the discipline:

> With regards to confidence and finding your voice within academic writing, at no point it is stressed that you're supposed to produce an argument that you believe in and that you want to argue for and then find evidence for.

There should be a bit more about building confidence around academic writing. Developing a style and lectures on style with writing that would be really useful. It could potentially be more engaging and incentivise people to work and enjoy their assessments more.

(Student, Sciences, 2020)

I went into the assessment not knowing how to write it: do I write it in first person? Do I write it in the present tense?

(Student, Humanities, 2011)

The challenge seems to be about developing students' conceptions of academic standards through explicit means like seeing, discussing, and teaching best practices, rather than assuming they will pick it up:

I'd never really been taught how to do an academic essay. It's just kind of expected that you pick it up.

(Student, Social Sciences, 2020)

You didn't get any help on how to write them. They just basically said 'Right, here's the essay questions. Go away and write them' and they didn't really offer any help with how to write them.

(Student, Social Work, 2010)

Seeing good and bad assessment performances helps students to build up a picture of what good looks like. However, students describe the potential of exemplars leading to simplistic and grade-oriented perceptions of quality and feeding formulaic perceptions about standards. This underlines the importance of 'taught, not caught' strategies to internalise standards which include discussion and critical engagement:

We were shown an example of a good one and a not so good one. So we could gauge what we were working towards and what we're trying to achieve. That was helpful.

(Student, Social Sciences, 2017)

We got given an example and a lot of people referred to that example, so we are like "yeah but ours is exactly like the example" and the example got like a b "so why is mine a c or why is mine a d or why did I get a really rubbish grade?"

(Student, Life Sciences, 2017)

But this also feels a bit like: 'tick box'; here's what we want to see. I'd like to have a bit more freedom instead of just being shown someone else's work.

(Student, Sports Science, 2018)

Students detect nervousness from staff about crossing the 'invisible line' between judging their work and helping them, along with fears that showing exemplars may not be institutionally supported, potentially leading to copying and less original work:

> The tutors have different opinions on if they feel like they're helping you too much, because they obviously don't want to cross that invisible line if you like, where they actually help you write it.
>
> (Student, Humanities, 2010)

> But then I remembered him saying, this is an example of a good essay. However, I'm not sure I'm really allowed to do this. Like he wasn't sure if he was supposed to be giving us an example of good work or if he wasn't.
>
> (Student, Humanities, 2011)

Deconstructing and discussing exemplars is clearly one way of helping students internalise standards. TESTA programmes have used other approaches to help students to see and come to know standards and develop their authorial voice and ownership in solving problems and crafting arguments. Here are some ideas from programme teams.

Actions to help students gain confidence in achieving standards

- Make space in the curriculum for activities which help students learn how to write, analyse problems, and use the skills of their discipline. These can involve peer review of short tasks, developing principles of how to write and solve problems elegantly, showing worked examples and working backwards to articulate best practice principles.
- Challenge received wisdom about using the passive and third person as standard formats. An objective language which hides agency is questionable. Find ways to encourage plain English, and the judicious use of authorial voice and agency (Sword 2013).

Theme #5: the value of formative feedback

Formative feedback is a key means for students to internalise standards. While its wider value is outlined fully in Chapters 5 and 6, in the context of this chapter, its chief good lies in helping students to develop a picture of what good looks like. It allows students to be novel and inventive without jeopardising their grades. Undertaking formative tasks and using formative feedback helps students become insiders in their discipline and its discourses.

Students describe formative assessment as helpful in clearing up confusion about expectations:

> Particularly in the first year, some form of formative assessment would be quite reassuring. I know in my first year I was just thinking 'I've absolutely no idea how I'm doing'. Apart from the assignment I genuinely don't know how I'm doing here.
>
> (Focus Group, Humanities, 2013)

> It was kind of meeting but as a presentation, so it was formative. If I didn't have that, I would have been so confused about the whole writing process.
>
> (Focus Group, Science, 2020)

Some light touch in-class formative peer review approaches really work:

> I barely even bother to look at the criteria because if I have the chance to get my work looked at during the lesson with the lecturer there and other people, I think that's got to give me enough clarification and judgement on whether I'm writing the right thing or not.
>
> (Focus Group, Creative Writing, 2010)

The crucial aspect of formative assessment is having sustained feedback so that students come to know over time what good looks like:

> The helpful few are giving you feedback all the time, not just inviting you to the office for ten minutes to discuss two pieces of work that you've written that your whole module is based on. I'd rather have more help spread out than one ten-minute session going biff, baff, boom, bye bye.
>
> (Focus Group, Humanities, 2010)

Actions to internalise standards through using formative feedback

- Invite first-year students to write a 500-word formative essay, on which you give feedback about how it can be developed. Design a summative assessment which requires students to rewrite their work based on the formative feedback, and with an accompanying reflection on how they have used the feedback. Mark the reflection in conjunction with reading the rewrite.
- Adopt rebuttal exercises to engage students in identifying which feedback resonates with their understanding, and which they disagree with or question. Using a cycle of drafting, receiving peer or teacher feedback, writing a rebuttal, and discussing areas of consensus and disagreement, and then redrafting, help students to take greater ownership over their work while refining it in response to feedback (Harland et al. 2017).

A brief synopsis

This chapter examines the influence of accountability and transparency mechanisms in mass higher education on students' capacity to internalise standards. It argues that the dominance of a transmission approach to acquiring standards leaves students unsure of how complex judgements are made. Positivist epistemologies obscure the complexity of making judgements about the quality of assessments. Student focus group data shows that students are confused by marker variation, they are ambivalent about the value of criteria, and they struggle to come to know what good looks like. Students appreciate interactive, dialogic approaches to internalising standards, and value formative feedback.

Note

1 102 focus groups with 552 students on 60 programmes in 14 universities over 12 years.

References

Ajjawi, R., and M. Bearman. 2018. Problematising standards: Representation or performance? (Ch 4, pp. 41–50). In D. Boud, R. Ajjawi, P. Dawson, and J. Tai (Eds.). *Developing Evaluative Judgement in Higher Education. Assessment for Knowing and Producing Quality Work.* London. Routledge.

Batey, J. 2018. *Expectancies, Marking and Feedback in Undergraduate Student Assessment.* Unpublished PhD Thesis. University of Winchester.

Baxter Magolda, M. B. 2004. *Making Their Own Way: Narratives for Transforming Higher Education to Promote Self-Development.* Sterling, VA. Stylus Publishing.

Bean, J. 2011. *Engaging Ideas: The Professor's Guide to Integrating Writing, Critical Thinking and Active Learning in the Classroom.* Second Edition. San Francisco, CA. Jossey-Bass.

Bloxham, S., P. Boyd, and S. Orr. 2011. Mark my words: The role of assessment criteria in UK higher education grading practices. *Studies in Higher Education* 36 (6): 655–670, DOI: 10.1080/03075071003777716

Bloxham, S., B. den-Outer, J. Hudson, and M. Price. 2016. Let's stop the pretence of consistent marking: Exploring the multiple limitations of assessment criteria. *Assessment & Evaluation in Higher Education* 41 (3): 466–481, DOI: 10.1080/02602938.2015.1024607

Carless, D., K. K. H. Chan, J. To, M. Lo, and E. Barrett. 2018. Developing students' capacities for evaluative judgement through analysing exemplars. (Ch.11, pp. 108–116). In D. Boud, R. Ajjawi, P. Dawson, and J. Tai (Eds). (2018a). *Developing Evaluative Judgement in Higher Education. Assessment for Knowing and Producing Quality Work.* London. Routledge.

Delandshere, G. 2001. Implicit theories, unexamined assumptions and the status quo of educational assessment. *Assessment in Education: Principles, Policy & Practice* 8 (2): 113–133.

Eisner, E. W. 1985. *The Art of Educational Evaluation: A Personal View.* Basingstoke. Falmer Press.

Erikson, M. G., and M. Erikson. 2019. Learning outcomes and critical thinking – Good intentions in conflict. *Studies in Higher Education* 44 (12): 22932303, DOI: 10.1080/03075079.2018.1486813

Freire, P. 1970. *Pedagogy of the Oppressed*. London. The Continuum Publishing Company.

Harland, T., N. Wald, and H. Randhawa. 2017. Student peer review: Enhancing formative feedback with a rebuttal. *Assessment & Evaluation in Higher Education* 42 (5): 801–811, DOI: 10.1080/02602938.2016.1194368

Havnes, A., and T. S. Prøitz. 2016. Why use learning outcomes in higher education? Exploring the grounds for academic resistance and reclaiming the value of unexpected learning. *Educational Assessment, Evaluation and Accountability* 28: 205–223. https://doi.org/10.1007/s11092-016-9243-z

Hinton, D. P., and H. Higson 2017. A large-scale examination of the effectiveness of anonymous marking in reducing group performance differences in higher education assessment. *PLoS One* 12 (8): 1–16.

Jessop, T., and C. Tomas. 2017. The implications of programme assessment patterns for student learning. *Assessment & Evaluation in Higher Education* 42 (6): 990–999, DOI: 10.1080/02602938.2016.1217501

Krawczyk, M. 2017. Do gender and physical attractiveness affect college grades? *Assessment and Evaluation in Higher Education*. 151–161. doi: 10.1080/02602938. 2017.1307320

Lincoln, Y. S., and E. G. Guba. 1985. *Naturalistic Inquiry*. Newbury Park, CA. SAGE Publications.

Mann, S. J. 2001. Alternative perspectives on the student experience: Alienation and engagement. *Studies in Higher Education* 26 (1): 7–19.

Nelson, R. 2018. Barriers to the cultivation of evaluative judgement: A critical and historical perspective (Ch. 5, pp. 51–59). In D. Boud, R. Ajjawi, P. Dawson, and J. Tai (Eds). (2018a). *Developing Evaluative Judgement in Higher Education. Assessment for Knowing and Producing Quality Work*. London. Routledge.

Nicol, D. J., and D. Macfarlane-Dick 2006. 'Formative assessment and self-regulated learning: A model and seven principles of good feedback practice. *Studies in Higher Education* 31 (2): 199–218.

NUS. 2008. Higher Education Campaign: Mark My Words, Not My Name [online]. Accessed May 20 2019. http://www.nus.org.uk/en/Campaigns/Higher-Education/Mark-my-words-not-my-name/

NUS. 2010. Charter on Assessment and Feedback (Online). Accessed online 20 August 2020. http://www.nusconnect.org.uk/asset/news/6010/FeedbackCharter-toview.pdf

O'Donovan, B. 2017. How student beliefs about knowledge and knowing influence their satisfaction with assessment and feedback. *Higher Education* 74: 617–633. https://doi.org/10.1007/s10734-016-0068-y

O'Donovan, B. 2018. *Assessment matters: a critical appraisal of assessment practice in higher education with a particular focus on enhancing student understanding of standards and criteria*. Unpublished PhD Thesis. Oxford Brookes University.

O'Donovan, B., M. Price, and C. Rust. 2008. Developing student understanding of assessment standards: A nested hierarchy of approaches. *Teaching in Higher Education* 13 (2): 205–217, DOI: 10.1080/13562510801923344

Orr, S. 2007. Assessment moderation: Constructing the marks and constructing the students. *Assessment and Evaluation in Higher Education* 32 (6): 645–656, DOI: 10.1080/02602930601117068

Palmer, P. 1993. *To Know as We Are Known: Education as a Spiritual Journey*. San Francisco, CA. Harper One.

Palmer, P., A. Zajonc with, and M. Scribner. 2010. *The Heart of Higher Education: A Call to Renewal. Transforming the Academy Through Collegial Conversations*. San Francisco, CA. Jossey-Bass.

Perry, W. 1981. 'Cognitive and ethical growth: The making of meaning' (Chapter 3, pp. 76–116). In Jossey Bass (Ed.). *The Modern American College*. San Francisco, CA. Jossey-Bass.

Pitt, E., and N. Winstone. 2018. The impact of anonymous marking on students' perceptions of fairness, feedback and relationships with lecturers. *Assessment & Evaluation in Higher Education* 43 (7): 1183–1193, DOI: 10.1080/02602938.2018.1437594

Polanyi, M. 1966. *The Tacit Dimension*. Chicago, IL. University of Chicago Press.

Rust, C., M. Price, and B. O'Donovan. 2003. Improving Students' learning by developing their understanding of assessment criteria and processes. *Assessment and Evaluation in Higher Education* 28 (2): 147–164, DOI: 10.1080/02602930301671

Sadler, D. R. 1989. Formative assessment and the design of instructional system. *Instructional Science* 18: 119–144.

Sadler, D. R. 2009. Indeterminacy in the use of preset criteria for assessment and grading. *Assessment and Evaluation in Higher Education* 34 (2): 159–179, DOI: 10.1080/02602930801956059

Shay, S. 2004. The assessment of complex performance: A socially situated interpretive act. *Harvard Educational Review* 74 (3): 307–329. https://doi.org/10.17763/haer.74.3.wq16l67103324520

Shay, S. 2005. The assessment of complex tasks: A double Reading. *Studies in Higher Education* 30 (6): 663–679, DOI: 10.1080/03075070500339988.

Shay, S. 2008. Beyond social constructivist perspectives on assessment: The centring of knowledge. *Teaching in Higher Education* 13 (5): 595–605, DOI: 10.1080/13562510802334970.

Sword, H. 2013. *Stylish Academic Writing*. Cambridge. MA. Harvard University Press.

Tai, J., R. Ajjawi, D. Boud, P. Dawson, and E. Panadero. 2018. Developing evaluative judgement: Enabling students to make decisions about the quality of work. *Higher Education* 76 (3): 467–481. https://doi.org/10.1007/s10734-017-0220-3.

Chapter 8

Reflections on TESTA's educational change process

Introduction

This chapter reflects on the theory of change that has evolved through conducting 'Transforming the Experience of Students through Assessment' (TESTA) with programme teams for more than ten years. It outlines some of the challenges of bringing about educational change in complex, distributed organisations with many competing and sometimes conflicting agendas. Drawing on the literature on academic development, organisational change, and academic cultures, it identifies strategies and principles of change that have made TESTA a valued process and led to its reach across the UK sector, and its influence elsewhere.

Reach is one measure of success for a change initiative. TESTA has reached 45 UK universities[1] known to the team, and a small number of universities in Australia, India, and Ireland[2] over a sustained period, having originally been funded for three years to work in four universities. It has been in demand as an approach since then, having been adopted as an enhancement measure in six of the seven universities in Scotland, embedded in quality assurance in three of them[3], and with investment following in more than a dozen researcher posts at universities across the UK. Wide reach suggests the value of TESTA's approach, which is an important indicator of success in an environment where pedagogic enhancements are seen by some academics as intrusive and wasteful:

> Most faculty see pedagogical improvement as a morass in which gains would be invisible if achieved and in which they can only lose time, money, and energy through vaguely configured efforts that create no enduring value. So the department preserves the individual space of the faculty member to teach unobserved and unmolested.
>
> (Tagg 2012, p. 12)

Impact is a further measure of success for a change initiative. Walker et al. (2017) examined whether programmes of study which had made assessment changes in the light of TESTA influenced students' retention on the programme. They were not able to demonstrate a significant relationship between

DOI: 10.4324/9780429347962-12

TESTA and student continuation rates. Instead, they found that students' backgrounds were more significant predictors of low retention, indicating the difficulty of measuring interventions in isolation from their context. However, TESTA did contribute to relatively good performance on whole institution assessment scores on the UK's National Student Survey (NSS) at the same university, having been undertaken on 157 programmes over five years (Walker et al. 2019). Smaller scale evidence from the University of Bristol shows modest improvements in assessment and feedback scores on programmes undertaking TESTA over three years (Gatrell 2023). However, using a metrics-based approach to assessing impact has limitations. Performance measures need to be interpreted in context and may not always be asking questions of pedagogic value, as evidenced in the analysis of feedback items on ten national surveys (Winstone et al. 2022).

This chapter takes a qualitative approach to understanding the value of the TESTA process and its impact on programme assessment patterns. It draws on the analysis of semi-structured interviews with 10 programme directors collected at the end of the funded period of the project (2012), and a further six interviews with programme directors undertaken in 2020. Chapter 1 outlines more fully the process of data analysis that was used. In contextualising these findings, this chapter reflects briefly on programme directors as key stakeholders; the changing role of academic development; the rationale for change; and the challenge of change. Finally, it distils principles from the TESTA change process which may be applicable to other academic development projects.

Programme directors as key stakeholders

TESTA's change process is dependent on programme directors. They act as go-betweens in the relationship between the university, academic developers, the programme team, administrators, and students. Their investment in the process comes through seeing some of the benefits of participating, in particular improved assessment design, more rewarding teaching, more balanced workloads, and greater student engagement in learning. TESTA's capacity to provide independent evidence about assessment is often a drawcard for them. Unsurprisingly, there can be wariness and caution in the beginning about the value of the process relative to the time and political capital it might expend with colleagues in their teams. Programme directors are often enthusiastic about enhancing education, but there may be a few members of the team who are more sceptical about change.

The informal leadership role of the programme director is complex, involving multi-layered relationships, and responsibilities (Lawrence et al. 2022). Programme directors are often expected to lead teams to enact decisions by senior managers (Moore 2022), and one of their key responsibilities is to oversee improvements in students' experience of education, evidenced through positive scores on metrics (Henri 2022). In this context, TESTA facilitators, who are usually academic developers, need to develop strong and positive relationships with programme directors, communicating the benefits of the approach and undertaking productive work with teams. More specifically, TESTA facilitators need to support programme directors to be enabling leaders, using strategies which help them to build connections with their teams, and follow through with commitments to collective action (Parkin 2022). Programme directors can move forward more effectively when the TESTA process has been collegiate, scholarly, and nudged members of the team to action, either through confirming intuition with evidence, or giving a fresh perspective.

The changing role of academic development

The nature of academic development has changed and its presence across universities in many countries of the world has grown as universities have admitted more students with more diverse educational backgrounds (Gibbs 2013). Student expectations of excellent teaching have risen in a marketised environment, and universities place more emphasis on performance metrics about teaching excellence and student satisfaction (Spence 2019). In the past four decades, universities in many countries have invested in central academic development centres, which have been the seedbeds for the scholarship of teaching and learning, and evidence-based practice (Gibbs 2013). Teaching in higher education is increasingly regarded as a profession with its own guild knowledge and expertise, with new lecturers being required to engage in training. Within this context, what does academic development look like, what has changed, and what is distinctive about TESTA's approach?

One of the most significant changes in academic development has been the shift from a focus on working with individuals to working with teams to encourage more systemic and sustained approaches to innovation (McGrath 2020, Gibbs 2013). This overcomes limits on individual teachers who struggle to "improve in effective ways if their colleagues and other courses do not" and it is more likely to secure "permanent change where the local culture and values are hostile to such change" (Gibbs 2013, p. 7). Related to this more context-sensitive form of academic development is the accompanying shift away from individualistic psychological theories about how students learn to more sociological ones about structure and agency (McGrath 2020, Roxå and Mårtensson 2017). TESTA embodies this new model of academic development with its focus on theories of alienation and engagement in students' experience in the context of their programme.

As academic development has evolved, so its approach has become more open to expanding the generic 'canon' of knowledge and theory underpinning it. This is challenging for a young field which has not secured a strong identity of its own in the academy. Its openness is shown in being respectful of, and curious about disciplinary practice. Increasingly, academic developers question generic and homogenising solutions, which lead to participants feeling suppressed or colonised (Manathunga 2006; Roxå and Mårtensson 2017). This is also pragmatic: "change processes that succeed in Law, flop in Engineering, and writing about teaching that engages Psychologists leaves Art Historians cold" (Gibbs 2013, p. 11). The role of academic developers in brokering change involves conversation and reciprocity about disciplinary and generic pedagogic practices. It entails asking 'what if' questions about alternatives, and nudging colleagues by sharing examples that have proven their worth elsewhere. TESTA's approach to academic development seeks to show this mix of openness, mutuality, and challenge as it works with different programmes: its aim is to listen and learn from disciplinary practices as well as to share expertise and guide teams in interpreting programme-level and student evidence (Walker et al. 2019).

TESTA research opens a conversation with students and academics about their everyday experience of assessment and feedback, anchors discussion in evidence and creates impetus for change. Conversation is central to its brokering work in recognition that the process of change is freighted with emotion and fears of managerialism. In conducting TESTA, teams have agency to make changes that arise from evidence, align with their disciplinary practice, and respond to students' feedback. However, in the context of markets and metrics, TESTA is caught between its developmental intent, and institutional drivers to improve performance measures in assessment and feedback. To that extent, programme teams recognise that their agency is bounded (McGrath 2020).

The rationale for change

Successful change projects are powered by their rationale. Persuading colleagues in universities to undertake educational changes requires a strong 'why' (Fullan and Scott 2009; Tagg 2012). It identifies 'who' the change is for and who stands to benefit from it. Different stakeholders in the process will see the 'why' from their own vantage point. In inviting teams to participate, TESTA academic developers set out a rationale which is about evidence, taking a programme approach, and stepping back to understand assessment patterns and students' experience of them. Programme teams participate in a facilitated process of change in which they have agency about their choices and actions. The benefits of TESTA follow from taking a programme approach to assessment design, informed by students' perspectives of their learning experience across different modules. TESTA enables sharing of innovations from within the team and from academic developers. It improves the student experience, and makes assessment, marking and feedback manageable and more rewarding for teachers and students (Hopwood-Stephens 2021).

In marketised higher education, the rationale for engaging in the TESTA process is linked to improving metrics about assessment and feedback. In the UK, universities invest in TESTA in response to pressures to enhance assessment and feedback scores on the NSS, which contributes to the Teaching

Excellence Framework (TEF) (Buckley 2021; Williams and Kane 2009). Persistently low assessment and feedback scores are a source of ongoing concern for universities, leaders with responsibility for education, and academics in general. The fear of being awarded a bronze rating in the TEF looms large. It has implications for a university's reputation, student recruitment, and particularly the attractiveness of programmes to international students. For universities, the financial implications are material.

The 'why' of TESTA also arises from a problem of diagnosis. Universities and academics are in 'imaginative gridlock' about how to improve students' experience of assessment and feedback and related performance measures (Friedman 2017, p. 17). Systems in gridlock are characterised by three common responses: trying harder at the same things, looking for answers rather than reframing questions, and either/or thinking that creates false dichotomies (Friedman 2017, p. 38). Imaginative gridlock plays out in responses to seemingly intractable assessment and feedback problems where individual academics, programme directors, and academic development teams 'try harder', developing inventive and time-consuming strategies to encourage students to find more meaning and value in their assessment and feedback. They write more feedback; they rewrite assessment criteria; they give more choices; they develop more varieties of assessment; they standardise feedback; they personalise it; they use audio feedback; they label every piece of correspondence with students as 'feedback', and they mark faster and faster in shorter periods of time. As Buckley (2021) comments, "relatively low scores tend to suck in the available attention and effort" (Ibid, p. 2009).

TESTA's rationale is to break the 'imaginative gridlock' by searching for answers outside of the existing modular paradigms, and beyond psychological theories of learning. The programme approach of TESTA enables a bird's eye view of assessment and feedback which resembles the experience of students taking several concurrent modules. Theories of alienation and engagement situate the problem of students' experience in the wider context of the programme, and in factors beyond the programme which influence students' learning. TESTA brings a deeper understanding of students' experiences. It provides a clear view of programme assessment patterns, leading to a more nuanced discussion of the problem at programme-level. It builds a shared understanding of the challenges, reducing the 'us' and 'them' false dichotomies between students and academics, and cutting through the language of blaming students for problems in assessment and feedback (see Quinn 2012).

The challenge of change

Resistance to educational change and teaching enhancement initiatives is common in higher education (Buller 2015; Fullan and Scott 2009; Quinn 2012; Tagg 2012). The reasons are complex. Universities are distributed organisations within which individual academics have high degrees of autonomy.

As Buller (2015) observes, 'members of distributed organisations tend to re-sist change more strongly because they view what's being discarded as part of themselves' (Ibid, p. 19). Autonomy and academic freedom often lead to greater personal engagement, with the consequence that any impetus to change how things are done appears to be an assault on the very identity of academics. Tagg (2012) frames academics' resistance to change as aversion to loss, and using the concept of the *endowment effect*[4] describes how the status quo is often more attractive to academics because many perceive what they have as more valuable than what they stand to lose through the risk of change:

> Changes in pedagogy and curriculum are offered as a way of making gains in student learning. But if it comes, and it always does, to a weighing of gains versus losses, loss aversion and the endowment effect will keep a thumb on the scale, leading losses to outweigh gains.
>
> (Tagg 2012, p. 9)

What do academics stand to lose through engaging with programmes of educational enhancement like TESTA? Quinn (2012) identifies academics' fears of loss of autonomy and intellectual freedom, and implicit in that, their loss of time. Spending time on educational activities is deemed wasteful, as "the time could be better spent conducting disciplinary research" (Ibid, p. 75). The prestige of research relative to teaching, with its autonomy, intellectual freedom, higher salaries, grants, and visible markers of accomplishment is one reason for departments isolating themselves from academic development initiatives (Tagg 2012). Another is the perception that academic development programmes and interventions are too generic to be of use in discipline-specific contexts and are either heavily laden with education theory or 'dumb down' the knowledge dimensions of the curriculum with skills and techniques. When interventions fail to deepen understanding and practice, these critiques may well have legitimacy (Quinn 2012, p. 75). A further strain of resistance comes from academics who see the purpose of the university as being to educate the elite and therefore hold a view that professional development to improve and diversify teaching approaches is unnecessary. According to this view, universities simply need to recruit students who are good enough to thrive and thereby enable academics to teach as they have always done (Quinn 2012).

There is no one single academic culture in universities, as Bergquist and Pawlak's study of six different cultures demonstrates (Bergquist and Pawlak, 2007). Academic cultures define the experience of their members, providing a shared purpose and an interpretive framework for them. They also help to contain anxiety, particularly in the face of external influences and internal changes. Cultures exist to ensure stability, especially when there is a high level of anxiety or stress in the organisation (Buller 2015). Inevitably though, collisions between various cultures occur, especially when the environment changes. Sparring between different academic cultures can be an impediment to change.

Bergquist and Pawlak (2007) identify six academic cultures which provide a way of understanding barriers and enablers of educational change in universities. However, any analysis of academic cultures will have limitations. These relate to contextual factors and to an implicit assumption that academics belong to only one culture when many are likely to identify with aspects of several different academic cultures. The interaction between exogenous changes in higher education and the stability of academic cultures poses a further limitation. Yet, while these cultural categories may lack nuance, they provide a heuristic for reflecting on the dynamics of educational change. For TESTA's change process, the most relevant cultures the authors identify are:

- the 'collegial' culture which sees disciplinary research and individual autonomy as paramount. It regards the purpose of universities as the generation and spread of knowledge alongside developing the values and character of their students. This culture is under enormous strain in mass higher education systems because it relies on small-scale classes and traditional educational practices. It is also the dominant culture in many research-intensive universities. The 'collegial' culture has strong overlaps with the 'tangible' culture, which is rooted in tradition, characterised by the pedagogic intimacy of human interaction, place, and historical symbols of campus life.
- the 'managerial' culture rivals the 'collegial' culture for dominance. It regards institutional performance and control as paramount, with success defined as meeting financial targets and improving metrics. It prizes accountability through measurable outcomes and sees the main purpose of universities as being to develop the knowledge and skills of students for success. Success measures include student satisfaction and the employability of graduates.
- the 'developmental' culture prioritises innovation, sharing ideas, and enhancement. It regards collaboration as paramount, viewing the purpose of higher education as the personal and professional growth of all, with the aim of encouraging student and staff potential. This culture introduces a positivity which can be at odds with both the 'managerial' and 'collegial culture' with their respective defining characteristics of measuring success and individual autonomy.
- The 'advocacy' culture prioritises access, human rights, and equity, with the aim of ensuring fair practices for staff and students. It sees the purpose of higher education as critiquing social structures and attitudes and aims for universities to exemplify emancipatory structures which address structural inequalities. The advocacy culture is most concerned about resources and staff workloads and seeks to secure fair practices through mediation and challenge. This culture is often in tension with the managerial culture. It can also regard the emphasis on educational enhancement within the 'development' culture as burdensome and a threat to fair staff workloads.

So how can understanding why academics resist change and the micro-cultures that permeate universities help educational change initiatives? Knowing and identifying the sources of resistance to change helps to contextualise individual and cultural issues so that academic developers can act with wisdom and insight. These insights support academic developers to challenge and counter discourses which keep educational enhancement at arm's length (Quinn 2012). They focus academic developers on addressing the challenges levelled at their practice, so that their work is "conceptualised as a critical engagement with theory and practice and implemented in ways that academic staff find useful" (Ibid, p. 81). In response to traditional conceptions of universities as the preserve of the elite, Quinn aligns with the 'advocacy' culture in invoking the purpose of higher education to be fundamentally emancipatory, and firmly concerned with equity and social justice. The tensions between this laudable purpose for higher education and the ideology of the market, with its managerialist orientation, mean that educational enhancement plays out on 'a field of contradictions' (Kvale 2007). Adopting theoretically informed approaches enables academic developers to offer nuance from a more rounded perspective of the issues.

Principles and practice of change from TESTA

TESTA's theory of change has emerged from facilitating change with programme teams over the duration of the project. In this section, data from interviews with 16 programme directors (ten in 2011, and six in 2021) provide insights into what has worked well in TESTA's approach to change. The role of programme directors is central to leading sustained change. This role usually relies on personal influence, rather than power and status in the academic hierarchy. The interviews illustrate the ongoing challenge of bringing about change. Barriers include tensions between research and teaching, protection of the status quo, and the increasing weight of expectation on academics to take on multiple roles in market-led, mass higher education (Berg and Seeber 2016; Quinn 2012; Tagg 2012). The following principles constitute key elements of TESTA's theory of change:

Change principle #1: evidence is a persuasive incentive for change

Programme Directors describe TESTA evidence as a powerful incentive to change. Empirical evidence from students, analysed by researchers external to the programme, adds impetus to previously anecdotal conversations about change. It strengthens and supports the desired direction set by programme directors:

> When you have the data in front of you, you can't put it on one side, so it's been very useful and has fed into the changes that are going on in the curriculum... which helps me go to the team and say 'Well, look, we've got the evidence now to be able to go ahead and do this' rather than it being on a whim...
>
> (Programme Director, Nursing, 2011)

It gives you data. It was always anecdotal before, but somehow without a framework, it didn't bring about change. TESTA gives you a framework which gives you a kind of justification.

(Programme Director, Humanities, 2011)

TESTA evidence empowers programme directors to lead changes with authority. The additional weight of institutional backing for TESTA adds to the power of evidence and persuades colleagues that they need to undertake changes. Programme Directors regard institutional commitment as an important factor in their repertoire of tactics to influence more reluctant colleagues to change their practice:

My strategy was to implement change little by little, demonstrate results and then within my term as Programme Director, manage to change everything. So, when TESTA came along, I jumped at the opportunity because I thought this is an excellent chance to get an external view on everything and then also get a bit of an impulse to change things faster and the institutional backing to do that as well.

(Programme Director, Engineering, 2021)

Listen gang, we have to do this, even if you think it's pointless, this is the way the wind is blowing and it's necessary for us to start taking this seriously, but also like a lot of my colleagues who felt similarly oriented towards teaching also felt empowered by it, and it was a really interesting process if you lean into it.

(Programme Director, Creative Industries, 2021)

Resistance to change is common. Programme Directors identify the sources of resistance as increased workload, infringement of autonomy, and protectionism of individual modular practices, even when the evidence might suggest otherwise:

The staff who weren't sold by the process to begin with remained unsold on a workload basis, which is reasonable. "We don't have time to do this. And we don't have time to do the outcomes."

(Programme Director, Arts, 2021)

I did actually have one lecturer say to me, I feel like you're stifling my academic freedom. I'm not - I just want you to use the same headings!

(Programme Director, Social Sciences, 2021)

I'm sure this is true everywhere in academia, but people can be very precious about the way that they do things in a particular way, but actually we're quite a diverse group of staff which we love and enjoy, but it also means that people have particular approaches to doing things, and any standardisation is a little bit resisted.

(Programme Director, Creative Industries, 2021)

Persuading colleagues to adopt findings from TESTA exposes divides in programme teams: between those who view themselves as the 'guardians of knowledge' and dismiss efforts to support students' learning as a form of spoon-feeding, and others who see the value of assessment *for* learning:

> The TESTA process exposed the habits of thinking and quite a large divide in pedagogy within academics. I was in one camp, with others who were well-disposed towards TESTA-like initiatives. On the other side of this, there are academics, who take what I might describe as a more traditional approach, which is "it's not my job to safeguard their feelings" and it connects to conversations about spoon feeding and handholding and personal memories of learning that people always have, this mythical idea of the essay covered in red pen. I find this very common and academics, they say "I learned so much from that first essay that came back with whole paragraph just crossed out, and the word "No" written in the margin."
>
> (Programme Director, Arts, 2021)

Programme directors recognise different forms of resistance, and value robust evidence from TESTA to persuade colleagues that changes are necessary:

> TESTA certainly gave us that focus, maybe a bit of rhetorical ammunition that we needed as well to really push things through at that moment.
>
> (Programme Director, Arts, 2021)

> It allows us to have the conversation with colleagues who are burying their head in the sand about things or slightly disregarding it all or weren't necessarily aware of what other colleagues were already doing, in any given area.
>
> (Programme Director, Creative Industries, 2021)

The combination of hard and soft data is powerful. Programme audit data enables teams to step back and see the assessment pattern from a student perspective:

> The sudden realisation that if I was a student that's how many I would do, and for those who were less surprised by that, I realised what they were saying was 'That's only two assessments per module'. And I was like 'Ah, but that's the point. This is a programmatic thing and you're used to thinking about a module'.
>
> (Programme Director, Humanities, 2011)

TESTA facilitators can counter scepticism about qualitative student comments with corroborating evidence from a wider sample of students who have completed the Assessment Experience Questionnaire (AEQ). Programme Directors attest to the robustness of the process:

> Staff find it very useful to have a credible external process. Sometimes internal quality processes are not in depth or robust enough. This felt bigger. More robust.
>
> (Programme Director, Arts, 2021)

They use the evidence to take a programme approach to designing assessments and feedback. The central idea within TESTA is that modules need to conform to programme decisions, even when that means sacrificing some modular autonomy for the greater good of the programme. For leaders, this means drawing lines in the sand with colleagues, and being prepared to take criticism:

> You can't have somebody ruin it. You can't have one unit be different, just because someone doesn't want to get on board. I think it's important for lines to be drawn. If it comes to it and, at the end of the day, the Programme Director is the person who has the overview of the Programme.
>
> (Programme Director, Engineering, 2021)

> We weren't particularly popular for a period of time.
>
> (Programme Directors, Creative Arts, 2021)

Change principle #2: setting an open and collegial tone helps teams grapple with evidence

Successful change initiatives are attentive to relationships: 'Change, like most things, gets managed through relationships, and strong relationships overcome bad design while good design and plans can't overcome bad relationships' (Bushe 2007, p. 3). Programme Directors attest to the collegial quality of relationships that ensure the process is meaningful and not managerial:

> TESTA is not about habit or form filling. I don't think it's just the tools. The tools are good, and they work really, really well, but I can imagine someone coming in and saying, 'We'll do this and wrap it up'. It's also the approach. It comes through a kind of collegiality.
>
> (Programme Director, Humanities, 2011)

A respectful and open tone is set at the start of TESTA debriefings. Participants are asked to reflect on their perceptions of what is going well and not so well in assessment and feedback on the programme before the case study is discussed. This invites and values staff perceptions and prompts discussion about best practices and areas of weakness; it surfaces common threads among the team. Staff perceptions often pre-empt and align with evidence in the case study. However, when there are fresh or contradictory insights from students, these stand out because assumptions have already been discussed:

> Something that just really jumps out at me from TESTA was that the formative versus summative piece, because at the time we were like "Oh there's loads of formative feedback, it's all over the place", but I certainly spotted a few units where students would really benefit from a proper formative assessment – and that is actually what they want.
> (Programme Director, Creative Industries, 2021)

Programme directors listen carefully to what the evidence tells them about the student experience of assessment and feedback, expressing empathy in their responses:

> It was a heart-sinking moment when they said, "When they give me feedback, I can't use it again". I was thinking "My word, that's so obvious". And we spent so much time on that primary teacher ethos giving this feedback and they said, "But it's not very useful because the next time I've got a poster" and I'm thinking "That's so obvious, why didn't I think of it?"
> (Programme Director, Social Sciences, 2011)

The TESTA case study is structured to privilege student voice in reporting focus group data, forming a narrative which helps staff to listen to what students are saying. The words of students are powerful catalysts for change and the in-depth nature of the data lends credibility to student voice:

> I remember how interesting it was to see some proper feedback from the students, because we struggle in getting substantive commentary from them about how things are going. Because they don't complete the unit evaluations, and engagement is very limited, so it was really interesting to get what felt like some quite rich qualitative data from at least some of the students. That was a positive, to see what they were actually thinking.
> (Programme Director, Arts, 2021)

Change principle #3: working together on co-creating solutions energises the change process

In describing a change in 'turnaround universities', Fullan and Scott (2009) make a case for building a consensus culture. Consensus implies dialogue, but they distinguish between 'consensus around the table' marked by endless rounds of meetings and 'consensus around the data' where evidence enables the dialogue to focus on committing to actions which will improve education (Ibid, p. 80).

TESTA initiates a generative process of co-creation where programme teams engage in a dialogue which stretches beyond the debriefing meeting.

Co-creation between external researchers and team members begins with the programme audit and extends through to debriefing about the data. The TESTA audit pieces together a shared understanding of the programme's assessment design in a discussion, drawing links between the context, teaching approaches, student demography, and outcomes for students. The purpose of the audit is to understand the planned curriculum. It is also to listen, clarify, come to shared understandings of concepts, and piece together the design of the whole assessment environment. As a conversation, it subverts the perils of desk-based research, which might only scrutinise the varnished version of a programme, written in the language of accountability. The audit captures a more provisional version of the programme, making sense of how different assessment tasks interact across the programme and their implications for students' learning.

Similarly, the TESTA debriefing negotiates meaning from complex evidence in the case study. It opens a conversation about assessment and feedback problems and innovations. The discussion is an informal and open-ended exercise in co-creating strategies which might work to enhance practice across the programme. Teams have plenty of their own ideas to contribute. TESTA academic developers 'listen with a menu' (Fullan and Scott 2009, p. 98), feeding in strategies, drawing out innovative practices from the team, and prompting ideas and actions for colleagues to take away and discuss later. A collaborative approach to designing assessment and feedback practices across the programme is more likely to lead to sustained and successful changes (McGrath 2020; Gibbs 2013). It is core to how TESTA unfolds:

> We then had probably two meetings subsequent to that big meeting, away days almost, to go through and thrash out as a team what we wanted to do with the programme as a whole, rather than "module leader, what do you want to do?" But actually "Let's all talk to each other and let's look at this and make it a nice coherent, carefully aligned programme".
>
> (Programme Director, Life Sciences, 2011)

> I've felt that it's been a collaborative thing in terms of working with you, but also then how everybody has been involved. It hasn't just been me working with you and saying to the team "We're going to do this". It's about "This is what they've found out folks. What are we going to do about it? How are we going to develop it? How will it best suit us?"
>
> (Programme Director, Social Sciences, 2011)

After the TESTA debriefing, the locus of action shifts to the programme team, to pursue ideas in relation to the evidence discussed and to co-create solutions:

> After we finished the TESTA, I got a slot in a department meeting and I put huge sheets of paper with all the units, and all the unit directors had to stick

post-its with all their formative and summative assessments for the unit, so that the whole department could look at what the students are seeing. Everybody was quite baffled when they saw what students are seeing at the cohort level, because it's very easy for a unit director to just keep visibility of their unit. That painted a picture with a lot of post-it notes, about 70 of them, mostly summative.

(Programme Director, Engineering, 2021)

Working as a team to co-create solutions reduces the risk for individuals who are keen to experiment because everyone takes responsibility for how ideas work out across the programme, celebrating successes and reflecting together on areas that need further revision. This liberates individuals from the risk of change and engages the collective wisdom and creativity of the team.

Change principle #4: sustainable change addresses the context and influences systems

Programmes are not designed in a vacuum. Assessment decisions are driven, in part, by context. For example, staff workload concerns in mass higher education drive patterns of assessment design, as do disciplinary ideas, large class sizes, tradition, or more loosely, 'the way we do things around here'. Institutional and faculty quality assurance mechanisms, and professional body accreditation requirements set parameters for assessment design, drawing real and imagined boundaries around what is deemed possible. Some programmes rely on myths about professional accreditation to perpetuate the status quo. Others espouse educational theories about learning outcomes or credit weightings to multiply summative assessments.

TESTA has had sector-wide success partly because of its emphasis on overcoming structural barriers to learning from assessment. It has deflected blame from academics for getting it wrong, to understanding wider influences, often structural, which prevent students from experiencing a coherent intellectual journey through their assessment. One Programme Director summed it up in this way:

While the team was more hesitant and resistant in the face of externality and in anticipation of it, when it happened, when it was revealed that it was in a way more systemic than personal, more pedagogic than personal, there was a sense in which they were able to engage more.

(Programme Director, Humanities, 2011)

In focusing on the situation, programmes and universities using TESTA have used systemic approaches advocated in the change literature. Changing the assessment environment that surrounds practice, for example, aligning written quality assurance mechanisms across a university to reflect TESTA principles is a powerful, yet simple way of enabling cross-institutional change. One university created a checklist of recurring assessment and feedback challenges from their TESTA research, which provided a simple way for teams and the whole institution to focus on areas of enhancement (Walker et al. 2019). Several universities have integrated TESTA into their routine quality assurance processes. This has led to system-wide changes in processes and paperwork which nudge teams to consider good assessment principles, for example, adding a compulsory category on module descriptor form to denote formative assessment highlights its value. Including a category for both formative and summative assessment also gives 'permission' to programmes to reduce summative assessment, while validating formative assessment and feedback.

Change principle #5: change is powerful when teams own it and exercise their agency

One of TESTA's central principles is to hand over the agency to programme teams to make choices and take actions based on their interpretation of the data (Walker et al. 2019). This builds ownership over the process and leads to sustained changes which prioritise areas of action. TESTA's role is to provide an external view of the assessment environment and to facilitate a productive discussion with the team. The team's role is to take forward actions which align with the evidence, and that they view as a priority. These features of TESTA's change process inspire and motivate teams to act in concert to bring about evidence-informed changes:

> I don't think I've ever seen our colleagues quite as energised and full of ideas; it's really given us the conviction that we can take ownership of our teaching and have the courage to be imaginative in what we're doing.
> (Programme Leader, Humanities, 2011)

After the debriefing meeting, the programme team take away the case study. A briefing note about follow-up actions discussed in the meeting is sent to the Programme Director. The final section of the case study provides a menu of options for teams to consider (Fullan and Scott 2009), nudging the direction of change without prescribing it (Heath and Heath 2010). Programme Directors value the autonomy to make decisions based on evidence and discussions with their teams:

> Already today I have seen some of yesterday's feedback being put into action across the team and we are feeling excited about the changes we are making.
> (Email correspondence from Social Work Programme Director, 2017)

Programmes are encouraged to focus on small things that will make a big difference to student learning from assessment. This may mean a uniform approach to feedback, as one programme instituted in response to student data on inconsistent feedback, at a time when they were using paper-based feedback:

> We had about ten of us and we said, "Let's put this down to just three action plans" and I said "Hang on, if we're going to do that, let's make it a tear-off sheet that they stick to the next one and say what they've done in response to it". We haven't fixed everything. But taking on three major things will have a knock-on effect with other things anyway.
>
> (Programme Director, Humanities, 2011)

It may mean releasing feedback without the grade so that students will book a tutorial to discuss their feedback before they receive their grades (see Black and Wiliam 1998) and engage in a dialogue about their next steps. It may mean substituting a formative assessment for a summative across each module on the programme. When these small changes begin to affect students' experience across the programme, they illuminate the way forward and give teams more incentive to make changes. Teams soon recognise that some changes work well straightaway, and these quick wins often seed further programmatic changes. Other changes may take longer and not work as well at first, or even at all, so it is important to build tolerance of risk into the discussions to create room for experimentation and encourage teams to work iteratively on changes, tweaking in response to feedback and experience. Programme Directors recognise their role in reassuring colleagues and encouraging measured risk-taking:

> That's what we've learned, you know, there's an anxiety, especially in colleagues who are new to teaching, that they need to give more and more feedback. It's not the case! it's less, and focused – that gives you the time to do your job better.
>
> (Programme Director, Creative Industries, 2021)

Agency is powerful. Teams feel like they have a stake in the process of change and can make a meaningful contribution to improving assessment and feedback, as illustrated here:

> The TESTA report-back was by far the most significant meeting I have attended in ten years of sitting through many meetings at this university. For the first time, I felt as though I was a player on the pitch, rather than someone watching from the side-lines. We were discussing real issues.
>
> (Email from a Senior Lecturer, Social Sciences, 2012)

A brief synopsis

This chapter reflects on a framework for change that has emerged through TESTA's work. It outlines two measures of success for educational change initiatives, reach and impact, and assesses TESTA's performance against these measures. In considering how academic development has evolved, it reflects on the movement from working with individual teachers to teams. TESTA has adopted a more sociological than psychological approach in line with developments in the field. This chapter examines resistance to change from the perspective of different academic cultures and in the context of exogenous changes to higher education. Finally, it uses qualitative interview data from programme directors to define five principles that have contributed to sustained change.

Notes

1 Aberdeen; Bath Spa University; Birmingham; Brighton; Bristol; Brunel University; Cardiff; Chichester; Christchurch Canterbury; Dundee; Durham; Edge Hill; Edinburgh; Edinburgh Napier; Exeter; Glasgow; Greenwich; Imperial College; Liverpool; London Metropolitan; Exeter; Imperial College; Keele; Kent; Liverpool; Liverpool John Moores; London South Bank University; Loughborough; Nottingham; Oxford Brookes; Portsmouth; Queen Mary University London; Robert Gordon; Roehampton; Sheffield Hallam University; Solent; Southampton; St Andrews; Strathclyde; Swansea; University College London; University of the West of Scotland; Winchester; Worcester; York.
2 University of New South Wales, Australia; Lady Irwin College, University of Delhi; Saurashtra University, Rajkot, Gujarat; Trinity College Dublin; University College Dublin; Dublin University of Technology.
3 Embedded in the University of Edinburgh; Dundee, and Strathclyde's enhancement and assurance processes: https://www.ed.ac.uk/institute-academic-development/learning-teaching/staff/assessment/leaf
https://www.dundee.ac.uk/academic-skills/for-staff/assessment-and-feedback-hub/testa/
https://www.strath.ac.uk/professionalservices/educationenhancement/innovationgoodpractice/testatools/
4 University of Chicago economist Richard Thaler (1980) (in Tagg 2012) defined the endowment effect as being that people will not take as big a risk to gain what they don't have as to keep what they do have. They see what they already have as more valuable.

References

Berg, M., and B. K. Seeber. 2016. *The Slow Professor: Challenging the Culture of Speed in Higher Education.* Toronto. University of Toronto Press.
Bergquist, W. H., and K. Pawlak. 2007. *Engaging the Six Cultures of the Academy.* San Francisco, CA. Jossey-Bass.
Black, P., and D. Wiliam. 1998. Assessment and classroom learning. *Assessment in Education: Principles, Policy & Practice* 5: 7–74.
Buckley, A. 2021. Crisis? What crisis? Interpreting student feedback on assessment. *Assessment & Evaluation in Higher Education* 46 (7): 1008–1019, DOI: 10.1080/02602938.2020.1846015
Buller, J. L. 2015. *Change Leadership in Higher Education.* San Francisco, CA. Jossey-Bass.
Bushe, G. R. 2007. Appreciative inquiry is not just about the positive. *OD Practitioner* 39 (4): 30–35.

Friedman, E. H. 2017. *A Failure of Nerve: Leadership in the Age of the Quick Fix.* New York, NY. Church Publishing.

Fullan, M., and G. Scott. 2009. *Turnaround Leadership for Higher Education.* San Francisco, CA. Jossey-Bass.

Gatrell, D. 2023. TESTA Impact Assessment. Unpublished Report. University of Bristol.

Gibbs, G. 2013. Reflections on the changing nature of educational development. *International Journal for Academic Development* 18 (1): 4–14, DOI: 10.1080/1360144X.2013.751691

Heath, C., and D. Heath. 2010. *Switch: How to Change Things When Change Is Hard.* Vauxhall, London. Random House Books.

Henri, D. 2022. Case study 8: Coordinating programme design through 'Assessment Therapy' (pp. 170–173). In J. Lawrence, S. Morón-García, and R. Senior (Eds). 2022. *Supporting Course and Programme Leaders in Higher Education.* Abingdon. SEDA Series, Routledge.

Hopwood-Stephens, I. 2021. TESTA: A formative evaluation of methodology and outcomes. Unpublished internal report. Bristol. University of Bristol.

Kvale, S. 2007. 'Contradictions of assessment for learning in institutions of higher learning'. In D. Boud and N. Falchikov (Eds). 2007. *Rethinking Assessment in Higher Education.* Abingdon. Routledge Taylor and Francis.

Lawrence, J., S. Morón-García, and R. Senior (Eds). 2022. *Supporting Course and Programme Leaders in Higher Education.* Abingdon. SEDA Series, Routledge.

Manathunga, C. 2006. Doing educational development ambivalently: Applying post-colonial metaphors to educational development? *International Journal for Academic Development* 11 (1): 19–29, DOI: 10.1080/13601440600578771

McGrath, C. 2020. Academic developers as brokers of change: insights from a research project on change practice and agency, *International Journal for Academic Development.* 25:2, 94–106, DOI: 10.1080/1360144X.2019.1665524

Moore, S. 2022. Empowering programme leaders: Developing relational academic leadership (pp. 124–135). In J. Lawrence, S. Morón-García and R. Senior (Eds). 2022. *Supporting Course and Programme Leaders in Higher Education.* Abingdon. SEDA Series, Routledge.

Parkin, D. 2022. Programme leaders as educational and academic leaders: A question of influence – Relationships, behaviour, and commitment (pp. 95–108). In J. Lawrence, S. Morón-García and R. Senior (Eds). 2022. *Supporting Course and Programme Leaders in Higher Education.* Abingdon. SEDA Series, Routledge.

Quinn, L. 2012. Understanding resistance: An Analysis of discourses in academic staff development. *Studies in Higher Education* 37 (1): 69–83, DOI: 10.1080/03075079.2010.497837

Roxå, T., and K. Mårtensson. 2017. Agency and structure in academic development practices: Are we liberating academic teachers or are we part of a machinery supressing them? *International Journal for Academic Development* 22 (2): 95–105, DOI: 10.1080/1360144X.2016.1218883

Spence, C. 2019. 'Judgement' versus 'metrics' in higher education management. *Higher Education* 77, 761–775. https://doi.org/10.1007/s10734-018-0300-z

Tagg, J. 2012. Why does the faculty resist change? *Change: The Magazine of Higher Learning* 44 (1): 6–15, DOI: 10.1080/00091383.2012.635987

Walker, S., D. McKenna, A. Abdillahi, and C. Molesworth. 2017. Examining predictors of retention with implications for TESTA@Greenwich. *The Journal of Educational Innovation, Partnership and Change* 3 (1): 122–134, DOI: 0.21100/jeipc.v3i1.607

Walker, S., E. Salines, A. Abdillahi, S. Mason, A. Jadav, and C. Molesworth. 2019. Identifying and resolving key institutional challenges in feedback and assessment: A case study for implementing change. *Higher Education Pedagogies* 4 (1): 422–434, DOI: 10.1080/23752696.2019.1649513

Williams, J., and D. Kane. 2009. Assessment and feedback: Institutional experiences of student feedback, 1996 to 2007. *Higher Education Quarterly* 63 (3): 264–286, DOI: 10.1111/j.1468-2273.2009.00430.x

Winstone, N. E., R. Ajjawi, K. Dirkx, and D. Boud. 2022. Measuring what matters: The positioning of students in feedback processes within national student satisfaction surveys. *Studies in Higher Education* 47 (7): 1524–1536, DOI: 10.1080/03075079.2021.1916909

Part IV

The future

New horizons and challenges

Epilogue
TESTA in a post-pandemic world

Introduction

In the opening chapter of this book, I set out four contributions that TESTA has made to thinking about assessment and feedback in higher education. The epilogue returns to these contributions and questions their relevance and evolution in a post-pandemic assessment environment. The introduction set out TESTA's contributions as:

- taking a *programme approach* to designing assessment and feedback adopting a shared philosophy and working as teams,
- focusing on designing assessment and feedback processes with a nuanced *understanding of students' experience*,
- drawing on sociological theories of *alienation and engagement* as an analytical approach,
- adopting an *evidence-based and systematic* approach to change to improve the design of assessment and feedback at a programme level.

The epilogue examines what has changed about assessment and feedback during the pandemic. It evaluates the extent to which TESTA's unique contributions remain pertinent moving into a post-pandemic future with the uncertainties that generative AI has unleashed on the world. Drawing on lessons learnt, it outlines tensions in assessment and feedback, and suggests three guiding principles for steering a course through them.

A virtual sea-change in assessment and feedback?

The pandemic prompted wide-scale educational change in higher education and led to new modes of assessment. Assessment changes were systemic and fast-paced, involving institutional shifts to online modes of assessment. Scholars are divided as to whether assessment and feedback practice changed at a deep level, reflecting the varied responses of universities in responding to an exogenous shock like a global pandemic. Some universities took top-down policy decisions to simplify and reduce assessment formats to ensure they were legible for students and functioned well online (Elkington 2021). Even in a context of these 'war-footing' policy decisions, the extent of change varied across universities and programmes, with some academics embracing innovative and authentic forms of assessment (Sambell and Brown 2021), treating the pandemic as an opportune moment of 'TINA' ('there is no alternative') (Fuller et al. 2020). Others transferred existing assessments 'as is' onto digital platforms with minimal change (Slade et al. 2021).

The pandemic initiated a trend towards more engaging, inclusive, and authentic assessment (Pitt and Quinlan 2021). Sambell and Brown's 'Covid-19 Assessment Collection' (2020), widely used in the UK and globally, illustrated the potential of authentic assessment, prompting a fresh wave of interest in it. Authentic assessment enables students to become insiders to the disciplinary discourse through using knowledge and skills in contexts and ways that resemble both professional and disciplinary practice (Villarroel et al. 2018). A philosophical interpretation of authenticity places emphasis on *why* authentic tasks matter for society, and how they shape students' 'sense of self, self-worth, and well-being' (McArthur 2023, p. 85). They have the potential to build students' confidence, enhance their skills, and extend the reach of theory to contexts beyond the academy. During the pandemic, academics made use of digital platforms and tools to engage students in authentic assessments, for example, using podcasts to bring environmental issues to life (Wakefield et al. 2022). These tasks respond to society's challenges, inviting students to contribute to society's conversations while at the same time enhancing their sense of self.

The pandemic highlighted the importance of inclusive assessment practice (Wilson et al. 2020). It presented enormous challenges for students with impairments; it exacerbated mental health conditions through isolation, and reinforced the digital divide for students with poor access to equipment, Wi-Fi, and lack of physical spaces to study (Killen and Langer-Crame 2021; Padden and O'Neill 2021; Wilson et al. 2020). In response to the exigencies of the pandemic, academics designed flexible learning opportunities, diversified assessment types and choices, and provided longer time frames than previously given in closed-book examinations (Buckley et al. 2021; Elkington 2021). Many of these measures gave more autonomy and agency to students in their preparation, choices, and uses of material. Scholars of inclusivity suggest that these radical shifts to assessment practice have opened the door to more systematic changes. They have raised universities' awareness of the value of inclusion beyond mere compliance (Padden and O'Neill 2021). Pandemic-related changes to assessment and feedback signal a watershed moment for inclusion:

Covid-19 has stimulated fast and effective progress. There are still areas to address but it is positive that many more people throughout HEIs are now considering inclusion. One particular area which has proved to be a real sticking point has been inclusive assessment. Now, the whole sector is beginning to see real progress in this area.

(Wilson et al. 2020, p. 13)

The use of digital platforms to engage students in discussion threads and enable them to contribute commentary, questions, and critique provided new opportunities for formative assessment and feedback. Online tools provide simple ways of incorporating formative tasks and can invigorate peer and tutor feedback as a routine process. The character and aims of online learning design and formative assessment are similar, encouraging 'sustained interactive collaboration among teachers and learners supporting them to engage productively and assisting them in the development of self-regulated learning dispositions' (Gikandi et al. 2011, p. 2334). This iterative and interactive quality of learning, scaffolded by teachers and peers, characterises both formative assessment and online learning design.

This particularly affected traditional examinations, which students sat under invigilated conditions, in silence, in physical rooms. The pandemic prompted a change in examinations. Social distancing meant that all assessments were conducted and submitted online, by students at home or in halls of residence. Previously, closed-book examinations constituted a central part of the assessment environment, especially for STEM subjects and in clinical disciplines. Exams have been criticised for the power they exert over students (Kvale 2007; Mann 2001); they provoke stress and anxiety (Jones et al. 2021); and they place undue focus on rote learning and memorisation (Gibbs and Simpson 2004; Sambell and Brown 2021). However, examinations are widely used because they are efficient, more secure than other formats, standardised, and easy to authenticate: 'we can say with relative certainty that we know who has undertaken an exam and the circumstances they were in' (Dawson 2016).

The closure of campuses left universities with two choices about examinations: either to replicate the format online or to deviate from the traditional closed-book format. Some universities invested in remote proctoring software to simulate exam conditions, with the intention of preserving the known aspects of examinations, in particular safeguarding academic integrity (Slade et al. 2021). In other universities, alternative online formats were devised, usually open-book, 'take-home' examinations where students had the opportunity to use resources in answering questions, often with more flexible timings (Buckley et al. 2021).

The large-scale use of open-book, online examinations presents a significant challenge to assuring the quality and standards of qualifications and authenticating their authorship. Concerns about cheating and breaches in academic integrity have increased and are widespread globally (Basken 2020; Janke et al. 2021; Lancaster and Cotarlan 2021; Reedy et al. 2021). Generative AI introduces a new level of challenge which entails a more fundamental rethink of assessment and academic integrity (Cotton et al. 2023). In a mass higher education system, the challenges of authentication are exacerbated by many students not being known by their lecturers. This is compounded by anonymous marking of summative assessment (Pitt and Winstone 2018) and low ratios of formative assessment (Wu and Jessop 2018). Many universities are weighing up academic integrity concerns against the learning benefits of alternative formats, especially their flexibility, and potential for being more inclusive (Bengtsson 2019; Elkington 2021). From an academic integrity perspective, there are significant challenges. From a learning perspective, open-book online examinations have pedagogic benefits and resemble authentic intellectual habits; students and staff see their potential (Elkington 2021). Their value is reflected in this blog of a final year student:

> For me, the alternative assessment was, without doubt, a far better learning experience. I could take a more thoughtful, measured approach to the questions, gained a much better understanding of what I was writing about, and did deliberate, relevant extra reading. Ultimately, I wrote what I feel was much closer to the best answer I could write, as opposed to the best answer I could cobble together with the scraps of information that happened to be at the forefront of my memory in an hour and a half exam. I was able to go really in depth as opposed to the sort of 'scattershot' approach I take before exams.
>
> (Roberts, 2020)

Changes made during the pandemic disrupted familiar assessment practices. While they have shown students and academics diverse and exciting ways of assessing students: authentic, inclusive, flexible, open-book, slower modes of assessment, they have raised problems and uncertainties about the extent of change to be embraced. There are tensions between authenticity and standardisation; between flexibility and presence; and between open-book formats and academic integrity. None of these are easily resolvable. What contribution can TESTA make to helping universities and programmes navigate post-pandemic assessment and feedback regimes, compounded and potentially overtaken by the disruption of generative AI?

Evaluating TESTA's unique contributions

This section examines the relevance of TESTA's approach in the face of changes brought about by the pandemic, using the claims about its unique contribution made in the opening chapter, which are discussed and evidenced throughout the book.

Contribution #1: taking a programme approach

In a context of wide-scale assessment change, TESTA's contribution to understanding programme assessment patterns is ever more relevant. Shaping a future for assessment that enables students to navigate their way through coherently designed degrees requires 'collaborative, programmatic, and institutional strategies and approaches' (Irish National Forum for Teaching and Learning Enhancement 2021, p. 2). A programme approach to assessment will support academics to move beyond fast-paced assessment changes to 'future-focused' changes which emphasise student learning, engagement, and agency across their programmes of study (Sambell and Brown 2020). In practice, this means identifying and analysing the following features of programme assessment design:

- the balance of different assessment types across a programme of study given their expansion during the pandemic
- patterns in the sequencing of online and in-person assessment types so that the programme is coherent for students, and they can act of their feedback
- new formative assessment and feedback practices and opportunities that relate to and extend beyond virtual environments
- changes in the weighting and prevalence of summative assessment
- the persistence of online open-book assessments, the place of proctoring, and the return of closed-book examinations post-pandemic
- models of programme assessment authentication for online assessments to synthesise and integrate learning and prevent breaches in academic integrity (Dawson 2020).

As the sector faces towards the future in a changing world, understanding and guiding changes at the programme level becomes increasingly important. In conversations with assessment leaders in the UK, McVitty (2022) found:

> A consistent theme was the value of taking a programme-level view of assessment, creating opportunities for students to experience different forms of formative and summative assessment at different points in their student journey, as well as addressing issues of assessment load and pinch points where assessments cluster that can create unnecessary stress and pressure. Achieving this requires investment in programme leaders and course teams, and encouraging teamwork across different course elements, as well as offering support for developing assessment literacy among individual staff.
>
> (McVitty, 2022)

Contribution #2: understanding students' experience of the programme

During the pandemic, external organisations and universities sought to understand students' individual experiences of teaching and assessment, mainly through large-scale surveys (Killen and Langer-Crame 2021; University of Bristol 2020). In contrast, TESTA's approach provides a contextualised perspective of students' whole programme experience of learning from assessment and feedback. Given the disruption of traditional assessment formats, the challenges of inclusion, and the adoption of more authentic and flexible modes of assessment and digital forms of feedback, understanding students' experience of their whole programme is even more important. It will answer questions about emergent patterns of assessment and feedback, and their influence on students' learning and engagement. These are the key questions that TESTA asks in a stable environment. In the aftermath of the pandemic, there is much to be learnt about the balance of different forms of assessment across programmes and how students are learning from and engaging with them (Irish National Forum for Teaching and Learning Enhancement 2021; McVitty 2022).

Students' use of generative AI tools such as ChatGPT for learning and assessment makes it even more important to understand how students are making sense of far-reaching changes in assessment and feedback. TESTA's evidence-based approach may be one way to gain a deeper understanding and work with students on identifying their human-centred elements (Sharples 2023).

Contribution #3: the explanatory power of alienation and engagement

Social isolation and meaninglessness (Seeman 1959) became more prominent during the pandemic. Systematic reviews have highlighted its effects on students' mental health and have identified isolation and withdrawal from social learning as factors which have accentuated mental illness and lowered student well-being (Pandya and Lodha 2022). The impact of an exogenous shock of this magnitude on students' learning and well-being has underscored the value of sociological theories of learning. Alienation and engagement theories provide a powerful heuristic for understanding students' learning in relation to the wider context.

Engaging students in learning which has wider social value and encourages their agency counteracts alienation. The process of engagement between lecturers and students has changed through using digital platforms. For some students, this has meant lecturers were more accessible to them, and content more digestible. For others, it has accentuated alienation. In responding to the new conditions, academics devised assessment strategies which were more flexible, inclusive, and authentic. Some of these approaches invited students to shape and take ownership of their learning and assessment in new ways, for example, enabling 'slow' and iterative forms of learning over longer duration in open-book online formats. Authentic assessment is a means to student engagement and agency (Wakefield et al. 2022). It has the potential to enrich and broaden students' learning, develop their employability skills, engender personal development, foster team-working, and fulfil wider social purposes. The digital disruption has demonstrated the possibilities for authentic and engaging forms of assessment, and their successful practice by academics from different disciplines.

TESTA's data gives insights into why students are feeling alienated and disengaged from their assessment and feedback across the programme. Students' sense of purpose may be profoundly disrupted as intellectual skills are supplanted by generative AI, introducing the potential for greater alienation. New ways of engaging students in intellectual pursuits which emphasise the human value they bring to intellectual and professional tasks are contingent on assessment design and relational forms of pedagogy and feedback. Principles of assessment and feedback which develop students' agency and 'dispositions to learn' will become increasingly important (Naidoo and Jamieson 2005, p. 278).

Contribution #4: using evidence to effect change

The pandemic years marked a sea-change in teaching, learning, and assessment. Many questions remain about whether innovative measures devised during an emergency have receded in significance as teaching and assessment have returned to more familiar in-person practices. TESTA adds value to emerging research about new approaches to assessment by providing evidence of students' experience across programmes. In a context of disruption, it provides programme teams with evidence to act upon, student voice data, and enduring assessment and feedback principles.

TESTA brings invaluable evidence to change models such as the UK's Royal Society for the Arts' (RSA) 'Future Change Toolkit' which seeks to enable organisations to categorise changes made during the crisis according to their fitness for purpose post-pandemic. The toolkit identifies four categories of change: temporary changes specific to the crisis; innovations which are game changers that should endure; activities which have ceased that may need to restart; and approaches which have been shown to be worth stopping permanently.

The TESTA process is helpful in identifying the new state of play of assessment and feedback on programmes; how students perceive their learning and the benefits of new forms of assessment, and enduring principles of assessment which aid systematic design and planning. Its change process enables programme teams to work collaboratively on holistic design of assessment and shared feedback principles, informed by evidence and student voice data. TESTA is increasingly relevant in a post-pandemic context through its capacity to help programmes to identify trends and challenges within disciplines and across universities.

The future of assessment and feedback

There are many uncertainties about the future of assessment and feedback as academics make sense of an unprecedented period of upheaval and innovation. The pandemic highlighted the potential of more inclusive, flexible, and authentic modes of assessment. It also underlined threats to academic integrity, to standards, and to ensuring fair assessment. Tensions between authenticity and standardisation, flexibility and fairness, and efficiency and personalisation are more prominent in the aftermath of the pandemic. Insights in this book suggest three guiding principles for beginning to resolve these tensions.

First, developing 'pedagogies of trust' with students through dialogue, respect, and creating pride in individual and group work to counteract breaches in academic integrity (Irish National Forum for Teaching and Learning Enhancement 2021). Engaging approaches to assessment and feedback, explored in this book, and exemplified through TESTA, help to create 'pedagogies of trust'. In practice, this means placing more emphasis on the *process* of students producing work, sharing ideas, and discussing feedback in informal ways as they develop assessment outputs and artefacts over time in class. It entails a deeper exploration of authentic assessment and formative processes which build student confidence and ownership. Designing assessment as part of a developmental trajectory with formative milestones creates possibilities for students to venture half-formed ideas in small groups, building towards their assessment outputs. It takes seriously learning, engagement, and the idea of student agency. In mass higher education, the place of seminars, small groups, tutorials, and problem classes is central to building these 'pedagogies of trust'.

Second, prioritising collaboration between teams of academics to develop strong pedagogies of assessment across programmes. A collaborative approach to programme assessment design in the context of familiar and experimental modes of assessment reduces the vulnerability of individual decision-making. It enables academics to take a proportionate approach to balancing and sequencing assessment across their programmes of study. Programme teams are in a better position than individual module leaders to identify a good mix of innovation, and to design assessment tasks which integrate learning from several modules. These should both challenge students to connect concepts from their studies and authenticate each student's work as original.

Third, tensions in assessment and feedback's 'field of contradictions' (Kvale 2007, p. 57) are best resolved in a dialogue between students and staff. This means sharing the tensions with students and working with them to develop equitable, engaging, and fair assessment strategies; enabling students to contribute to the shape of their assessment and to recognise the social value of authentic assessments, especially in an era of generative AI (Cotton et al. 2023; Rudolph et al. 2023). It means encouraging students to become agents of their learning, to take pride in their work, and to use digital tools appropriately and critically.

References

Basken, P. 2020. Universities say cheating exploding in Covid era. Article published 23 Dec 2020. Available at: https://www.timeshighereducation.com/news/universities-say-student-cheating-exploding-covid-era Accessed 20 January 2022.

Bengtsson, L. 2019. Take-home exams in higher education: A systematic review. *Education Sciences* 9(4): 267–285. **https://doi.org/10.3390/educsci9040267**

Buckley, A., D. Brown, O. Potapova-Crichton, and A. Yusuf. 2021. Sticking plaster or long-term option? Take-home exams at heriot-watt university (pp. 127–137) in Baughan, P (ed) *Assessment and Feedback in a Post-Pandemic Era: A Time for Learning and Inclusion*. York. Advance HE.

Cotton, D. R., P. A. Cotton, and J. R. Shipway 2023. Chatting and cheating. Ensuring academic integrity in the era of ChatGPT. Preprint. https://doi.org/10.35542/osf.io/mrz8h

Dawson, P. 2016. Five ways to hack and cheat with BYOD e-exams. *British Journal of Educational Technology*, 47: 592–600. https://doi-org.bris.idm.oclc.org/10.1111/bjet.12246

Dawson, P. 2020. *Defending Assessment Security in a Digital World: Preventing E-Cheating and Supporting Academic Integrity in Higher Education*. Abingdon. Routledge.

Elkington, S. 2021. Scaling up flexible assessment (pp. 31–39). In Baughan, P (ed) *Assessment and Feedback in a Post-Pandemic Era: A Time for Learning and Inclusion*. York. Advance HE.

Fuller, R., V. Joynes, J. Cooper, K. Boursicot, and T. Roberts 2020. 'Could COVID-19 be our 'There is no alternative' (TINA) opportunity to enhance assessment? *Medical Teacher* 42 (7): 781–786.

Gibbs, G., and C. Simpson. 2004. Conditions under Which Assessment Supports Students' Learning. *Learning and Teaching in Higher Education*. 1:3–31.

Gikandi, J. W., D. Morrow, and N. E. Davis 2011. 'Online formative assessment in higher education: A review of the literature. *Computers & Education* 57 (4): 2333–2351.

Irish National Forum for Teaching and Learning Enhancement. 2021. Ten things we have learned about assessment. Next Steps Project. Available at: https://www.teachingandlearning.ie/wp-content/uploads/Ten-Things-D2.pdf Accessed on 17 February 2023.

Janke, S., S. C. Rudert, Ä Petersen, T. M. Fritz, and M. Daumiller. 2021. Cheating in the wake of COVID-19: How dangerous is ad-hoc online testing for academic integrity? *Computers & Education Open*, 2, Article 100055. https://doi.org/10.1016/j.caeo.2021.100055.

Jones, E., M. Priestley, L. Brewster, S. J. Wilbraham, G. Hughes, and L. Spanner 2021. Student wellbeing and assessment in higher education: The balancing act. *Assessment & Evaluation in Higher Education* 46 (3): 438–450, DOI: 10.1080/02602938.2020.1782344 OI: 10.1080/02602938.2016.1194368

Killen, C., and M. Langer-Crame 2021. JISC Student digital experience insights survey 2020/21: UK higher education findings. Published online 7 September 2021. Available online at: https://beta.jisc.ac.uk/reports/student-digital-experience-insights-survey-2020-21-uk-higher-education-findings Accessed on 14 February 2023.

Kvale, S. 2007. 'Contradictions of assessment for learning in institutions of higher learning', in D. Boud and N. Falchikov (Eds). 2007. *Rethinking Assessment in Higher Education*. Abingdon. Routledge Taylor and Francis.

Lancaster, T., and C. Cotarlan. 2021. Contract cheating by STEM students through A file sharing website: A covid-19 pandemic perspective. *International Journal for Educational Integrity*. 17, 3. https://doi.org/10.1007/s40979-021-00070-0

Mann, S. J. 2001. 'Alternative perspectives on the student experience: Alienation and engagement. *Studies in Higher Education* 26 (1): 7–19.

McArthur, J. 2023. Rethinking authentic assessment: Work, well-being, and society. *Higher Education* 85, 85–101 (2023). https://doi.org/10.1007/s10734-022-00822-y

McVitty, D. 2022. Building back learning and teaching means changing assessment. WonkHE. 24/01/22. Available at: https://wonkhe.com/blogs/building-back-learning-and-teaching-means-changing-assessment/ Accessed on 15 February 2023.

Naidoo, R., and I. Jamieson 2005. Empowering participants or corroding learning? towards a research agenda on the impact of student consumerism in higher education. *Journal of Education Policy* 20 (3): 267–281, DOI: 10.1080/02680930500108585

Padden, L., and G. O'Neill 2021. Embedding equity and inclusion in higher education assessment strategies: Creating and sustaining positive change in the post-pandemic era (pp. 138–147). In Baughan, P (ed) *Assessment and Feedback in a Post-Pandemic Era: A Time for Learning and Inclusion.* York. Advance HE.

Pandya, A., and P. Lodha 2022. Mental health consequences of COVID-19 pandemic among college students and coping approaches adapted by higher education institutions: A scoping review. *SSM - Mental Health.* 2. https://doi.org/10.1016/j.ssmmh.2022.100122.

Pitt, E., and K. Quinlan 2021. The impact of covid-19 on assessment and feedback practice: From the emergency phase to the preparation phase and beyond (pp. 22–30). In Baughan, P (ed) *Assessment and Feedback in a Post-Pandemic Era: A Time for Learning and Inclusion.* York. Advance HE.

Pitt, E., and N. Winstone. 2018. The impact of anonymous marking on students' perceptions of fairness, feedback and relationships with lecturers. *Assessment & Evaluation in Higher Education.* 43(7): 1183–1193. DOI: 10.1080/02602938.2018.1437594

Reedy, A., D. Pfitzner, L. Rook, and L. Ellis 2021. Responding to the COVID-19 emergency: Student and academic staff perceptions of academic integrity in the transition to online exams at three Australian universities. *International Journal for Educational Integrity* 17(9): 1–32. Pre-print. https://doi.org/10.1007/s40979-021-00075-9

Roberts, T. 2020. Putting the 'Ex' in Exams? Blog post for the Bristol Institute for Learning and Teaching. 16 July 2020. Available at: https://bilt.online/putting-the-ex-in-exams/Accessed 4 January 2022.

Royal Society for the Arts. https://www.thersa.org/globalassets/living-change/rsa-future-change-toolkit.pdf Accessed 2 January 2022.

Rudolph, J., S. Tan, and S. Tan 2023. ChatGPT: Bullshit spewer or the end of traditional assessments in higher education. *Journal of Applied Learning & Teaching* 6(1): 1–23. https://doi.org/10.37074/jalt.2023.6.1.9

Sambell, K., and S. Brown 2020. Covid-19 Assessment Collection. Available at: https://sally-brown.net/kay-sambell-and-sally-brown-covid-19-assessment-collection/ Accessed on 18 February 2023.

Sambell, K., and S. Brown 2021. Changing assessment for good: Building on the emergency switch to promote future-oriented assessment and feedback designs (pp. 11–21). In Baughan, P (ed) *Assessment and Feedback in a Post-Pandemic Era: A Time for Learning and Inclusion.* York. Advance HE.

Sharples, M. 2023. Presentation on Generative AI to Russell Group PVC Education Network. 23 April, UCL East. London.

Seeman, M. 1959. 'On the meaning of alienation. *American Sociological Review* 24 (6): 783–791.

Slade, C., G. Lawrie, N. Taptamat, E. Browne, K. Sheppard, and K. E. Matthews 2021. Insights into how academics reframed their assessment during a pandemic: Disciplinary variation and assessment as afterthought. *Assessment & Evaluation in Higher Education* 47 (4): 588–605, DOI: 10.1080/02602938.2021.1933379

University of Bristol 2020. Education Pulse Survey. Available at: https://www.bristol. ac.uk/students/updates/student-surveys/pulse-survey/ Accessed on 14 February 2023.

Villarroel, V., S. Bloxham, D. Bruna, C. Bruna, and C. Herrera-Seda 2018. Authentic assessment: Creating a blueprint for course design. *Assessment & Evaluation in Higher Education* 43 (5): 840–854, DOI: 10.1080/02602938.2017.1412396

Wakefield, A., R. Pike, and S. Amici-Dargan 2022. Learner-generated podcasts: An authentic And enjoyable assessment for students working in pairs, *Assessment & Evaluation in Higher Education*, DOI: 10.1080/02602938.2022.2152426

Wilson, L., J. Conway, N. Martin, and P. Turner. 2020. *Covid-19: Disabled students in higher education: Student concerns and Institutional challenges.* Report by the National Association of Disability Practitioners, Aylesbury, England. URL: https://nadp-uk. org/covid-19-resources-for-members-and-colleagues/Accessed 16 February 2023.

Wu, Q., and T. Jessop 2018. Formative assessment: Missing in action in both research-intensive and teaching focused universities? *Assessment and Evaluation in Higher Education* 43 (7): 1019–1031, DOI: 10.1080/02602938.2018.1426097

TESTA case study

BA (Hons) X: Poppletown University

TESTA BACKGROUND

TESTA is an evidence-led approach to understanding assessment patterns on whole degree programmes. The purpose of TESTA is to help programme teams identify enhancements for student learning based on evidence and assessment principles. TESTA uses three methods to gather evidence about the typical assessment experience of students:

- Programme audit (evidence from documents and the team).
- Assessment Experience Questionnaire (based on established assessment principles).
- Focus groups with students.

This case study summarises the evidence from these three methods, and is for use and discussion by the programme team. More about TESTA on www.testa.ac.uk

The programme audit

Defining the cohort

This Single Honours has 184 students: 64 in both Year 1 and Year 2, and 56 in Year 3. There are six full-time faculty members, four fractional staff and teaching assistants, and one practice co-ordinator. Most of the students are British (above 90%); 50% of students are 18 to 21 years old, and the remaining students are between 22 and 54 years. The male–female ratio is about 1:9.

The average attendance of students is about 60%, and the retention rate is particular problematic in first year.

There are 6 × 20 credit modules in Year 1. In both Year 2 and 3, there are 3 × 20 credit modules plus 1 × 60 credit module (70 and 100 days of Placement in Year 2 and 3, respectively). In Year 3, there is one 20 credit optional module. Year 2 and 3 include two and three Recall Days, respectively.

Year			Modules			
Year 1	20	20	20	20	20	20
Year 2	20	20	20	60		
Year 3	20	20			60	20

Summary categorisation of assessment

The audit showed the following patterns of assessment across the whole programme:

Variable	BA (Hons) X
Total number of assessments	41
Number of summative tasks	17
Number of formative tasks	24
Varieties of assessment	12
Proportion of exams	0%
Time to return	3–4 weeks
Volume of written feedback	7,193 words (360 words per script)

Comparison with other TESTA undergraduate programmes

A comparison of the BA (Hons) X data with 73 TESTA programmes in 14 UK universities:

Variable	BA (Hons) X	TESTA bachelors (n= 73)	Mid-quartile range on n=73 programmes
Total assessment	41	49	n/a
Number of summative	17	36	33–48
Number of formative	24	13	1–19
Varieties of assessment	12	13	8–15
Proportion of exams	0%	13%	10–30%
Time to return	3–4 weeks	19 days	n/a
Volume of written feedback	7,193 words (360 words per script)	8,021 words (222 words per script)	3,800–7,900

The BA (Hons) X has a lower number of summative assessment tasks (17) than the mid-range means (33–48). The number of formative tasks (n=24) is almost double compared to the average score of TESTA Bachelor programmes (n=13). The total number of assessment tasks (41) is lower than the average number of assessment of the TESTA Bachelor programmes (49). There is a similar number of varieties of assessment to the TESTA sample (12). Students receive feedback within a similar span of time compared to the TESTA sample.

Modules audited to represent a 'typical' pattern

Level	Types of assessment	Varieties	Summative	Formative	Exams	Oral Feedback	Written Feedback	Return times
4	Presentation (group), Essay (analytical and reflective case study), Video Conversation with Service Users, Reflective Essay based on Video Conversation, Video, Brochure, Portfolio, Real-Time Evaluation	8	8	6	-		NA	3–4 weeks
5	Essay (theory-based critical review), Report (case analysis), Portfolio (observation, reflection, mid-way review)	+2	4	9	-		NA	3–4 weeks
6	Portfolio, Poster Conference, Essay (literature review), Essay (experiential case study)	+2	5	9	-		NA	3–4 weeks
Totals		**12**	**17**	**24**	**-**		**NA**	**3–4 weeks**

Features of BA (Hons) X from audit discussion

a   The number of formative assessment types (24) is significantly higher than summative ones (17). Even when compared to the sample of other TESTA Bachelor programmes, the number of formative assessments is very high. This should predict high scores for internalising standards on the AEQ, with well-distributed and high levels of effort and engagement across the course.

b   Students encounter more varieties of assessment in their first year (8) than in the second and third years. Many assessment varieties are repeated as students then progress through the degree. These are likely to help students gain mastery of different learning and assessment processes.

c   The course is largely practice-oriented. The placement units provide opportunities for hands-on, experiential, and self-directed learning through real-life cases. Units contain practical elements which may enhance students' essential skills and knowledge relevant to their future career.

d   Portfolios, particularly the ones in the second and third years, involve a comprehensive record of students' observation and reflection on professional practice. Students need to gain these academic and technical skills in their initial years so that during the placement units and in final year essays, they can appropriately exploit them.

e   Professional skills workshops and recall days are helpful for students in understanding professional practices and learning content of the discipline. However, the attendance in these sessions is low. New engagement strategies are needed to reach out more students.

f   Several tasks in BA (Hons) X have strong elements of RIT embedded within them, such as Reflective Essay based on Video Conversation and Poster Conference. The placement units have potential to be an excellent field for both students and faculty members to practise RIT.

Assessment experience questionnaire

Forty students from BA (Hons) X completed the Assessment Experience Questionnaire (AEQ 4.0). The AEQ helps understand what impact the assessment environment is having on student learning behaviours. The AEQ contains five scales. The scales relate to conditions of assessment which promote student learning. Students answer on a five-point Likert scale where 1 = strongly disagree; 2 = disagree; 3 = neutral; 4 = agree; and 5 = strongly agree. A high mean score on the AEQ is 4=agree.

BA (Hons) X has higher scores in How Students Learn (Mean = 3.70; Median = 3.71), and Student Effort (Mean = 4.21; Median = 4.33). Formative Assessment (Mean = 2.81; Median = 2.83) and Internalising Standards (Mean=2.59; Median 2.67) scores are much lower than expected given the relatively high number of formative tasks. Quality of Feedback (Mean=3.39; Median 3.25) score is also low compared to TESTA sample (Mean=3.69).

The table below shows BA (Hons) X Mean and Median AEQ scores. As AEQ data is not on a normal curve, the median is considered to be more accurate.

Scales	How Students Learn	Formative Assessment	Internalising standards	Student Effort	Quality of Feedback
Mean scores n=40 students	3.70	2.81	2.59	4.21	3.39
Median scores n=40 students	3.71	2.83	2.67	4.33	3.25
TESTA mean n=10 programmes n= 510 students	3.67	3.27	3.17	4.00	3.69

Focus group data

We conducted one focus group with four final year students on 10 March 2017. The conversation of the session was recorded and transcribed. All the text data were analysed using thematic coding. While reporting the research, the word 'students' is used, not to represent all students on the BA (Hons) X, but to reflect pertinent issues raised by students in the focus group. Focus group data provide an explanation for the numbers in the AEQ data. Transcripts have been thematically analysed to reflect the following emphases in the student voice data.

a **Feedback**

Headline 1: Students find oral feedback on placements useful

We have supervision and I'd go through my bit of work that I had given in the previous week and she'd (the lecturer) write comments on the bottom and also we would talk through it so that was helpful. I can't think of any from the actual university lecturer.

I had fortnightly supervision and it's all about your work and yourself, that was like an hour and half to talk about whatever I wanted to talk about, work-related, so I would bring in my work and she was really at given me feedback and we'd go through it straight away and talk about what was good, what was better, what could be done better.

Headline 2: They value increased access to tutorials with lecturers

But sometimes where you're reading it and you don't understand what they've meant

I1: Do you have any way to contact the tutors?
R4: You can contact them.
R1: Yeah, when I've had grades that haven't been that good, I've set up tutorials with teachers and they've been happy to that.

The lecturers are putting on tutorials a lot more this year, they're putting booking slots on the system where you can actually book so they're advertising it.

Headline 3: But finding a convenient tutorial slot is not always easy

[Availability of tutorials ...] depends if the tutor has previously been able to fit them in, for example, if I went to my tutor, cause my tutors have changed, so if I go to my tutor and then they can't fit in for weeks, I'm not going to keep asking them cause it's pointless.

... if you want to speak to them (the lecturers), you have to make an appointment, but sometimes they aren't available and sometimes you don't have the time, especially if you're in Placement.

Headline 4: Students describe inconsistent feedback

We all had feedback at the end and everyone was just so positive. I almost looked forward to writing the assignment, because I was so clear on what we had to do and that's what should be consistent but we've got another module and no one has any idea, like people are having breakdowns.

Sometimes you don't understand what they are saying [in feedback]. Not in all of them because some are really good. But sometimes where you're reading it and you don't understand what they've meant.

Headline 5: Students say that inconsistency drives a conservative approach

Where there is a lack of consistency with the lecturers, if peer feedback was encouraged, it would add to that inconsistency... This has been an ongoing issue throughout our degree, so actually I think the reduction in any feedback had been encouraged, unless it's for an official assignment, they don't encourage it

Headline 6: Students want to know how to improve their work

The feedback we get, sometimes is very constructive and we can reflect on it, but it's then where do we go from there because we then don't have the further guidance to then improve for next time.

Last year I got told that my work wasn't structured very well, I kept going off on tangents in the middle of my essay and I was told I needed to structure it a bit more so it kind of flows, but I was like 'how do I do that?'. [Lecturers] say this but don't offer ways on how to do it.

b How students learn

Headline 1: Students put a high value on X placements

The way I've learnt the most, and I think you guys will agree, is being on placement. Our placement experience, which is completely away from the university, has actually been the most useful.

You learn so much from that, and I'm grateful we got to do that, because if we didn't do placement, I would not be able to go into the job.

We had to write an essay on what model we used in practice which I think was good, it helped practice and influence my essay, and I felt confident in that, because I've done it.

I was really able to understand how I implemented risk and how I managed it, and it was a lot clearer for me and I feel like I'm learning while I'm writing it.

Headline 2: They endorse the need for studying theory

In individual study, you're forced to read and look at theories. It is helpful for placement wise, learning the theory and the law, it's really useful for that, but most assignments, I'm not going to go back and look over them.

Our first year, it was very theory-based and you learn a lot more of like law, so although they're relevant, you then truly develop as you go on because it prepares you knowledge wise, for the actually physical practice, when you go out on placement. I would say it has developed in that sense but I think the way they've done the assessments is perhaps, could have been better.

Headline 3: Students find it difficult to learn when assessments are bunched

In our first year we had 4 assignments due in within 2 weeks, and I'm not very good at managing two things at once, so I found it really stressful, and I didn't do very well in them because I was rushing to get one done, then I've got to do another one, I was all other the place.

I know third year is meant to be harder, but with placement it escalates more than what other third years have on their degree course. I think maybe they could have spaced out the assessments a little bit more that would have been really useful.

Headline 4: They are grateful for recent changes to the distribution of tasks

They have taken that on board haven't they, because we had our reflective essay's as well as our university assignments all while we were on placement, so we were doing a CD which is a reflective essay once a week, as well as an assignment, plus being working full time, but we have fed that back and they have changed it now so they've put university assignments before or after the course, then just for portfolio while you're on placement.

Headline 5: Students are critical of the timing and levels of some tasks

Some [assessments...] would have been more appropriate earlier on in our academic degree, so we just did about one risk and responsibility and it's good because it's based on our own experience, however, if you can't write that essay now, there's an issue, because you should be able to know about those sorts of things, so it would have been better if we did it earlier.

What we're having now, would be more useful at the beginning of the course, we're all stressing out because we need to know what is expected of us, and we're just getting guest speakers and it's really a bit frustrating, and I'm like 'why would I come in? I could have been at home doing the essay.

I know third year is meant to be harder, but with placement it escalates more than what other third years have on their degree course. I think maybe they could have spaced out the assessments a little bit more that would have been really useful.

Headline 6: They feel that some enrichment activities could be better timed

R1: Like we're doing our final essays but we're not being told or taught what we actually have to do. We're doing like an hour of mindfulness yesterday.

R2: So, we did meditation yesterday we've got an assignment on children with families, and we just had a seminar on that module, nothing to do with the assignment. Everyone is coming into uni to learn and for guidance on how to do the assignment cause we're on our last hurdle now but the seminars we've got, there's barely anything to do with the assignments.

Headline 7: Students question the alignment between teaching and assessment

I don't think the assessments help us to learn more than just actually doing the work in the classroom because quite often we seem to do a roundabout with teaching, so in our seminars we have a conversation which isn't necessarily relevant to the work and I don't feel like we learn well, because we've only done assignments really.

We did [a course] yesterday. We've got an assignment and we just had a seminar on that module, nothing to do with the assignment.

R4: We're doing like an hour of mindfulness yesterday.
R2: So, we did meditation yesterday we've got an assignment on children with families and we just had a seminar on that module, nothing to do with the assignment.

Headline 8: They would like a more person-centred approach from academics

They (the lecturers) try to make it (the reflective task) sound like it's a very personal experience, like our tutors know us and understand our situations, but I beg to differ really, I feel like a lot of work lacks the person-centred approach that we we're expecting.

For a midway meeting, we're meant to get our university tutor and then our work-based supervisor and educator, but this year, the tutors wouldn't come to the midway and they're expected to cover three meetings. They don't have to do much. But they're like 'We don't need to come to this'. You're marking our grade, but you're not coming to see what we're doing. So, it's very inconsistent.

c Internalising standards

Headline 1: Students rely on clear assessment briefs to internalise standards

We always get assignment briefs, and on that it will show you what to get and it had a little paragraph about to get an A you need to do this, but a B would be a good understanding of the topic, but who judges what a good understanding of the topic is?

In this one brief, [the lecturer] took the assignment criteria and he wrote two separate paragraphs on what he wants and described this and tell me why you think this ... and this is the layout you should have, and it's not even that big of an essay really, but he's really pulled it to pieces so you completely understand.

Headline 2: They value approaches which seek to ensure consistency

In our risk topic, the one lecturer is marking all of them, and then another will look at the grades they gave and re-mark them. I love that they do that because it's actually consistent.

Headline 3: But they regard consistency as the exception rather than the rule

Linking that with your question on assessments, our information that we receive is so inconsistent, between lecturers, and it is the most nerve-racking experience, because we're so close, if anything happens now and we trip up, then our whole degree could be jeopardised. It's just the inconsistencies. It adds to the stress and adds to our anxiety and frustration. It's been a nightmare.

The same things are being brought up every year, the same issues that people are bringing up and it just never seems to be like, inconsistent marking; inconsistent lectures. Like we're doing our final essays but we're not being told or taught what we actually have to do.

So, you have four lecturers marking different ones, and that's why it's so inconsistent, because one person may feel like this is good understanding and the other think it's just ok.

I: What one thing would improve the assessment and feedback?
  Group: Consistency.

Headline 4: Students do not trust the marking process

I went and showed a bit of work to a lecturer couple of weeks back, and she told me that my whole plan wasn't very good, and I needed to change it all, but then I spoke to another lecturer and he was like "this is a great idea and fantastic". So, what do I do, because either of them could be marking my work?

The thing is, with the fact of inconsistent marking, if we show something to one person they might think it great, but then the person that actually marks it then they may think it's horrible.

I remember once, I went and spoke to a lecturer about my portfolio, it was a practice first year one, and they said it was really, really good and that I would pass, but I failed.

Once I had a lecturer tell me little things like, not to include my reference list in my poster, so I changed it all and then my other lecturer said "No it's fine, you can". I understand it's not feasible for one person to mark 50 essays, but if they all sat in a room and were clear on what the criteria were…

R1: All the lecturers need to be in one room, and talk to each other. I don't think anyone talks to each other. One person says one thing; the other person says something completely different.

R4: There's such a lack of communication

Headline 5: They are not confident in the grades they receive

For me, my grades, have been so inconsistent over the last 3 or 4 years, I've got top A2s to fails, so that's why I feel like the marking is very inconsistent, because I can't get my head around how you go from that bad to that well, in the space of weeks, it doesn't make much sense.

Headline 6: In addition, there is a perception of a theory-practice divide

You could have your practice, work-based supervisor who you're working with every single day saying 'the student is amazing, she's going to be a great Xer, I want her to have an A' but they don't have any contribution to what your grade is going to be at the end of it, it's all down to the written work.

d   **Integration of research**

Headline 1: Research elements are embedded in the course

We have portfolio which includes reflective essays and observations.

For our research, we've chosen topics so each one is different and then we have to look at the research we can find on that topic and then we just critique that research and where's there're gaps.

That (video interview) conversation we had with a service user but, in my seminar, we watched it back as a whole seminar group and the students were able to comment and give feedback as well.

Headline 2: But may cause a bit of panic

It's only now on this one topic where they've said to research and everyone is panicking because we've only read books.

Headline 3: Partly linked to lack of formal guidance on research methods

I don't think we've had any guidance [on conducting research]. They're just like go choose a topic and go find some research and then you've got to analyse it. There's no guidelines on what you should look at. They haven't gone through with us how to get the research.

e   **Student effort**

Headline 1: Student effort changes across levels and units

In my first year, I was a lot more studious, in that I would pick up a book and think that was kind of interesting, I would never do that now, because I don't have the time.

[In Placement] … you work Monday–Friday, 9–5, and I worked the weekends as well, If I picked up a book just because it was interesting, it was a waste of time because it wouldn't be necessarily be relevant. I'd say this year, I only study if I have to. If I can avoid it then I do.

On placement I didn't want to go to the library in the evenings because I'd get back late, so I think it (student effort) changes, so I have more time now, so I can go more in depth with things.'

Headline 2: Students express the need for more recognition of hard work

It feels a bit patronising in some ways, especially now cause we're dedicating so much of our time, cause we're not on placement and we're at university, we really throw our hearts and souls into this and they're like 'you'll be alright', and we're like "Will we though?" And it's just been so stressful, because we've really been working hard and I don't feel like they're (lecturers) giving us enough credit for the efforts we've put in.

INTERPRETING THE DATA: WHAT'S GOING ON?

The section below explores questions which arise from the datasets for discussion about enhancements.

1 *Why do students give the BA (Hons) X a low score for formative assessment (2.83)?*

The low score for formative assessment on the AEQ is surprising, given that the audit shows a high number of formative tasks (24). It is possible that the design of formative tasks does not encourage uptake because too many assessment types create confusion, or because they are not seen to connect well enough with summative tasks, or they need to be more aligned with professional theories and practices. Well-designed formative tasks provide feedback which feeds forward to a summative task to support deep learning. In the focus group data, oral feedback on formative tasks is discretionary, whereas written format of feedback dominates the process. Giving regular oral feedback could be a powerful mechanism for improving the student learning experience. This may have the double benefit of personalising learning for students and building relationships.
  Some ideas:

- Develop multi-stage formative tasks which link to the summative ones allowing students to build and refine with helpful feedback. In this regard, students can receive peer and tutor feedback at different phases.
- Incorporate personalised and verbal feedback to help students explore their individual strengths and weaknesses. It is also beneficial to monitor how students address the feedback in their tasks.

- Design formative tasks which are personally and professionally meaningful, drawing on the real-world dimensions of the BA (Hons) X degree. Although the present number of formative tasks is very high, some of them can be modified to allow students to take risks, think outside of the box, and learn deeply.
- Connect the assessment types across units and levels so that students can gradually accomplish more complex academic tasks in the later stages. For example, Students need to apply rigorous observation and reflection skills in the placement phase. Therefore, they should be oriented with these academic and technical skills in the early stage of the degree programme.

2 *Why do students give a low score for internalising standards (2.67)?*

In both the AEQ and focus groups, students indicate difficulties in understanding what quality looks like in their assessment tasks. They talk about inconsistencies and the absence of a culture of shared practices in marking and feedback among lecturers. As a result, they are surprised by grades, confused by mixed messages in criteria, and say they get contradictory advice from different lecturers. Assignment briefs are one tangible source for students to get information about marking standards, but students describe these as lacking consistency.

There is a relatively high variety of assessment types (12), which may cause confusion. However in most cases, students undertake essays, reports, or written work. The audit describes quite a few technical reports with templates for students to fill in which are more likely to result in boredom than confusion, so it is surprising that there is such a strong perception of inconsistency. However, there are no peer review processes, mock marking exercises, or co-creation of criteria which could help them better understanding of the standards of marking. The low take-up of formative tasks goes some way to explaining the low scores for internalising standards as students learn about expectations from formative tasks.

Some ideas:

- Discuss examples of student work with students.
- Engage students in exercises which help them to judge the quality of work.
- Develop students' appreciation for marking processes through co-creation exercises involving criteria, assessment questions, and learning outcomes.
- Encourage students to self-assess their own work in writing at the time of submission.
- Use formative tasks to help students fine-tune their understanding of standards through using and discussing feedback.
- Develop uniform marking standards through regular calibration exercises.
- Investigate whole course assessment design to ensure there is coherence, sequencing, and logical progression through levels.
- Ensure assessment briefs have a common approach.

Assessment experience questionnaire (V3.3)

By filling out this questionnaire, I understand that I am agreeing to participate in a research study

Please respond to every statement by circling 1 = strongly disagree; 2 = disagree; 3 = neutral; 4 = agree; and 5 = strongly agree to indicate the strength of your agreement or disagreement

Programme of Study: ....

Biographical Data: (please tick as appropriate)

Male ....   Female..........

Age   (17–21.....)   (22–30).........   (31 +......)

Average achievement on this course: (1st......); (2:1.......); (2:2.......) (3.......)

	Please respond with respect to your experience so far of the programme named above, including all its assessment components	Strongly disagree	Disagree	Neutral	Agree	Strongly agree
1	I used the feedback I received to go back over what I had done in my work	1	2	3	4	5
2	The feedback I received prompted me to go back over material covered in the course	1	2	3	4	5
3	I received hardly any feedback on my work	1	2	3	4	5
4	You had to study the entire syllabus to do well in the assessment	1	2	3	4	5
5	The assessment system made it possible to be quite selective about what parts of courses you studied	1	2	3	4	5
6	The way the assessment worked you had to put the hours in regularly every week	1	2	3	4	5
7	It was always easy to know the standard of work expected	1	2	3	4	5
8	I paid careful attention to feedback on my work and tried to understand what it was saying	1	2	3	4	5
9	The teachers made it clear from the start what they expected from students	1	2	3	4	5

10	The staff seemed more interested in testing what I had memorised than what I understood		1 2 3 4 5
11	It was possible to be quite strategic about which topics you could afford not to study		1 2 3 4 5
12	It was often hard to discover what was expected of me in this course		1 2 3 4 5
13	On this course it was necessary to work consistently hard to meet the assessment requirements		1 2 3 4 5
14	Too often, the staff asked me questions just about facts		1 2 3 4 5
15	I didn't understand some of the feedback on my work		1 2 3 4 5
16	Whatever feedback I received on my work came too late to be useful		1 2 3 4 5
17	The way the assessment worked on this course you had to study every topic		1 2 3 4 5
18	To do well on this course all you really needed was a good memory		1 2 3 4 5

These questions are about the way you go about your learning on the course

19	When I'm reading I try to memorise important facts which may come in useful later		1 2 3 4 5
20	I usually set out to understand thoroughly the meaning of what I am asked to read		1 2 3 4 5
21	I generally put a lot of effort into trying to understand things which initially seem difficult		1 2 3 4 5
22	I often found myself questioning things that I heard in classes or read in books		1 2 3 4 5
23	I find I have to concentrate on memorising a good deal of what we have to learn		1 2 3 4 5
24	Often I found I had to study things without having a chance to really understand them		1 2 3 4 5

Learning from the exam (only to be completed if there were exams on the course)

25	Doing exams brought things together for me		1 2 3 4 5
26	I learnt new things while preparing for the exams		1 2 3 4 5
27	I understood things better as a result of the exams		1 2 3 4 5

Overall satisfaction

28	Overall I was satisfied with the quality of this course		1 2 3 4 5

Comments you would like to make:

Scales

Quantity of effort (alpha = 0.69)

6 The way the assessment worked you had to put the hours in regularly every week

13 On this course it was necessary to work consistently hard to meet the assessment requirements

Coverage of syllabus (alpha = 0.85)

4   You had to study the entire syllabus to do well in the assessment
5   The assessment system made it possible to be quite selective about what parts of courses you studied (negative scoring)
11   It was possible to be quite strategic about which topics you could afford not to study (negative scoring)
17   The way the assessment worked on this course you had to study every topic

Quantity and quality of feedback (alpha = 0.61)

3   I received hardly any feedback on my work (negative scoring)
15   I didn't understand some of the feedback on my work (negative scoring)
16   Whatever feedback I received on my work came too late to be useful (negative scoring)

Use of feedback (alpha = 0.70)

1   I used the feedback I received to go back over what I had done in my work
2   The feedback I received prompted me to go back over material covered in the course
8   I paid careful attention to feedback on my work and tried to understand what it was saying

Appropriate assessment

10   The staff seemed more interested in testing what I had memorised than what I understood (negative scoring)
14   Too often, the staff asked me questions just about facts (negative scoring)
18   To do well on this course, all you really needed was a good memory (negative scoring)

Clear goals and standards

7   It was always easy to know the standard of work expected
9   The teachers made it clear from the start what they expected from students
12   It was often hard to discover what was expected of me in this course (negative scoring)

Surface approach

19   When I'm reading I try to memorise important facts which may come in useful later
23   I find I have to concentrate on memorising a good deal of what we have to learn
24   Often, I found I had to study things without having a chance to really understand them

Deep approach

20 I usually set out to understand thoroughly the meaning of what I am asked to read.
21 I generally put a lot of effort into trying to understand things which initially seem difficult
22 I often found myself questioning things that I heard in classes or read in books

Learning from the examination (alpha = 0.78)

25 Doing the exams brings things together for me
26 I learn new things while preparing for the exams
27 I understand things better as a result of the exams

Satisfaction

28 Overall, I am satisfied with the teaching on this course

Assessment experience questionnaire (V4.0)

By filling out this questionnaire, I understand that I am agreeing to participate in a research study.

Please respond by circling 1 = strongly disagree; 2 = disagree; 3 = neutral; 4 = agree; and 5 = strongly agree

Programme/course of Study: ....

Please respond to your experience of assessment and feedback on the programme/course above.

Over the duration of my programme/course...	Strongly disagree	Disagree	Neutral	Agree	Strongly agree
1 Feedback helped me to understand things better	1	2	3	4	5
2 I was able to apply learning from my assessments to new situations	1	2	3	4	5
3 Assessments helped me develop skills for graduate work	1	2	3	4	5
4 The assessment demands meant that I had to study hard	1	2	3	4	5
5 I had to put the hours in regularly every week if I wanted to do well	1	2	3	4	5
6 Assessments developed my problem-solving skills	1	2	3	4	5
7 I rarely undertook ungraded assessment tasks	1	2	3	4	5
8 I could see from my feedback what I needed to do to improve	1	2	3	4	5
9 I had to study regularly if I wanted to do well	1	2	3	4	5
10 My feedback was personal to me	1	2	3	4	5
11 Assessments enabled me to explore complex problems facing the world	1	2	3	4	5
12 I did the bare minimum for ungraded tasks	1	2	3	4	5
13 I felt the assessment expectations were always changing	1	2	3	4	5
14 I only studied things that were covered in graded assessments	1	2	3	4	5
15 I often found the assessment criteria confusing	1	2	3	4	5
16 I only valued work that counted	1	2	3	4	5
17 It was difficult to understand the assessment expectations	1	2	3	4	5
18 Assessments challenged me to think differently	1	2	3	4	5

Comments you would like to make:

Scales

The AEQ includes five factors, each of which is described below, with associated items identified.

How students learn (Cronbach's alpha = 0.833)

Students' perceptions of how the assessment environment influences their depth of understanding

2. I was able to apply learning from my assessments to new situations
3. Assessments helped me develop skills for graduate work
6. Assessments developed my problem-solving skills
11. Assessments enabled me to explore complex problems facing the world
18. Assessments challenged me to think differently

Internalisation of standards (Cronbach's alpha = 0.805)

Students' perceptions of the quality of work required

13. I felt the assessment expectations were always changing (R)
15. I often found the assessment criteria confusing (R)
17. It was difficult to understand the assessment expectations (R)

Quality of feedback (Cronbach's alpha = 0.682)

Students' perceptions of the value of qualitative comments on their work

Feedback helped me to understand things better
8. I could see from my feedback what I needed to do to improve
10. My feedback was personal to me

Student effort (Cronbach's alpha = 0.749)

Students' perceptions of how hard they work relative to assessment demands

4. The assessment demands meant that I had to study hard
5. I had to put the hours in regularly every week if I wanted to do well
9. I had to study regularly if I wanted to do well

Formative assessment (Cronbach's alpha = 0.836)

Students' perceptions of ungraded work intended to improve learning

7. I rarely undertook ungraded assessment tasks (R)
12. I did the bare minimum for ungraded tasks (R)
14. I only studied things that were covered in graded assessments (R)
16. I only valued work that counted (R)

Appendix D

Assessment experience questionnaire (V5.1)

By filling out this questionnaire, I understand that I am agreeing to participate in a research study.

Please respond by circling 1 = strongly agree; 2 = agree; 3 = neither agree nor disagree; 4 = disagree; and 5 = strongly disagree

Programme of Study: ....

Level of study (e.g. 1st year, 2nd year, 3rd year; 4th year): ....

Thinking about the whole of my course, my experience has been that...	*Strongly agree*	*Agree*	*Neither agree nor disagree*	*Disagree*	*Strongly disagree*	*Not applicable*
1 Assessments encourage me to study concepts in depth	1	2	3	4	5	N/A
2 Feedback helps me to understand how to improve	1	2	3	4	5	N/A
3 Feedback on work that does not count helps me to learn	1	2	3	4	5	N/A
4 Links between assessments on different units are not always clear to me	1	2	3	4	5	N/A
5 Assessments help me to deepen my understanding of concepts	1	2	3	4	5	N/A
6 The assessment demands mean that I need to study hard to do well	1	2	3	4	5	N/A
7 There is not enough time between assessments to make use of the feedback	1	2	3	4	5	N/A
8 I learn a lot from assessment tasks which do not count	1	2	3	4	5	N/A
9 It does not matter if I forget about what I have learnt on a unit after I have passed it	1	2	3	4	5	N/A

10	I need to put the hours in regularly every week if I want to do well	1	2	3	4	5	N/A
11	I often skip assessments which do not count	1	2	3	4	5	N/A
12	Assessments do not usually develop my problem-solving skills	1	2	3	4	5	N/A
13	Assessments seem to test the same things across different units	1	2	3	4	5	N/A
14	Some assessments require me to evaluate different arguments or evidence	1	2	3	4	5	N/A
15	My feedback is personal to me	1	2	3	4	5	N/A
16	Assessments encourage me to rethink my ideas	1	2	3	4	5	N/A
17	I do not understand how to do well in my assessments	1	2	3	4	5	N/A
18	Some assessments encourage me to explore real world problems	1	2	3	4	5	N/A
19	I do the bare minimum when assessments do not count	1	2	3	4	5	N/A
20	My feedback feels quite generic	1	2	3	4	5	N/A
21	I am clear about what is expected for assessments	1	2	3	4	5	N/A
22	I feel well prepared for new methods of assessment	1	2	3	4	5	N/A
23	I only value work that counts	1	2	3	4	5	N/A
24	I often revisit content from previous units to get to grips with new material	1	2	3	4	5	N/A
25	I understand more because of the feedback I receive	1	2	3	4	5	N/A
26	The standard required to do well on an assessment is not always clear	1	2	3	4	5	N/A
27	Some assessments require me to bring together knowledge and skills from different units	1	2	3	4	5	N/A
28	I only read academic texts when there is an assessment coming up	1	2	3	4	5	N/A
29	Preparing for exams helps me to see connections between aspects of the course	1	2	3	4	5	N/A
30	I pay careful attention to my feedback	1	2	3	4	5	N/A
31	I struggle to learn in depth when there are too many assessments	1	2	3	4	5	N/A
32	Some assessments require me to apply my learning to new situations	1	2	3	4	5	N/A
33	When preparing for assessments, I rarely use learning from other units	1	2	3	4	5	N/A
34	Assessments which do not count are just a distraction	1	2	3	4	5	N/A
35	I can usually predict which topics I need to study when it comes to exams	1	2	3	4	5	N/A
36	I can see from my feedback what I need to do to improve	1	2	3	4	5	N/A
37	When there are lots of assessments, I don't bother with ones that don't count	1	2	3	4	5	N/A
38	I usually receive feedback in time to act on it	1	2	3	4	5	N/A
39	I only study the things I am assessed on	1	2	3	4	5	N/A
40	I am never sure what is expected with new methods of assessment	1	2	3	4	5	N/A

Scales

How students learn

Assessments encourage me to study concepts in depth
5. Assessments help me to deepen my understanding of concepts
12. Assessments do not usually develop my problem-solving skills (neg)
14. Some assessments require me to evaluate different arguments or evidence
16. Assessments encourage me to rethink my ideas
18. Some assessments encourage me to explore real-world problems
32. Some assessments require me to apply my learning to new situations

Formative assessment

8. I learn a lot from assessment tasks that do not count
11. I often skip assessments that do not count (neg)
19. I do the bare minimum when assessments do not count (neg)
37. When there are lots of assessments, I don't bother with ones that don't count (neg)
23. I only value work that counts (neg)
34. Assessments that do not count are just a distraction (neg)
39. I only study the things I am assessed on (neg)

Internalisation of standards

17. I do not understand how to do well in my assessments (neg)
21. I am clear about what is expected for assessments
26. The standard required to do well on an assessment is not always clear (neg)
22. I feel well prepared for new methods of assessment.
40. I am never sure what is expected with new methods of assessment (neg)

Influence on student effort

6. The assessment demands to mean that I need to study hard to do well
10. I need to put the hours in regularly every week if I want to do well
28. I only read academic texts when there is an assessment coming up (neg)
35. I can usually predict which topics I need to study when it comes to exams

Quality of feedback

2. Feedback helps me to understand how to improve
3. Feedback on work that does not count helps me to learn
15. My feedback is personal to me
20. My feedback feels quite generic (neg)

25. I understand more because of the feedback I receive
30. I pay careful attention to my feedback
36. I can see from my feedback what I need to do to improve
38. I usually receive feedback in time to act on it

Integrated assessment design

4. Links between assessments on different units are not always clear to me (neg)
7. There is not enough time between assessments to make use of the feedback (neg)
9. It does not matter if I forget about what I have learnt on a unit after I have passed it (neg)
13. Assessments seem to test the same things across different units (neg)
24. I often revisit content from previous units to get to grips with new material
27. Some assessments require me to bring together knowledge and skills from different units
29. Preparing for exams helps me to see connections between aspects of the course
31. I struggle to learn in depth when there are too many assessments (neg)
33. When preparing for assessments, I rarely use learning from other units (neg)

Appendix E

TESTA Focus Group questions

1. ASSESSMENT IN GENERAL: Tell me about how you are assessed on your course/programme. What assessments have you learnt the most/ and the least from and why? How well do the assessment tasks connect and develop across the course?
2. FORMATIVE/SUMMATIVE: Do you ever do assessed tasks which do not count? If you do, how do they help you to learn? What sort of tasks? What is the feedback like? Does everyone do them?
3. RESEARCH-BASED ASSESSMENT: What does research mean to you and what does doing research look like in your subject? Do any of your assessed tasks involve you doing research? What form do they take? How does doing research influence how you learn?
4. FEEDBACK: Tell me about the feedback you get. Can you give an example of really powerful feedback you have received which developed your learning? What about feedback which hasn't really helped you? How do you get your feedback? What is your experience of peer feedback? How does feedback help you learn?
5. STUDY HABITS AND BEHAVIOUR: How does assessment influence how, how much and when you work? How does it affect what you pay attention to, what you ignore? How does assessment influence your approach to learning?
6. GOALS AND STANDARDS: Tell me about how you have come to know what good work looks like, and how you know what is likely to get good marks or to pass or fail?
7. SUMMING UP: Overall how does assessment on your course help you learn? What one thing would improve assessment and feedback?

Index